# Redeeming Laughter

# Redeeming Laughter
## The Comic Dimension of Human Experience

PETER L. BERGER

WALTER DE GRUYTER
NEW YORK • BERLIN

# About the Author

**Peter L. Berger** is a University Professor at Boston University. He is the author of many books in sociology and religion, including *The Social Construction of Reality* (with Thomas Luckmann), *The Sacred Canopy, A Rumor of Angels* and, most recently, *A Far Glory: The Quest for Faith in an Age of Credulity*.

**Library of Congress Cataloging-in-Publication Data**
Berger, Peter L.
    Redeeming laughter : the comic dimension of human experience / Peter L. Berger.
        p.      cm.
    Includes bibliographical references and index.
    ISBN 3-11-015562-1 (cloth : alk. paper)
    1. Comic, The—Religious aspects—Christianity.   2. Wit and humor—Religious aspects—Christianity.      I. Title.
    BR115.C63B47 1997                                                          97-12095
    233—DC21                                                                          CIP

**Die Deutsche Bibliothek - CIP-Einheitsaufnahme**
Berger, Peter L.:
Redeeming laughter : the comic dimension of human experience /
Peter L. Berger. - Berlin ; New York : de Gruyter, 1997      DBN: 95.027928.5⊗
    ISBN 3-11-015562-1                                                          SG: 11

**British Library Cataloguing in Publication Data**
Berger, Peter L.
    Redeeming laughter : the comic dimension of human experience
    1. Comic, The - Religious aspects   2. Comic, The - Psychological aspects
    I. Title
    152.4 ' 3
    ISBN 3-11-015562-1

Manufactured in the United States of America
10  9  8  7  6  5  4  3  2  1

To the Memory of My Father
George W. Berger

# Table of Contents

# Prefatory Remarks, Self-Serving Explanations, and Unsolicited Compliments

People who work in bookstores tend toward a pessimistic worldview, or so I have observed. This is very understandable, given both the quantity and (mostly) quality of the merchandise they are obliged to sell. And then there is the problem of classification: just where in the store is a particular book to be located? I can foresee that this book will raise this question in a particularly irritating fashion, thus contributing to the malaise already afflicting what I consider to be one of the more honorable occupations in our generally depressing age. Is this book to be placed in the humor section? In religion? In sociology? The predominance of Jewish jokes might suggest Judaica, the defense of Oscar Wilde gay and lesbian studies. By currently fashionable principles of literary theory, the author is the very last person to say how a book is to be understood. Nevertheless, if a choice is to be made, I would suggest a division: some books under humor, some under religion. It is certainly about humor; and the underlying argument as well as the finale are religious, and the title intends to make this clear from the beginning.

People who review books are, of course, even more pessimistic than those who sell them. As someone once observed, even-handed malice is the cardinal virtue of the critic. This book will provide ample opportunity for the exercise of this virtue. It takes its material from many fields, in most of which I have no professional competence. I have made an effort to use my sources responsibly, and I have taken some advice, but I'm confident that there are misinterpretations and, more important, omissions at various points of my argument. This knowledge has caused periodic attacks of anxiety during my work on the book. I have consoled myself with two thoughts. First, the literature about the nature of the comic, while vast, is singularly unsatisfactory in answering some of the basic questions about the phenomenon, partly because so few authors have been willing to step beyond the boundaries of their professional competencies; in other words, the comic is a subject that cries out for unprofessional treatment. Second, I have reached an age, tottering on the edge of senility, where I can afford to be reasonably nonchalant about what people say about me. However, I will say this much in my defense: I have no delusions about being some sort of Renaissance man; I do have certain obsessions. I have been obsessed with the question of the nature of the comic all my life, ever since my father, an inveterate teller of jokes, encouraged me to tell my own about the time when I entered kindergarten, where according to reliable sources I made a nuisance of myself as I faithfully followed the paternal mandate. Sooner or later, I had to write this book.

It is easy to say what this book is *not*. It is not a jokebook, though I very much hope that readers will occasionally laugh. Put differently, it is a book about humor, but not primarily a humorous book. It is not a treatise in any of the intellectual disciplines from which it draws, and my own discipline of sociology is not at all central to my main argument. And, while it draws mainly on works of literature to illustrate the different modes of the comic, it is not a work of literary criticism.

This book is a prolonged reflection about the nature of the comic as a central human experience. Its main argument can be stated succinctly: Humor—that is, the capacity to perceive something as being funny—is universal; there has been no human culture without it. It can safely be regarded as a necessary constituent of humanity. At the same time, what strikes people as funny and what they do in order to provoke a humorous response differs enormously from age to age, and from society to society. Put differently, humor is an anthropological constant *and* is historically relative. Yet, beyond or behind all the relativities, there is the *something* that humor is believed to perceive. This is, precisely, the phenomenon of the comic (which, if you will, is the objective correlate of humor, the subjective capacity). From its simplest to its most sophisticated expressions, the comic is experienced as *incongruence*.

Also, the comic conjures up *a separate world*, different from the world of ordinary reality, operating by different rules. It is also a world in which the limitations of the human condition are miraculously overcome. The experience of the comic is, finally, a promise of redemption. Religious faith is the intuition (some lucky people would say the conviction) that the promise will be kept.

Even if the main argument of this book is stated in such a brief form, it must be clear that it cannot be sustained within any given intellectual discipline. Philosophy would be the only plausible candidate but, as becomes clear quickly, philosophers have been of only modest use in the exploration of the comic phenomenon. Having started on the argument, I had to improvise as I went along. I had no foolproof method at hand (the word *foolproof*, come to think of it, is very appropriate here). The aforementioned kindergarten stood in Vienna, which may be of methodological relevance. If I have a method at all here, perhaps it could be called a baroque one. It is based on the assumption that there are hidden connections and a hidden order behind the near-infinite richness of the empirical world, and that the order is ultimately God-given and salvific. Therefore, it does not matter where one begins an exploration or which path of inquiry one takes: the underlying realities will disclose themselves in one way or another. Put in baroque terms, the shortest distance between two points is the circle. Finally, when one gets there, one will laugh.

My editors, who are naturally worried, have advised me that, in view of the complicated character of this book, I should give the reader some kind of preview or overview of the contents. Fair enough. So here goes: The book begins naively (or, which is more or less the same thing, phenomenologically) by just *looking at* the experience of the comic as it appears in ordinary life, without recourse to any academic disciplines. Overall, the book is divided into three parts. Part I deals with what could be called the anatomy of the comic—that is, with the question of just what it is. So as not to induce in the reader a state of unbearable suspense, let me say right away that no conclusive answer will be forthcoming (though some excellent reasons for why such an answer is not possible). Nevertheless, as one looks at the findings and the speculations coming out of different approaches, a clearer picture of the phenomenon does emerge. The approaches surveyed are those of philosophy, physiology (a passing glance only, since I'm not only incompetent but *monumentally* incompetent in this area), psychology and the social sciences. There are two interludes, tangents off the main argument. While my own education forced me to rely mainly on Western sources, it is important to keep in mind the universality of the comic phenomenon; one interlude, then, deals with humor in East Asia. The other interlude is a reflection on Jewish humor, which uniquely illustrates some of the points I want to make here.

Part II is a *tour d'horizon* of different genres, or forms of expression, of the comic. These are mostly illustrated by examples from literature. Of course, there is no intention here of presenting the authors of these works in any depth; they are simply used here as what Max Weber called "clear cases"—cases, that is, of the different comic genres. The comic forms of expression discussed (not necessarily an exhaustive list) are benign humor, tragicomedy, wit, satire, and (most important for the main argument) the strange counterworld of what the Middle Ages called "folly." Authors used by way of illustration are, among others, P. G. Wodehouse, Sholem Aleichem, Oscar Wilde, and Karl Kraus. (An odd collection, no doubt. If there is a comic section in the hereafter, I wonder how they get on together. The mind boggles at some of the possibilities.) I regret that I could not use any visual expressions of the comic here, but to do so would have made this book inordinately expensive and my editors even more worried.

Part III is my attempt to pull together the religious implications of the argument. It is, so to speak, an exercise in lay theology. (I am a Lutheran, of a rather heterodox sort, and I believe in the priesthood of all believers, ipso facto in the right of all believers to think theologically.) One chapter deals with the relationship of folly and redemption. An interlude tries to face up to the question of why it is that most theologians are such a humorless lot. The final chapter, looking at the comic as a signal of transcendence, narrowly avoids the charge of being a sermon. I conclude with the wonderful poem of Gilbert Keith Chesterton about the donkey on which Jesus rode into Jerusalem.

Some acknowledgments are in order. If I were to thank all the individuals who have helped me think about the nature of the comic (mostly, by first making me laugh), I would have to go on for many pages, and my editors would pass from worry to rage. I should mention my oldest friend, Wolfgang Breunig, who was with me in the kindergarten where I first made a pest of myself as a teller of jokes, who still lives in the same house on the Petersplatz where he lived then, and who has endured my jokes ever since with admirable patience. This particular book was started (without malicious intent, I stipulate) by Ann Bernstein, who visited Boston a few years ago and, as intellectuals are wont to do, asked me what I was working on. When I answered that I wasn't working on anything in particular, she said, "Why don't you write a book on humor? You tell so many jokes." I replied that this was a ridiculous idea. Some three hours later it struck me that, of course, this is what I should do.

As I proceeded with this (literally) ridiculous project, a number of friends and colleagues made helpful suggestions. First among them is Anton Zijderveld, one of the very few sociologists who has done important work on humor. I would also like to thank Ali Banuazizi, John Berthrong, Noel Perrin, Christopher Ricks, and Ruth Wisse. I would very much like to say that any faults of this book are entirely due to them, while I am solely responsible for its merits.

Brigitte Berger has listened, patiently *and* critically, to my writings for almost as long as she has been listening to my jokes. This book, too, owes very much to her attention and suggestions. Diya Berger, whose smile becomes ever more knowing, has taught me much about the origins of humor in the wonders of childhood (see Chapter 4, note 9).

Finally, I want to thank my editors, Bianka Ralle and Richard Koffler. They have been greatly supportive.

# Prologue

Amid the variety of human experiences of reality, or of what appears to be reality, the experience of the comic occupies a very distinctive place. On the one hand, it is ubiquitous. Everyday life is full of comic interludes, of occasions for humor, of little jokes as well as more elaborate ones. What is more, the experience of the comic is universal. While its expression differs greatly from one culture to another, there is no human culture without it. On the other hand, the experience of the comic is highly fragile, fugitive, sometimes hard to remember. What seems funny in one moment may suddenly take on a tragic quality in the next moment, a joke may be so subtle that it barely reaches the level of full attention, and this is why only a short time later it may be difficult to recall just why something evoked amusement. The fragility of the comic becomes particularly evident as soon as the attempt is made to analyze it intellectually, as anyone knows who has ever tried to explain a joke. All of this means that the comic is something of a mystery. Just what is this experience, and how does it relate to other human experiences?

Human beings make judgments about truth, about goodness, about beauty, and philosophers have been worrying for some three millennia how the validity of such judgments can be established. Yet the comic does not fall under any of these primeval categories. Take the joke, that most succinct form of verbal humor. It makes little sense to ask whether a joke is true. To be sure, it may refer to situations that, in terms of one's knowledge of the world, could not have occurred—say, a joke about a political figure involved in an event that in fact took place before or after the time when this individual was in power. But this error, this "untruth," may have little bearing on whether the joke is funny or not; indeed, the point of the joke could actually be this empirically false juxtaposition of person and event. The comic effect of a joke also bears little relation to the realm of moral judgment. Of course it is possible to make moral judgments about the *context* in which a joke is told and about the *intentions* of the joke-teller. Proverbially, one should not tell tales about gallows in the house of someone who was hanged, and the insensitivity of someone who does merits moral condemnation. The same goes for jokes that are intended to denigrate this or that group of people—racist jokes, anti-Semitic jokes, and so on. It is even possible to say that the very *contents* of a particular joke are immoral—as with the sort of hatred-inspired jokes just mentioned, or with jokes that seem to extol cruelty or are based on blasphemy. Yet, while stipulating all these moral points, there remains the disquieting fact that, after one has fully explained why this joke is morally reprehensible, *it may still be funny*. More than that, one of the important social functions of humor seems always to have been to outrage conventional moral sentiments. While humor can clearly be used for good or evil purposes, the comic as such appears to be strangely beyond good and evil. Finally, it makes just as little sense to ask whether a joke is beautiful or ugly. There is a realm of esthetic experience and a realm of comic experience, but the two seem to be quite independent of each other.

There is, of course, an enormous literature about different manifestations of the sense of the comic—books on comedy as a dramatic form, on irony and satire, on the sense of humor of different nationalities and regions, on different categories of jokes, on social roles embodying the comic such as court jesters and clowns, and on festivals based on humorous merriment such as the carnival. However, there is a relative paucity of writings about the nature of the comic as such, certainly if compared to the libraries of books about the nature of truth, goodness, and beauty. Few philosophers have bothered to think seriously about the funny. Undoubtedly this has something to do with the aforementioned fragility of the comic experience. Try to grasp it, and it dissolves. How many jokes could survive treatment by philosophers? But there is also the widely assumed notion that the serious and the funny exclude each other. After all, one cannot simultaneously pray and joke, declare one's love and joke, contemplate mortality and joke—or at least such simultaneity would require a very big effort, one likely to be misunderstood by most people. There is a good word for the inappropriate insertion of humor into a serious situation—the word is *frivolity*. It is frivolous to make jokes during a religious ceremony, a proposal of marriage, or a funeral. Conventionally, then, the comic appears to be banned from all truly serious occasions. This social fact has led many to the view that the comic is a superficial or marginal aspect of human life, in which case it would be perfectly understandable that serious thinkers have not paid much attention to it. The present book is grounded in the conviction that such a view is very much mistaken.

This is a book about the comic, that mysterious component of reality that is detected, or believed to be detected, by what is commonly called a sense of humor. Again, in common usage it is said that someone *lacks* a sense of humor if he or she is unable to detect the presence of the comic. Writing a book about the comic could be construed as prima facie evidence of such humorlessness. Conversely, the witness to such an endeavor may well find it funny in the extreme. It calls out for a humorous antithesis, as occurs when a philosopher lecturing on metaphysics loses his pants or has a visible erection or an irrepressible attack of the hiccups—the physical taking comic revenge on the pretension of the metaphysical. In other words, people who write books on the comic are legitimate targets for parody, satire, and other aggressive modes of the humorous response to intolerable seriousness.

I know all this, and it makes me very nervous. It is not so much that I'm anxious that others may make fun of this enterprise. Much more nervous-making is the suspicion that my own sense of the ridiculous will make it impossible for me to proceed for very long. How can one take apart something that is so fragile? Or hold up for scrutiny what is inherently fugitive? Is it not ludicrous to expect that, after having thoroughly *examined the structure of comic experience*, one will with a serious face declare to the world *what it is*? In (probably futile) self-defense—and that means, mainly, defending myself against my own sense of humor—let me say at the outset: I have no such expectation. Also, as will become clearer later on, I would have to be mad to hold such an expectation, for, if I'm right in my intuitions about the comic, if I could ever say, *This* is what it is, I would be in possession of the innermost secret of existence. The comic, because of its elusive nature, can only be approached both circumspectly and circuitously. One must be very, very careful, or the thing will break before one's eyes. One cannot attack it directly, one must go around it, round and round, again and again. Perhaps then it will not be frightened away. Perhaps then it will stand still long enough to yield a slightly better glimpse of what it may be underneath its many guises. This much I can say with great assurance: No certainties will emerge from this particular exploration.

> Around the turn of the century a newly ordained rabbi was sent out from his yeshiva on the lower East Side of New York to become the first rabbi to minister to a congregation in Alaska. His old teacher bid him farewell, blessed him, and said, "And remember, my son, always remember—life is like a cup of tea."
>
> The young rabbi went out to Alaska, and he was very busy there, but every now and again he would think of what his teacher had said, and he would wonder what this saying meant. After seven years his congregation let him take a vacation. He went back to New York, visited the yeshiva, and went to see his old teacher. "I've always wanted to ask you this," he said. "When I left the yeshiva, when you gave me your blessing, you said to me—'life is like a cup of tea.' Tell me rebbe, what did you mean?"
>
> "Life is like a cup of tea?" asked the old man. "I said this?"
>
> "Yes, you did. What did you mean?"
>
> The old man thought for a while, then he said, "*Nu*, maybe life is *not* like a cup of tea."

There is an, as it were, Hinduized version of the same story. The difference is nuanced, but the nuance makes it worth telling.

This young American was traveling in India, looking for the meaning of existence. He was told that way up there, on one of the most inaccessible peaks of the Himalayas, there was a holy man who was supposed to know the answer. The young American spent many weeks wandering, enduring great hardship, and finally reached the place where the holy man resided. There he was, sitting immobile, his eyes fixed on the distant peak of Mount Everest.

"My name is John P. Shulze," said the young American. "I'm from Cleveland, Ohio, and I'm looking for the meaning of existence. I'm told that you know. Can you tell me?"

The holy man, without moving his gaze from the distant peak of Mount Everest, intoned solemnly, "Life is like the lotus flower."

The young American said nothing, pondering this profound saying. There was a long silence. Then a slight frown crossed the holy man's brow. He looked away from the distant mountain and, in a worried tone, said to the young American, "Do you have any other suggestions?"

And this story leads, for whatever reason, to another. It is not clear that there is any connection.

Mrs. Shapiro, from Brookline, Massachusetts, was also traveling in the Himalayas, in search of a holy man who lived on one of the most inaccessible peaks of that mighty mountain chain. After many weeks of travel, enduring great hardship, she finally reached that place. A young disciple of the holy man received her and told her, "The holy man is very busy. Today is Tuesday. He can see you on Friday, at three in the morning. In the meantime you can stay here in this cave."

Mrs. Shapiro stayed in the cave from Tuesday evening until very early Friday morning. It was very cold, she had to sleep on the ground, and there was nothing to eat except for wild berries and churned yak milk. On Friday, just before three in the morning, the young disciple came to pick her up. He led her to another cave. And there sat the holy man. Mrs. Shapiro went right up to him. She said, "Marvin, come home!"

I have told three jokes. Two of them are Jewish and the third one, if one may put it this way, has a Jewish undertone. This should not be surprising. Some of the best jokes are Jewish. Much has been written about Jewish humor. Why are there so many Jewish jokes? There are many reasons that can be given. Historical reasons: jokes are stories that must be cleverly told, and Jewish culture (for profoundly religious reasons) is probably the most verbal in human history. Psychological reasons: jokes relieve suffering, and what people have endured more suffering over the centuries than the Jews? Sociological reasons: through much of their history the Jews have existed on the margins of societies, and marginality makes for a comic perspective. And then there is the most profound reason, a theological one: the Jews are the people who have invented God (or, if you will, who have discovered Him—or, if you really will to think theologically, whom He has invented). But *that* is a story that will come much later in these ruminations.

Come to think of it, I have now adumbrated most of the major themes with which I intend to deal in this book. As I go round and round my effervescent topic, I must discuss some history, some psychology, some sociology, and in the end I will find myself asking some theological questions. Perhaps I should stop right now, stop with the adumbrations. The joke would then be on me, certainly not on the reader, for then there would be no reader. A Chinese sage is reputed to have said, "If you have a choice, it is better that the joke be on someone other than yourself." I take this as an encouragement to go on.

Though I cannot resist the temptation to tell yet one more Jewish story. It is a classical one, which was alluded to in the title of the late Irving Howe's autobiography.

> In the old days, somewhere in Eastern Europe, a traveler arrived in a *shtetl* in the middle of winter. There, outside the synagogue, an old man sat on a bench, shivering in the cold.
>
> "What are you doing here?" asked the traveler.
>
> "I'm waiting for the coming of Messiah."
>
> "That is indeed a very important job," said the traveler. "I suppose that the community pays you a good salary?"
>
> "No, not at all," said the old man. "They don't pay me anything. They just let me sit on this bench. Once in a while someone comes out and gives me a little food."
>
> "That must be very hard for you," said the traveler. "But even if they don't pay you anything, surely they must honor you for undertaking this important task?"
>
> "No, not at all," said the old man. "They all think that I'm crazy."
>
> "I don't understand this," said the traveler. "They don't pay you. They don't respect you. You sit out here in the cold, shivering, hungry. What kind of a job is this?"
>
> The old man replied: "It's *steady work.*"

# I

# Anatomy of the Comic

# 1

## The Comic Intrusion

As we begin our circling around the phenomenon of the comic, a number of general questions at once suggest themselves: What is it? Where is it? How is it used? What does it mean? Given our circuitous approach (which is, or so it seems, dictated by the nature of the phenomenon), it will not be advisable to attempt answers to these questions in a rigorously systematic way. But it does make sense to make a preliminary stab, at least, at tackling the first question: What *is* this thing we are talking about?

An English-speaking individual with a measure of higher education is likely to start by taking out that great philological monument, the *Oxford English Dictionary*. Even if one is not interested at the moment in the ways a word has been used all the way back to *Beowulf* and the *Canterbury Tales*, one hopes at any rate to get an idea of current usage from the OED. Here, then, are some relevant definitions. Under *comic*: "Calculated to excite mirth, intentionally funny." And a second definition: "Unintentionally provocative of mirth; laughable, ludicrous." This seems a bit awkward: Why not simply say that the comic is something that, whether intentionally or not, is perceived as funny? In any case, this does not get one very far. Not to put too fine a point to it, what is really said here is that the funny is something that is seen to be funny. Then under *humor*: "That quality of action, speech or writing, which excites amusement, oddity, jocularity, facetiousness, comicality, fun." And a B definition: "The faculty of perceiving what is ludicrous or amusing, or of expressing it in speech, writing, or other composition; jocose imagination or treatment of subject." Added to these wonderfully imprecise if not circular definitions is the curious comment: "Distinguished from wit as being less purely intellectual, and as having a sympathetic quality in virtue of which it often becomes allied to pathos."

This does take one a little further. It makes a useful distinction between a *quality* of certain human realities and the *faculty* of perceiving that quality. Phenomenologists get at the same distinction by talking about the *noematic* and the *noetic* aspects of a phenomenon. The distinction will be useful later on in these ruminations, as it will protect against the confusion of the comic phenomenon as such with its physiological foundations or its social-psychological functions. The OED also makes clear that the comic (or, as here, the "humorous") can be found in actions, in speech, or in written materials. Beyond that, one is again left with a good deal of confusion. What is the difference between *jocularity* and *facetiousness*? Between *comicality* and *fun*? One would think that *comic* and *humorous* are synonyms in their adjectival form. Or perhaps one might say that the sense of humor is that faculty which perceives the comic (or, if one prefers, comicality). One could go on. *Comedy:* "That branch of the drama which adopts a humorous or familiar style, and depicts laughable characters and incidents." *Joke:* "Something said or done to excite laughter or amusement; a witticism, a jest; jesting, raillery; also, something that causes amusement, a ridiculous circumstance." One *could* go on; I think not.

I have been using the second edition (1991) of the Compact OED. That is the one that weighs a ton, or so it seems, and that one can only read with the help of a magnifying glass thoughtfully provided by the publisher. After quite a short time one's eyes hurt; at least mine did. The discomfort provoked a fantasy. I have no idea how the OED is composed. I imagine that there must be committees of scholars. Do they meet? I visualize them as small groups of fussy dons, the men in frayed tweed jackets, the women wearing sensible shoes, all staying within walking distance of the British Museum in one of those splendidly uncomfortable bed-and-breakfast places in Bloomsbury. Would there be a committee on mirth and jocularity? If so, is it too fanciful to think that these people, indulging in the witty malice that is at the core of the English academic ethos, might play some jokes of their own? "We'll show those bloody Americans who buy the OED . . . " Chuckle, chuckle . . .

Let us, for now, shelve the question of just what the comic is. Inevitably, we will have to return to it. Instead, let us turn to the second question that suggested itself: *Where* is it? Or more precisely: Where amid the vast panoply of human experiences does the comic manifest itself? In approaching this question, one can employ a useful distinction made by Max Weber in the case of religion: he distinguished between the religion of the "virtuosi" and that of the "masses" (such as, for instance, between the Catholicism of Teresa of Avila and that of the ordinary people showing up for mass on Sunday morning). A similar distinction can usefully be made here. There are "virtuosi" of the comic—not just great comic writers (Aristophanes, Shakespeare, Molière, etc.), but great jesters and clowns and stand-up comedians, or the great joke-tellers such as once inhabited the coffeehouses of Central

Europe. But there is also the comic of the "masses," and this is what we should look at first.

As soon as we do this, we are struck by one overwhelmingly evident fact: *The comic is ubiquitous in ordinary, everyday life.* Not all the time, of course, but weaving in and out of ordinary experience. And it is not the virtuosi of the comic that we have in mind here, but quite ordinary people—specimens, if you will, of *l'homme comique moyen.* Let us visualize a day in the life of such people—we will call them John and Jane Everyperson, an ordinary American couple. They wake up in the morning. John is one of those people who wake up instantly, jump out of bed, and are ready to go. Jane is of the other kind, the one who wakes up slowly, reluctantly, not out of laziness but because waking reality seems quite implausible as she reencounters it. She wakes up, sees John prancing about (perhaps he does morning push-ups, or perhaps he is just purposefully going about his *toilette* and the serious task of getting dressed), and the sight seems quite ludicrous. Perhaps she laughs, or perhaps she suppresses laughter out of marital delicacy (after all, this absurdly active individual has just emerged from *her* bed and is *her* husband), but the fact is that the first conscious thought in her mind that day is a perception of the comic. John, let us assume, comes to the comic a little more slowly (activists usually do). But he does make a joke at breakfast, perhaps about the toast he has just burned, or about the couple in the adjacent apartment (the walls are thin) who can once again be heard making love in the early morning. Then the Everypersons' young children come in, pretending to be the monsters they saw on a television show last night, and now everyone is laughing. Then John and Jane read the newspaper; he laughs at a cartoon; she makes a sarcastic comment about the latest folly of the government. All these expressions of the comic—and, mind you, they haven't even finished breakfast yet!

It would not be difficult to pursue them in equal detail throughout the day. John's boss engages in heavy, sadistic irony in berating a subordinate at a staff meeting; in revenge, John and his colleagues enact a parody of the boss safely while he is away during lunch. Jane is blessed (or afflicted) with colleagues at work who are compulsive joke-tellers; during their lunch hour they vie with each other in this activity: "Have you heard this one?" "I think I can top yours!" "Do you know the latest Al Gore story?" And so on. Perhaps Jane has her own jokes to tell; perhaps she is that wish fulfillment of every compulsive joke-teller—the patient listener who always laughs when the punch line comes, because she has forgotten the joke although she has heard it before more than once. In either case, she participates in yet another experience of what our OED authors would call jocularity. Needless to say, the afternoon and the evening are not immune to these reiterated appearances of the comic. Perhaps John and Jane spend the evening actually attending a performance by one of the currently available virtuosi of the comic—a Woody Allen movie, say, or a Jackie Mason show. Without going into any further details, it is clear that the comic appears and reappears throughout their waking hours. It is even conceivable that one of them *dreams* of a joke, laughs in the dream, and then wakes up laughing.

Unless John and Jane are philosophically inclined, they have probably never reflected on the nature of the comic. They recognize it when they see it, at least most of the time (once in a while their sense of humor deserts them), and at least within their own sociological context (we can leave aside for the moment the problem they would encounter in recognizing humor if they were suddenly transported into a very different context—say, a Chinese village where a group of peasants are telling each other funny stories). To say that they recognize the comic when they see it is to say that there is a sector of reality that, in their perception, is separated from other sectors, precisely the sector of the comic, to which laughter is the most appropriate response. This sector may be entered for an extended period of time, as on the occasion of watching a comedy film or attending the performance of a comedian, or even of participating in a protracted joke-telling session (these are the times when they may observe that their jaws are beginning to hurt from laughing). Mostly, however, this comic sector is less long-lasting, momentary, even fugitive. Recognizably different though it is, it weaves in and out of the rest of reality as experienced in the course of the day. A joke is told in the midst of a conversation about, say, business matters; having told the joke, the individual may return to the previous topic by saying something like, "But now, *seriously*." At the same business meeting one of the participants suddenly burps audibly; the others are amused by this eruption of incongruous physicality amid the serious activity of negotiating a multimillion-dollar contract; but precisely because the business at hand is so serious, they quickly suppress their sense of humor.

In ordinary, everyday life then, the comic typically appears as an *intrusion*. It intrudes, very often unexpectedly, into other sectors of reality. These other sectors are colloquially referred to as serious. By implication, then, the comic is unserious. We will later on have reason to question this interpretation of the ontological status of the comic; indeed, we may even dare to propose that the comic is the most serious perception of the world there is. For the moment, though, let the conventional distinction stand: The comic is posited as an antithesis to serious concerns. This perception of an antithesis is commonly expressed when people are trying to take the edge off a humorous observation that might offend, when the joke has "gone too far." The conventional formula by which this is done is the statement, "But it was only a joke!" Put differently, "This was not meant to be taken seriously!" Those to whom this explanation is made—that is, those who were the butts of the joke—are then expected to acknowledge that no offense was intended and that none is taken. If they make this concession *grudgingly,* they implicitly testify to the fact that the conventional line between serious and unserious discourse is not as clear as is generally assumed. In other words, they are probably correct in suspecting that the joke that "went too far" touched a raw reality and therefore is much more than *only* a joke.

In trying to become clearer about the empirical location of the comic, we can make use of two authors, Alfred Schutz and Johan Huizinga, a philosopher and a historian, respectively. Neither was particularly concerned about the comic as such, but some of their ideas can be helpful at this juncture of our reflections.

One of Schutz's major contributions was his delineation of different sectors of what human beings experience as reality, most succinctly in his essay "On Multiple Realities."[1] He was particularly interested in the relation between the reality of ordinary, everyday life, which he called the "paramount reality," and those enclaves within the latter, which he called "finite provinces of meaning." The reason for the first term is quite clear: This reality is paramount because it is the one that, most of the time, is most real to us—in his words, "the world of daily life which the wide-awake, grown-up man who acts in it and upon it amidst his fellow-men experiences within the natural attitude as a reality."[2] The second term is less felicitous; perhaps Schutz would have been better advised to use a term of William James, which he cites in the beginning of his essay—"subuniverses." In any case, finite provinces of meaning or subuniverses are experienced as the individual temporarily "emigrates" from the paramount reality of everyday life. The latter is perceived, most of the time, as most real because it is the reality within which we engage in actions with palpable consequences and which we share with the largest number of other human beings. Its accent of reality is strongest and most enduring, so that the other zones of experience exist, so to speak, as islands within it. Yet these other experiences, while they are attended to, have their own "accent of reality." As one shifts from the paramount reality to one of the finite provinces of meaning and then back again, each transition is experienced as a kind of shock. Examples of such finite provinces of meaning are the worlds of dreams, of the theater, of any intense esthetic experience (say, of being drawn into a painting or a piece of music), of a child's playing, of religious experience, or of the scientist engaged in a passionate intellectual pursuit. And, indeed, Schutz gives an additional example (not elaborated upon): ". . . . relaxing into laughter if, in listening to a joke, we are for a short time ready to accept the fictitious world of the jest as a reality in relation to which the world of our daily life takes on the character of foolishness."[3]

Is the comic a finite province of meaning in Schutz's sense, and if so, how does it differ from other finite provinces of meaning?

Each finite province of meaning, according to Schutz, has a number of characteristics: A specific "cognitive style," different from that of everyday life; a consistency within its specific boundaries; an exclusive sense of reality, which cannot be readily translated into that of any other finite province of meaning or of the paramount reality, so that one can only enter or leave it by means of a "leap" (here Schutz employs the term of Kierkegaard to denote the passage from unbelief into religious faith); a different form of consciousness or attentionality; a specific suspension of doubt (or *epoché,* to use the phenomenological term); also, specific forms of spontaneity, of self-experience, of sociality, and of time perspective (here Schutz uses Henri Bergson's term *durée*).

These characteristics may at first seem overly abstract. Let us concretize by applying them to what is perhaps the most universal finite province of meaning—the world of dreams. As we dream, we are clearly moving in a world whose rules are radically different from those of awake everyday life; a different logic prevails, as it were. Things that are impossible in the one world are taken for granted in the other. For example, we can be in two places simultaneously, we can enter another person's thoughts, we can move forward and backward in time, we can communicate with dead people. Yet all these things, which would be dismissed as illusions in the paramount reality, are experienced in a matter-of-course, taken-for-granted way in the world of a dream. While it lasts, the dream is real, indeed *more* real than the awake world; we suspend doubt for its duration. We move spontaneously in this dream world, as if we had always known it. And, obviously, our sense of self, of other people, and of time differs sharply from the manner in which these exist in the awake world. Most revealingly, the transition from one world to the other is experienced as a sort of shock, or leap. This becomes very evident in the experience of waking up from an intense dream. We then return to reality in distinctive stages, the reality at issue being, of course, precisely the paramount reality of everyday life; as we leap out of the dream, the contours of the everyday world at first appear unreal—the bed on which we lie, the furniture of the bedroom, the plans for the day ahead. We may then engage in various more or less ritualized activities in order to shift back the accent of reality to this other world. We look at the clock to see what time it is (it is morning in the "real world"; it was evening in the dream). We look out of the window (this is Boston; in the dream it was Vienna). We get up, get something to eat perhaps, speak with someone in person or on the telephone (this is my wife here, not the dead grandfather in my dream). And so on. Gradually or quickly, depending on temperament, the paramount reality reasserts itself (Jane Everyperson, as we have seen, returns gradually; John manages the transition in one energetic jump). If all goes well, by breakfast time the reality of the dream will have faded and the clamorous world of everyday life (newspaper, noisy children, the agenda for the day) will have reasserted itself. We may then (though sometimes it is difficult to put into words) tell others about our dream. But we will reassure them and ourselves that it was, after all, only a dream.

Both the similarities and the differences between the reality of dreaming and of the comic are readily evident. One can compare a dream with, say, a joke that may itself have a certain dreamlike quality. Imagine a dissident in the former Soviet Union, who has a dream in which he tells off the most powerful Communists—a case of wish fulfillment par excellence. Then, later on that day, he sits with a group of fellow dissidents and tells an anti-Communist joke. Soviet-dominated Europe was a great producer of jokes, as oppressive political situations often are (we will have occasion later on to look at the political uses of humor). The following is taken, more or less at random, from a rich reservoir of such jokes:

> Gorbachev wakes up and looks out of the window at the sun.
> "Good morning, sun," he says. "Do you have a message for me?"
> "Yes, Comrade President," replies the sun. "It is dawn over the Soviet Union."
> At midday Gorbachev looks out of the window again and says, "Well, sun, do you have another message for me?"
> "Yes, Comrade President," says the sun. "It is high noon over the Soviet Union."
> In the evening Gorbachev looks out once more and asks the same question.
> The sun replies, "I'm in the West now. Go to hell, Mike!"

The similarities are there: Both the dream and the joke are enclosed worlds within which the reality of everyday Soviet life is suspended. Different logics apply, both in society and in nature—the docile citizen becomes a defiant rebel, a man can converse with the sun. The categories of time and space, the relation to oneself and to others, are all different. And there is the shock upon reentering the world of everyday life. The dissident wakes up, looks at his watch, has breakfast, reads the newspaper (the same old *Pravda*—alas), and the massive reality of everyday life in the Soviet Union reasserts itself. His rebellious encounter with the regime was, unfortunately, only a dream. Similarly, having told his joke, the dissident finds himself jolted back to the paramount reality. A likely side effect of this shock is the sudden suspicion that one of the listeners may be an informer. He may then laugh apologetically and say, "Of course, this is only a joke." This may or may not impress the authorities to whom the informer reports.

But there are also differences: Most obviously, the dream is a solitary experience, the joke-telling a social one. This is related to the fact that the world of the dream is more self-enclosed, with (while it lasts) a stronger accent of reality. The little world of the joke is much more loosely inserted into the world of everyday life, is therefore more fugitive, more vulnerable. Also (though this is less important), the dream is a passive experience, it "happens" to the individual. The joke-telling is a deliberate act; the individual "makes it happen." (This is true in this instance, as in all instances of joke-telling; it is less important for a general understanding of the comic, because there are many instances where the comic also happens to an individual, where it, so to speak, overcomes the individual just as a dream does.)

Take one more example, this time a joke with no obvious political content (though, conceivably, it could have political undertones in certain situations):

> This optimist has died and wakes up in hell. It turns out that hell is a vast ocean of feces in which the damned are submerged up to their chins. The optimist looks around and addresses the person next to him who has evidently been around for a longer time: "So, this is what hell is? A big ocean of feces?"
>
> "Yes," says the neighbor. "This is what it is."
>
> The optimist thinks for a moment, then says, "Well, at least we're only buried up to our chins."
>
> At this moment a strange noise is heard in the distance. *Putt-putt. Putt-putt.*
>
> "What is this noise?" asks the optimist.
>
> His neighbor replies, "*That* is the devil in his motorboat."

Here, indeed, is all the stuff for a nightmare—death, hell, an ocean of feces, being buried, the devil. The aforementioned similarities and differences between a dream of hell and a joke involving hell pertain here as well, but there is an additional, significant difference. The dream of hell, we may assume, is one of pure terror. In the joke, however, the terror is, as it were, suspended or bracketed. The joke has a benign quality that the nightmare absolutely lacks. Perhaps this is the "sympathetic quality" mentioned in their description of humor by the OED lexicographers chuckling away in their Bloomsbury bed-and-breakfast.

One may say now that there are different types of finite provinces of meaning, the difference consisting in the degree of emigration from the reality of everyday life. The dream is probably the most completely enclosed type, the dreamer having emigrated completely from the paramount reality. It is not possible to be simultaneously awake and asleep (though, of course, in the transition there are intermediate stages). There are experiences of the comic that have a very similar quality—for example, sitting in a darkened theater and being completely absorbed in the comedy being enacted on the stage. Most of the time, however, the comic is experienced in a less total, less enclaved manner. It appears within everyday life, momentarily transforms the latter, then quickly disappears again. It may even be a sort of "subtext" within everyday life, a *pianissimo* accompaniment to the "serious" themes to which one must attend in the "real world." The comic, then, definitely constitutes a finite province of meaning in a Schutzian sense, but it is a finite province of meaning with quite distinctive traits.

It may be further useful to compare the experience of the comic with two other realms of experience that also, clearly, constitute finite provinces of meaning—the experiences of the esthetic and of sexuality. They too are capable of creating realities that, for a time, are exclusive and fully enclosed. Thus one may be totally absorbed in esthetic contemplation or in a particularly intense sexual scene. Schutz (who was from Vienna, that most theatrical of cities) liked to refer to the experience of the theatergoer; As the lights go out and the curtain rises, the reality of everyday life fades away and what goes on up there on the stage seems to be the only reality there is. And as the curtain falls and the lights go on again, one returns to the allegedly more real world, typically in stages. *Mutatis mutandis* (the nontheatergoer might be tempted to exclaim, *"vive la difference!"*), the same might be said of an intense sexual experience: The clothes come off, and for a while there seems to be nothing more real than what the two (or the several) naked bodies are doing to each other. As the clothes are put back on again, or even earlier, the reality of everyday life will reassert itself in its full nonsexual repertoire of themes and roles. This is not to say that these two "worlds of phantasms" (Schutz's phrase) may not be rudely interrupted. There may be a fire alarm in the theater, or an irritated neighbor may bang on the wall of the love nest. Indeed, a sudden eruption of one's sense of humor may critically disturb either experience and suddenly deprive it of its unique reality: One of the actors on the stage may forget his lines and utter a hilarious spoonerism, or one of the participants in the orgy may slip and fall off the bed. But, after all, even the most intense dream can be suddenly interrupted by something that happens in the real world.

All the same, what the comic has in common with esthetic and sexual

experience is precisely the aforementioned fugitive or subtextual quality. In the middle of a business negotiation one may suddenly be overcome by the beauty of the view from the window and, for a moment, the
serious business at issue may fade out. Similarly, one may find oneself
mentally undressing the person with whom one is negotiating this particular business transaction and, for a moment, this angle on the situation may be more interesting than the business deal being negotiated.
The serious business person will, of course, quickly suppress these situ-
ationally irrelevant intrusions and return attention to the ongoing negotiation. Still, there are unserious individuals who will forget themselves
and give in to their esthetic or erotic impulses; such individuals (unless,
perhaps, they are already at the very top) are unlikely to have a brilliant
business career.

Like the esthetic and the sexual realities, the reality of the comic can
relate to everyday life in nuanced ways. It may lead one to escape
everyday life, for a moment at least, perhaps for longer periods of time,
in some cases permanently. It may also challenge the reality of everyday
life; the example of the political joke (subversive by definition) well
illustrates this possibility. Also, it may even enhance everyday life if it
appears in a nuanced, moderate form: A light joke may actually facilitate
the ongoing business negotiation, as may the esthetically pleasing decor
of the board room or the mild *frisson* of sexual attraction. In these cases,
of course, the comic, the esthetic, and the sexual are experienced in a
highly controlled, domesticated form. They are not allowed to interfere
with the mundane business at hand. The mores and manners of society
are always available for such containment. The paramount reality of
everyday life always defends itself against the ever-present danger of
being swept away by those other realities lurking behind its facades. In
this sense, the comic, the esthetic, and the sexual realities are always, at
least potentially, subversive. If allowed to emerge in their full force, they
are capable of inundating the serious concerns of everyday life with their
alien logics. The artist and the libertine are potentially dangerous figures; so is the virtuoso of the comic. But, of course, the danger of
subversion is mutual. Everyday life is threatened by the finite provinces
of meaning; conversely, it in turn poses a constant danger to the fragile
reality of every finite province of meaning. In the normal course of
events, everyday life is the stronger party.

Before we conclude this preliminary exploration of the comic intrusion into everyday life, we may usefully compare the comic with a
related but distinct phenomenon that is also seen as antithetical to
seriousness—the phenomenon of play. On this we can use as a guide
the by-now classic work *Homo Ludens* by the Dutch historian Johan
Huizinga.[4]

Huizinga's book proposes a daring and far-reaching thesis, namely, that all human culture, beginning with language, has its origin in play. This thesis, convincing or not, does not have to preoccupy us here. But Huizinga's delineation of the ludic phenomenon is so close to our present topic that we ought to take it into account. From the beginning of his argument Huizinga insists on the autonomous, the *sui generis* quality of play. He actually starts out by comparing play with laughter and the comic, then insists that it is different from either: Play does not usually provoke laughter among either the players or any possible spectators, and there is usually nothing funny about people at play. But neither does play fit under other categories of human experience: "Play lies outside the antithesis of wisdom and folly, and equally outside those of truth and falsehood, good and evil. Although it is a non-material activity it has no moral function. The valuations of vice and virtue do not apply here."[5] And, Huizinga adds, play is also different from esthetic experience, though there are some affinities. For our purposes, though, Huizinga's most important observations are to the effect that, if one were to use the Schutzian category once more, play is clearly a finite province of meaning to which individuals can emigrate from the reality of everyday life: "Play is not "ordinary" or "real" life. It is rather a stepping out of "real" life into "a temporary sphere of activity with a disposition all of its own." It is "an intermezzo, an *interlude* in our daily life." And again: "Play is distinct from "ordinary" life both as to locality and duration. This is the third main characteristic [after the previously mentioned ones of freedom and disinterestedness] of play; its secludedness, its limitedness. It is "played out" within certain limits of time and place. It contains its own course and meaning."[6]

The similarities with the comic are obvious. The comic too is an *interlude*—literally, an in-between playing or in-between game. In between *what*? Well, clearly, in between the serious, mundane activities of everyday life. This quality, as Huizinga develops at great length, applies to all forms of play, from the simplest to the most complex—a child playing alone with some pebbles or with toys, a group of children playing a game together (Jean Piaget and George Herbert Mead have shown how crucial such playing is in the socialization process), and adults playing any number of games—poker or chess, soccer or baseball, all the way to the sacred games of religious and political ritual. In every one of these activities the players step out of ordinary life into a separate reality with its own logic, rules, distribution of roles, and coordinates of space and time. As the players reenter ordinary life—say, winners and losers shake hands—they may also say, as after a dream or a joke, "It was only a game."

But the dissimilarities are also important. Perhaps most important: The comic is more exclusively human than play. Animals play; animals do not laugh or joke. Also, *homo ludens* has a greater capacity to create an enclosed reality than *homo ridens*. To repeat the terms we have used before, the comic is more fugitive, more interwoven with the fabric of everyday life; conversely, play is less likely to be a subtle subtext, rather requires a more deliberate separation from ordinary activities. Playing, it seems, must always be deliberately initiated (this is what Huizinga means by its freedom); it is made to happen. The comic can also be deliberately constructed, as in the telling of a joke or the staging of a comedy, but very often it simply happens to or befalls the individual. Conceivably, the experience of the comic is rooted in the human propensity to play. It may even be describable as a form of playfulness, but if so, it is a very distinctive form. Perhaps this distinctiveness is disclosed by the fact that only human beings laugh, while they share with animals the capacity to play. Finally and very significantly, while there are perceptions of all sorts involved in playing, the latter remains primarily *a form of action*. By contrast, while the comic may be represented by specific acts, it is primarily *a form of perception*, a uniquely human one. The comic is perceived as the perception of an otherwise undisclosed dimension of reality—not just of its own reality (as a player perceives the reality of a game), but of reality as such. The comic intrusion is the occurrence of this perception in every possible realm of experience.

The comic is an exclusively human phenomenon. It is also universally human. It goes without saying that the experience of the comic differs as between human cultures. To paraphrase Pascal, what is funny on one side of the Pyrenees is not funny on the other side. The same can be said, though, of esthetic experience or sexual attractiveness, and indeed (as the original statement by Pascal had it) of convictions of truth and error. This cultural relativity of the comic experience is important, but it tells us little if anything about the cognitive validity of its alleged perception. And it leaves us with the question we shelved some pages back: the question of just what it is that is supposedly perceived.

## Notes

1. Alfred Schutz, "On Multiple Realities," in *Collected Papers,* Vol. I (The Hague: Nijhoff, 1962), 207ff.
2. Ibid., 208.
3. Ibid., 231.
4. Johan Huizinga, *Homo Ludens: A Study of the Play-Element in Culture* (Boston: Beacon, 1955).
5. Ibid., 6.
6. Ibid., 8f.

# 2

# Philosophers of the Comic, and the Comedy of Philosophy

The history of Western philosophy begins with a joke: This is only a slight exaggeration. In the dialogue *Theaetetus*, Plato puts the following anecdote into the mouth of Socrates:

> [T]he jest which the clever witty Thracian handmaid is said to have made about Thales, when he fell into a well as he was looking up at the stars. She said that he was so eager to know what was going on in heaven that he could not see what was before his feet.[1]

And Plato adds the observation that this mockery applies to anyone who gets involved in philosophy. Actually, the anecdote has an earlier version. Plato took it from Aesop's *Fables*, where the fall is attributed to an anonymous astronomer. But why Thales? And is there any reason why the handmaid (who, in some versions of the story, is described as being pretty as well as clever) should be from Thrace?

Attributing the prototypical pratfall to Thales places it at the very dawn of Greek philosophy. Thales of Miletus was one of the early pre-Socratics, living from the mid–seventh to the mid–sixth century B.C.E. Herodotus puts him at the top of his list of Seven Sages. Thales is known, among other things, for his belief that water is the primal element and for his statement that the world is full of gods. He predicted a solar eclipse in 585 B.C.E., a feat that, no doubt, necessitated a lot of sky-gazing. If Plato wanted to suggest that the philosophical enterprise lends itself to being laughed at, he could not have chosen a better philosopher to make his point. It is less clear why the clever (and, one would like to think, pretty) handmaid should come from Thrace. Unencumbered by the weight of classical scholarship, one may speculate. Thrace, it so happens, is the land where the cult of Dionysus is supposed to have originated. If this speculative interpretation is given credence, the little anecdote confronts the protophilosopher with the proto-comedian, throwing light on the origins of Greek comedy as well as Greek philosophy.

Classical scholars, of course, disagree about almost anything. But there is widespread agreement to the effect that both comedy and tragedy originated in the cult of Dionysus.[2] The former, one may suppose, has the more profound Dionysian roots. Aristotle states that the word *comedy* derives from *komodia*, the song of the *komos*, which was the frenzied crowd participating in the Dionysian rites. Classical literature is full of descriptions of these rites—ecstatic, orgiastic, violating all conventional decencies in both words and deeds, and for all these reasons eminently dangerous. Dionysus is the god who violates all ordinary boundaries, as do his devotees, who become satyr-like creatures, a grotesque hybrid of humans and animals. Comedy retains these Dionysian features, even when in later times they are toned down—domesticated or defanged, as it were. The comic experience is ecstatic, if not in the archaic sense of a frenzied trance, in a mellower form of *ek-stasis*, "standing outside" the ordinary assumptions and habits of everyday life. The comic experience is orgiastic, if not in the old sense of sexual promiscuity, in the metaphorical sense of joining together what convention and morality would keep apart. It debunks all pretensions, including the pretensions of the sacred. The comic, therefore, is dangerous to all established order. It must be controlled, contained in some sort of enclave. It could be said that comedy as a performing art is already such a containment of the comic experience, ritualizing it in socially acceptable forms and confining it within the boundaries of the dramatic stage. The spectators laugh in the theater, and that may keep them from laughing in and laughing *at* the solemn performances of religion and the state.

In Greek mythology and religion, Dionysus, the god of darkness and primeval passions, is commonly counterposed to Apollo, to the god of sunlight and reason. This counterposition was made famous in modern philosophy by Nietzsche, in *The Birth of Tragedy out of the Spirit of Music*, and Nietzsche's distinction between the Dionysian and Apollonian elements in human culture has been widely applied. Yet the two gods, though opposites, are also linked—as are comedy and tragedy. It was at Delphi, Apollo's principal sanctuary, that Dionysian rites were incorporated into the worship of the god of sunny reasonableness.[3] It is not difficult to imagine how this might have come about; indeed, it is possible to imagine how a piquant comedy could be written around this event. Imagine the priests engaged in the decorous ceremonies honoring the presiding deity of the Delphi sanctuary, and then imagine their annoyance whenever a Dionysian *komos* would barge in and disrupt the orderly proceedings with its obscene shrieks and ecstatic convulsions. Then one day a wise and somewhat Machiavellian priest had a bright idea. "Look," he said to his colleagues, "we clearly cannot get rid of these terrible people. Let us instead put them on the payroll and give them a safe place in the program." And so the Dionysian comedians were allocated their own slot in the sanctuary's agenda—say, Tuesday and Thursday, from three to five in the afternoon. During those times they could shriek and convulse to their hearts' content, leaving the non-Dionysian staff to go about their serious business the rest of the week. The basic formula here is that incorporation entails containment. It is, by the way, an excellent formula for containing all sorts of revolutionaries, but that is another story.

Both philosophy and comedy came to bloom in fifth-century Athens. Socrates probably lived from 469 to 399 B.C.E.; Aristophanes' first play was performed in 427 (and, of course, Aristophanes had some very nasty things to say about Socrates in a later play). But before comedy was established as a separate dramatic form, it was a part of tragic dramas—if you will, it had its own slot within the tragic program. That slot was a so-called satyr play, Dionysian in style, which followed the tragic performances as a kind of postlude. In the most literal sense of that phrase, it provided comic relief. Relief from what? Well, relief precisely from the utmost seriousness of tragedy. After the tears came laughter. This laughter did not annul or deny the emotions evoked by the tragic spectacle. But presumably it made these emotions more bearable, permitting the spectators to leave the theater and to return to their ordinary pursuits with a modicum of equanimity. Thus the domestication of the comic ecstasy was both psychologically and politically useful.

Given the ubiquity of the comic in human experience, one would expect that philosophers paid a lot of attention to it. Surprisingly, this is not the case—not in Greek philosophy, and not since then. Perhaps this is a case of Thales failing into the well over and over again. Still, the manner in which philosophers have both dealt and failed to deal with the comic experience does help to advance an understanding of the phenomenon. In other words, the present chapter has some justification.

Plato's *Theaetetus* does not primarily deal with the comic; the anecdote about Thales and the Thracian handmaid is more in the nature of an aside. Plato did write another dialogue, the *Philebus*, in which comedy is dealt with at some length.[4] The overall question discussed here is whether a life of pleasure is to be preferred over a life of intelligence; Philebus (literally "Loveboy") argues for the former, Socrates for the latter. The topic of comedy is raised in the context of Socrates' argument that there can be combinations of pleasure and distress. The audiences at both tragedy and comedy enjoy their tears and their laughter. But the pleasure derived from comedy is of a particular kind: it is based on malice, at enjoyment over the misfortune of others. Comedy ridicules those who think that they are richer, stronger, more handsome, or more intelligent than in fact they are, and the audience enjoys these discrepancies. Socrates and Philebus had agreed earlier that malice is a form of distress (not very convincingly, one may say), so that the enjoyment of the audience could be seen as supporting Socrates' view that pleasure and distress can be combined. This issue may not be terribly interesting, but the *Philebus* does point to the debunking theme in the comic experience, a theme that was to arouse enduring interest in later analysts of the phenomenon. The pratfall, as it were, is pointed to as a central element in the comic experience. The notion of malice as underlying the enjoyment of comedy was also to continue in later discussions. Since malice is hardly an admirable quality, this also raises an ethical issue: Is there something morally reprehensible about comic laughter? Plato, it may be said, was obsessed with the importance of order, a most serious business. It stands to reason, then, that he would have his doubts about laughter.

Aristotle had a good deal to say about both tragedy and comedy, mainly in his *Poetics*. Unfortunately, the second book of that work, in which there was an extended treatment of comedy, has been lost (a fact that is made much of in Umberto Eco's novel *The Name of the Rose*). But here is one passage from the extant text of *the Poetics* that, at any rate, gives some clues as to Aristotle's view:

> As for comedy, it is . . . an imitation of men worse than the average; worse, however, not as regards any and every sort of fault, but only as regards one particular kind, the Ridiculous, which is a species of the Ugly. The Ridiculous may be defined as a mistake or deformity not productive of pain or harm to others; the mask, for instance, that excites laughter, is something ugly and distorted without causing pain.[5]

Comedy here is seen as an "imitation" (*mimesis*), that is, as a specific representation of reality. "The Ugly", "mistake", "deformity"—all these terms refer to a basic discrepancy, a rupture in the fabric of reality. The comic representation discloses the discrepancy; again, one may say, the pratfall appears as a primal comic experience. These themes are also present in Plato. Aristotle adds another point: Different from tragedy, comedy allows the contemplation of these aspects of life in a painless manner. Aristotle's idea about the purging quality, the catharsis, of tragedy is well known: tragedy purges its spectators by pity and fear. Did Aristotle believe that there was also a comic catharsis? If so, would it be a purging by pity *without* fear? Eco is not the only one who would like to know. In any case, there is an interesting and probably correct insight here: The comic experience is painless, or at least relatively painless as compared with tragedy, because it undertakes a greater *abstraction* from the empirical reality of human life. Aristotle seems to believe that, because of this, comedy is more harmless than tragedy. If so, in this he would have been in error.

The themes raised by Plato and Aristotle apparently resonated throughout classical antiquity, whenever authors looked at the phenomenon of the comic. Cicero may be taken as representative of this continuity. Here is a key formulation from his treatise on oratory:

> [T]he seat and as it were province of what is laughed at . . . lies in a certain offensiveness and deformity; for these sayings are laughed at solely or chiefly which point out and designate something offensive in an inoffensive manner.[6]

Cicero is concerned with public speaking rather than with the theater (and not only in this treatise; he was, after all, primarily a lawyer and politician), which somewhat shifts the emphasis. Again, though, there is mention of deformity, of an underlying discrepancy. But Cicero's interest in the present context is mainly practical. He advises caution in the use of ridicule by an orator, since it might offend the feelings of his audience in a way that will undermine the intended purpose of the oratory. He discusses a long list of jokes used in speeches by various Roman public figures (most of these jokes require elaborate footnotes to be comprehensible today and very few will be taken as funny by a modern reader). Here once more the ethical question is raised: Are there occasions when one should not use ridicule? Beyond such moral and practical matters, Cicero adds another perspective on the comic phenomenon: The most common kind of joke, he maintains, is when we expect one thing and another is said. Ambiguity, that is, is an important element of the comic. Cicero also discusses what he calls "ironic dissimulation," when one says the reverse of what one means. Cicero would certainly have appreciated the irony in Shakespeare's rendition of Mark Antony's oration on the occasion of Caesar's funeral—"I come to bury Caesar, not to praise him" (though Cicero, a staunch republican of the old Roman type, was hardly in sympathy with Mark Antony's politics).

The classical approach to the comic, essentially sour and troubled by moral scruples, continues in early Christian and medieval thought.[7] Neither the patristic authors nor the scholastics had much good to say about laughter, which was frequently interpreted as a reprehensible diversion from the proper Christian task of weeping over the sins of this world and getting ready for the joys of the next world. Needless to say, this does not mean that there was no laughter and no sense of the comic during all this time. If nothing else (and there was much else), there was the exuberant comic explosion of the carnival, a festival in true apostolic succession from the Dionysian orgy. We will have to look at this later in this book. The Christian philosophers had little to add in this area to the perceptions of their pagan predecessors. It is only with the coming of modernity that some new themes appear in the writings on the comic by Western philosophers.[8]

At the very beginning of the modern era stands a comic masterpiece, Erasmus's *The Praise of Folly.* Itself an extended joke, it takes its form from the medieval carnival, which was also known as the Feast of Fools. The idea of the book occurred to Erasmus in the summer of 1509 while riding across the Swiss Alps on a journey from Italy to England. He wrote the book while staying with his friend Thomas More in London (there is a word play in the title, alluding to More's name—the Greek word for folly is *moria*). Erasmus was ambivalent in his later attitude toward this work, and defended himself against its critics by saying that he did not really mean what he wrote there, that the book was intended to be an innocent jest. If so, the joke was finally on him, since it is this book rather than any other of his many writings that posterity has come to consider his greatest accomplishment.

The book is a long sermon by personified Folly (Stultitia) herself, dressed in the cap and bells of the fool's professional attire. Folly proclaims herself as a divinity, "fountain and nursery of life," and argues at length that all good things in life depend on her. It is through Folly that men can live spontaneously, unreasoningly, and it is only in this way that life can be tolerable. Through the words of Folly (if you will, in her comic perspective), all the pretensions of mankind are unmasked. Erasmus, who had had unpleasant experiences with academics, especially those from the University of Paris, takes particular delight in debunking the pretensions of philosophers and other intellectuals (whom he describes as "those who strive for eternal life by issuing books"):

> People still make much of that celebrated saying of Plato, that the state will be happy when philosophers become kings or kings become philosophers. In fact, if you consult the historians, you will find that no prince ever played a state more than when the scepter fell into the hands of some pseudophilosopher or devotee of literature.[9]

And here is Erasmus's characterization of the philosophers:

> How delightfully they are deluded as they build up numberless worlds; as they measure the sun, the moon, the stars and their orbits as if they were using a ruler and plumb line; as they recite the causes of lightning, winds, eclipses, and other unfathomable phenomena, without the slightest hesitation, as if they were confidential secretaries to Nature herself, the architect of all things, or as if they came to us straight from the council chamber

of the gods. At the same time, Nature has a grand laugh at them and their conjectures. For that they have actually discovered nothing at all is clear enough from this fact alone: on every single point they disagree violently and irreconcilably among themselves. Though they know nothing at all, they profess to know everything.[10]

The same passage goes on to say that these philosophers, who claim to see universal ideas, sometimes cannot see a ditch or a stone in their path. The English translator footnoted this with a reference to Aesop and to the *Theaetetus:* Thales rides—or rather, pratfalls—again.

Folly ranges across a wide swath of human life and thought in her sermon. Much of the satire continues to bite more than four centuries later, and therefore continues to give pleasure. But for the present considerations Erasmus's book is important for another reason: Perhaps for the first time, here is the presentation of what could be called a full-blown *comic worldview*. It is that of a world turned upside down, grossly distorted, and precisely for that reason more revealing of some underlying truths than the conventional, right-side-up view.

Erasmus' modern compatriot, Anton Zijderveld, has pointed to the same worldview in the title of his book on the sociology of the Fool— *Reality in a Looking-Glass* (a work that will be examined later in this book). Erasmus, as it were, summarized and canonized the perceptions of the world that a long line of jesters, court-fools and comic actors has adumbrated before. Perhaps for the first time, Erasmus suggests that the comic experience (which is just what Folly personifies) can provide an alternate and possibly more profound view of the nature of things.

Descartes, whose work falls into the first half of the seventeenth century, is frequently considered to be the first modern philosopher (there are other candidates for this title, but an adjudication of the several claims is hardly the concern of this book). He had some things to say about laughter in his *Passions of the Soul;* they are mildly interesting. Descartes thought that laughter is a kind of physiological malfunction (a view that, with some reformulation, may still be valid today) and that what happened when people laugh is a sudden acceleration in the flow of blood (this may have to be dismissed as erroneous). Somewhat more interesting than Descartes' fanciful physiology is his view of what causes the bodily mishap of laughter: The shock caused when one comes on something surprising and possibly dangerous; he calls this "a surprise of admiration":

> "It is when we encounter an object that surprises us, which we judge to be new or different from things we know or different from what we suppose that it should be. This results in our admiring it and being astonished by it."[11]

This suggests two aspects of the comic experience that were to be elaborated in later interpretations: the distinctive interaction of mind and body in the act of laughing, and the sensation of shock that triggers the act. These are valid insights, whatever the scientific status of Descartes's ideas concerning human physiology.

For whatever reasons, the seventeenth and eighteenth centuries witnessed an explosion of interest in the phenomenon of the comic across Europe. In France this coincided with the appearance of Molière's comedies. The premiere of his *Tartuffe* was performed in Paris in 1664 and was followed by a vociferous controversy. It was attacked as being morally dangerous and harmful to religion, and Catholic circles kept it from the stage for five years. Molière defended himself in the preface to a new edition of the comedy in 1669. The key sentence of this defense stated that "the usefulness of comedy is that it corrects the vices of men."[12] In direct contradiction with the long line of pagan and Christian critics of the comic, there came now a spirited defense of comedy as a moral enterprise.

The classical skepticism as to the moral status of the comic, however, had not disappeared. In England, Thomas Hobbes, in *Human Nature* (1640) and *Leviathan* (1651), had some nasty things to say about laughter. Echoing Plato, he sees laughter as one of man's worst attributes, its purpose being to boost self-esteem at the expense of the less fortunate. This negative view was much criticized, especially by the Earl of Shaftesbury (*An Essay on the Freedom of Wit and Humor*, 1714), who sees wit, if in good taste, as a means of differentiating between truth and falsehood, and between virtue and vice. Wit, therefore, is socially useful, indeed has a philosophical and ethical significance. The debate continued throughout the eighteenth century.[13] In 1776, in *On Laughter and Ludicrous Composition*, James Beattie opined that laughter is caused by "an uncommon mixture of relation and contrariety, exhibited or supposed to be united, in the same assemblage." Laughter, he thought, became increasingly refined—due, among other things, to the increasing influence of women in polite society. This, he believed, was a very good thing. Somewhat earlier, Francis Hutcheson (*Thoughts on Laughter*) put forth what became the key term in the evolving theory of the comic—laughter, he argued, is the response to a perception of *incongruity*.

In the German-speaking world, as in France, the debate was closely related to disagreements over the moral status of comic dramas. Particularly at issue were the popular harlequin (*Hanswurst*) comedies, which derived from the medieval tradition of Folly and provided the occasion for more or less open criticisms of established institutions. Thus in 1770 the Austrian government banned all *Hanswurst* performances in Vienna, with only partial success. But the debate over the moral and political dangers of comedy inevitably led to reflections about the intrinsic nature of the comic. In other words, ethics led to epistemology: Is the comic experience a moral good? But what *is* it in the first place? [14]

Moses Mendelsohn (*Philosophical Writings*, 1761) thought that laughter is caused by the contrast between perfection and imperfection, though he also emphasized the subjectivity in the perception of such contrast—what makes one person laugh, saddens another. Justus Moeser (*Harlequin, or Defense of the Grotesque-Comic,* 1761) saw laughter as a fundamental human need, caused by the spectacle of size without strength:

> A man falls to the ground. Next to him a child also falls. One laughs at the former, because one would attribute strength to his size, enough strength to prevent his fall. By contrast, the child's fall evokes pity. [15]

Kant, who wrote about everything, also wrote about laughter. Significantly, he did so in the context of an esthetic theory, that is, a theory about the nature of the beautiful. This allocation of the comic to the field of esthetics was going to continue in philosophy for a while. It is significant because, however grudgingly, it concedes the epistemological status of the comic experience: It is not just a physiological or psychological process, but also involves a distinct perception of reality. Thus in his *Critique of Judgment* Kant defines beauty as the object of a representation "without concepts." [16] Presumably Kant would not have been happy with this reformulation, but one might say that the comic experience, like esthetic experience (and perhaps as a variant of the latter), provides a perception of reality different from that provided by reason. To use Pascal's famous phrase, the comic would then appear as a form of the "reason of the heart." In his extended discussion of laughter, Kant follows Descartes in describing what he thought to be its physiology. [17] This one may safely omit. He also stresses the medicinal use of laughter: It comes out of a feeling of health, it furthers the business of living (*Lebensgeschaeft*) of the body, and thus shows that the soul can become a physician for the body. But when he gets to the epistemological question—the question of what it is that provokes laughter—Kant expands on Hutcheson's key concept of incongruity: Laughter is caused by the perception of "something contradictory" and (this is Kant's original contribution) by the "sudden transformation of a tense expectation into nothing." To illustrate this "sudden transformation . . . into nothing" (*"ein Affekt aus der ploetzlichen Verwandlung einer gespannten Erwartung in nichts"*), Kant tells a number of stories (or, if you will, jokes):

> An American Indian watches an Englishman open a bottle of ale, which flows out in the form of foam. The Indian cries out in astonishment. When the Englishman asks what there is to be astonished about this, the Indian

replies, "I'm not astonished by the foam coming out of the bottle, but by how you managed to put it into the bottle in the first place."

The heir of a rich relative wants to give him a festive funeral and hires professional mourners. He complains, "The more money I give them to look sad, the happier they look."

Someone tells a story of a man whose hair, because of a great grief, turned gray overnight. Someone else, upon hearing this story, tells another—about a merchant, who returned from India with a ship full of valuable goods, which he had to throw overboard to save the ship in a heavy storm. He was so upset that his wig turned gray overnight.

One may conclude that telling jokes was not a forte of the Sage of Koenigsberg. But he certainly grasped a central element of every joke, and thus possibly of the comic experience in general: A grotesque incongruity, perceived suddenly in the face of a quite different expectation. In the telling of jokes, this perception is delivered in what in English is called the punch line, a phrase that nicely conveys Descartes's idea of the shock that causes laughter. In German the phrase is *die Pointe*—the point at which, in Kant's understanding, the expectation collapses into nothing.

An influential critic of Kant's view of the comic was Jean Paul (*Aesthetics*, 1804), the nom de plume of Jean Paul Richter, a copious author of humorous and satirical works.[18] Jean Paul thought that Kant's view was too narrow: The comic comes not only when a strained expectation is reduced to nothing; the opposite can provoke it—when something suddenly comes out of nothing. But he is also critical of the, as it were, epistemological thrust of the Kantian view. Like Mendelsohn, he stresses the subjectivity of laughter. One man weeps at what another laughs about. The comic always resides in the subject, has no objective status. Still, Jean Paul too cannot avoid altogether the question of what, psychology apart, the comic perception is in itself. It is, he thinks, the contrast between what someone tries to be and what in fact he is. The comic, once again, is understood as an experience of incongruity. Its social usefulness lies in its debunking power. But Jean Paul, unlike all the philosophers, not only analyzed the comic but actually produced comic literature. It should not surprise, then, that he says that finally humor has no purpose beyond itself; it should be enjoyed for itself.

As one looks at the development of this discussion through the seventeenth and eighteenth centuries, one sees how the epistemological question, as to what the comic is in itself, increasingly comes to the fore over and beyond the moral question of what it may be good for. As far as the latter question is concerned, one also discerns an increasingly positive view of the comic as against the pejorative bias of classical antiquity and the Christian tradition. The development of comedy as a dramatic genre in all the major European countries certainly accounts in part for the increasing interest in the comic. It is possible to speculate that there may also be a connection with the emergence of modern consciousness. The genius of modernity (whether one views it as a good or an evil spirit) is to disaggregate, to debunk, to look behind the facades of the social order. This inevitably results in a vision of all sorts of incongruity. The affinity with the comic perspective is plausible.

The gigantic figure of Hegel stands astride the entire history of philosophy in the nineteenth century. What he had to say about the comic, regrettably, is somewhat less than gigantic. He too discussed the phenomenon under the general rubric of esthetics.[19] Comedy, Hegel states, displays a world without substance, and because of this it negates any purposes that may arise within it.[20] It is, as it were, a parallel world— somehow weightless, made of air, in which actions can be lightly begun and just as lightly ended. Hegel differentiates the ridiculous from the comic. The ridiculous is, literally, that which produces laughter, and virtually anything can do that. One may laugh out of benevolent wisdom, or in mockery and contempt, or out of despair. Comic laughter— that is, laughter provoked by the comic—is defined more narrowly. It is the result of actions within that parallel world in which anything can happen:

> Here pretty and worthless purposes are accomplished with an appearance of great seriousness and after elaborate preparations. Yet, after these purposes collapse, their author can rise up from his fall in free cheerfulness, just because his purposes were so negligible that nothing is really lost when they fail.[21]

If one tries to associate this (not exactly weightless) prose with an image, one can easily visualize a clown jumping up after a pratfall. Whether Hegel was *thinking* of a clown or not, the image is helpful in understanding what he intended to convey.

But Hegel also follows what by his time had become a tradition: conceptualizing the comic in terms of incongruity. The comic arises out of contradictions, and these can be of different kinds. Hegel mentions the contradiction between effort and result (this is perhaps the clownish contradiction, between capacity and ambition, between purposes and external accidents). All these are perceived as ridiculous and can lead to a comic resolution (*komische Aufloesung*). Most generally, the comic arises out of the contradiction between human subjectivity and the substance of reality (*das Substantielle*)—if you will, between the real world, which is very heavy indeed, and the light, weightless world to which the human spirit aspires. It is possible, however, that this last sentence overinterprets Hegel (which is not necessarily troubling).

It is a well-known fact (though perhaps a regrettable one) that some people, after being subjected to even a very minor quantity of Hegelian prose, feel urgently in need of comic relief (or, if you will, *komische Aufloesung*). And, speaking of incongruity as a key theme in the philosophers' contemplation of the comic, one may plausibly give some thought to elephants. Since the extinction of the dinosaurs, the elephant has been the largest animal on earth. Its huge size is awe inspiring. But, like all huge things, it becomes comic when confronted by the puny. Man himself, of course, is puny when compared to the elephant. In the following episode, one may speculate that the mouse, a puny animal indeed, stands in for man:

> A mouse meets an elephant. The mouse is male, the elephant female. The elephant is in a good mood and looks down benevolently upon the little mouse, "Hello, little mouse. I am so big and you are so small. That is very funny. I like you, little mouse." The mouse is encouraged by this and. says, "Oh, Miss Elephant. Allow me to tell you a wish I have had for many years. I have always wanted to make love to an elephant. Will you let me?" The elephant laughs uproariously, slaps her hind legs with her trunk, and says, "Why not? Just go ahead, little mouse." The elephant lies down under a coconut tree and accommodates herself to the mouse as best as she can. And the mouse gets busy fulfilling his old wish, amid great efforts. [See Hegel, above, on effort and result, not to mention capacity and ambition.] While the mouse exerts himself, the elephant hardly notices what is going on. Indeed, she falls asleep. But then a gust of wind moves through the trees, a coconut falls off and hits the elephant on the head. She wakes up and exclaims, "Ouch!" Whereupon the mouse says solicitously, "Oh, I'm sorry. Did I hurt you?"

One may also speculate that the discrepancy between mouse and elephant, man and elephant, adumbrates the fundamental discrepancy between man and the elephantine enormity of the universe. In that case, the ambition of the human mind to understand the universe is remarkably akin to that of a mouse wishing to make love to an elephant. Could one think of a better metaphor for the intrinsic incongruity of the philosopher's enterprise?

> There was once an international congress of philosophers. An Indian philosopher is talking to an American: "You Westerners have a completely wrong idea about the universe. You believe that the earth is a globe going around the sun. That is a mistake. The earth is a flat disc supported on the back of an enormous elephant."
> "Very interesting," says the American. "But what supports the elephant?"
> "There is a second elephant underneath the first," says the Indian.
> "And what supports the second elephant?"

"Ah yes, there is a third elephant supporting the third."

And before the American can ask another question, the Indian philosopher says, "My good chap, you may as well face it. There are elephants *all the way.*"[22]

Karl Loewith once characterized nineteenth-century philosophy as the slow decomposition of the gigantic carcass of the Hegelian system. The image is not very attractive, but it is pertinent. According to Loewith, the three principal actors in this drama were Marx, Kierkegaard,and Nietzsche.[23] Of those three, Kierkegaard had most to say about the comic, in observations scattered throughout his opus. Kierkegaard's main interest, of course, was religious, and his particular focus was on irony as a precursor of religious insight. The word *irony* comes from the Greek for dissembling: The ironist plays a game of pretending with his audience. He always means something else than what he says—more than he says, or less so, or at any rate something different. In this sense, almost all of Kierkegaard's opus is an enormous exercise in irony, one work after another appearing under different pseudonyms, each pseudonym representing a different position—a game of masks or, if you will, of peekaboo, behind which the author hides and from which he sporadically reveals himself. Only at the very end of the opus, and indeed of his life, did Kierkegaard emerge from the pseudonymous masks with his passionate attacks on the established church of Denmark, written under his own name.

An important discussion of the comic occurs in the *Concluding Unscientific Postscript*, which appeared under the pseudonym Johannes Climacus.[24] Here are two key formulations:

What lies at the root of both the comic and the tragic . . . is the discrepancy, the contradiction, between the infinity and the finite, the eternal and that which becomes.[25]

The tragic is the suffering contradiction, the comical, the painless contradiction.[26] Both statements recall earlier philosophical formulations that were discussed previously in this chapter. The former statement recalls Pascal's description of man as the midpoint between the infinite and the nothing, and, as with Pascal, the context is clearly religious. The incongruity is, so to speak, cosmic. It is precisely for this reason that the comic can be seen as a sort of antechamber to religious faith.

There is a certain irony in the fact that the latter statement is followed by a long footnote that is a miniessay on the nature of the comic. Should every ironist produce ambiguous texts and put his most developed thoughts into footnotes? This one actually consists of a long list of jokes, each one containing a contradiction that is putatively painless: A child of four turns to a child of three-and-a-half and says patronizingly, "Come now, my little lamb." A man in a restaurant eats salad with his fingers, then says to the waiter, "Ah, I thought it was caviar." A baker says to a poor person, "No, mother, I cannot give you anything; there was another here recently whom I had to send away without giving anything; we cannot give to everybody." Are these stories really painless? Perhaps, but there are situations in which these and similar jokes could illuminate quite painful realities.

For instance, the last of the jokes in the preceding paragraph is reminiscent of a joke told in East Germany at the time of the Communist regime:

> A man enters the haberdashery department of an HO, which was the acronym for government stores. He asks to see some undershirts. "I'm sorry," says the salesperson. "You are in the wrong place. You have to go to the next floor. There they have no undershirts. Down here we have no shirts."

But Kierkegaard was not primarily interested in the nature of jokes. He saw humor as the last existential stage before faith, as a sort of incognito faith. These are insights that will have to be taken up again toward the end of this book. For now, it is enough to point out that Kierkegaard too stands squarely in what can be called the incongruity school in the philosophical treatment of the comic.

Probably the most important philosophical work on the comic in the twentieth century is Henri Bergson's *Laughter* (*Le Rire*), originally published in 1900.[27] Before Bergson gets to his central thesis he discusses a number of important issues connected with the phenomenon. He emphasizes that laughter is a purely human phenomenon. Other animals may evince laughterlike symptoms, but only human beings truly laugh. Specifically, only human beings laugh because someone or something strikes them as funny (apes may grin, but it is unlikely that they do so because they have just heard a good joke). Also, according to Bergson, laughter is a group phenomenon and thus has social functions (this is debatable: surely there is such a thing as solitary amusement—but let that pass for now). More important, Bergson discusses a rather puzzling aspect of the phenomenon: The emotional texture of the comic experience. In order to laugh at what strikes one as funny, one has to curtail whatever strong emotions one might otherwise have in the situation, be it pity, or love, or hatred. Put differently, the comic occurs in a strangely antiseptic sector of perception, purged of emotions, and thus very similar to the mind-set of theoretical contemplation:

> The comic demands something like a momentary anesthesia of the heart. Its appeal is to intelligence pure and simple.[28]

This is a significant observation. It can easily be put in the Schutzian language used in an earlier chapter: The experience of the comic occurs in a finite province of meaning. This entails an abstraction from the meanings that the same events or persons would otherwise have in everyday life. And in that respect, at least, it is similar to what Schutz called the "theoretical attitude"—that is, the abstraction that must be performed if one is to subject a phenomenon to intellectual analysis.

Take two cases: An individual about whom I greatly care suddenly falls flat on his face. If I allow myself to laugh at this pratfall—that is, if I let myself perceive it as comic—I must for the moment bracket my feelings of pity or concern, because these would prevent me from laughing. But suppose that I'm a physician. My interest now is to diagnose my friend's condition, and to that end I must also bracket my personal feelings. In other words, both the act of comic perception and the act of medical diagnosis require an abstraction from the web of meanings and emotions that constitute what Schutz called the paramount reality of everyday life. And, come to think of it, my laughing at the pratfall could also be called a kind of diagnosis. (One may reflect here that the Greek word literally means "knowing through" or, if you will, "seeing through": to perceive the comic or to perceive an underlying medical condition it is necessary to see through the surface of events.)

Two images succinctly illustrate Bergson's central thesis. One is the pratfall, already discussed exorbitantly ever since Thales of Miletus fell into his well. The other is that favorite children's toy, the jack-in-the-box. In both instances what occurs is a kind of automation. Something living is reduced to something mechanical, and it is precisely this reduction that strikes one as funny. Bergson sums up a discussion of various comic gestures:

> The attitudes, gestures and movements of the human body are laughable
> in exact proportion as that body reminds us of a mere machine.[29]

Put differently, we laugh when the sheer physicality of an individual overwhelms his social or moral pretensions: The philosopher falls into a well. The professor fails to notice that his nose is dripping. The prophet farts.

Bergson too is in the incongruity tradition of explaining the comic, but he defines the incongruity rather narrowly. Specifically, his central thesis is that the comic incongruity is that between mind and body, or between life and matter. This explanation makes wider sense in the context of Bergson's philosophy of life, of the *élan vital* that for him defines humanity, but this need not be of concern here. Bergson's thesis goes a considerable distance in explaining the phenomenon, but its universal applicability may be questioned. To be sure, it points up very well one important case of comic incongruity, but the phenomenon is not exhausted by that case. Thus, for an important example, Bergson's approach helps one to understand the very large place occupied by sexuality in the universe of humor. The sexual drive, more than any other, consists of an intrusion of the merely physical into the pretensions of social roles—body over mind, if not exactly matter over life: the philosopher, in the midst of pronouncing on an intricate problem of epistemology, has an involuntary erection (of which he may not even be aware). But there are large areas of humor that cannot be made to fit into this scheme. Take political humor, for example. Whatever the incongruity is here, it is not that between mind and body, life and matter. The same goes for humor dealing with the alleged qualities of different ethnic or social groups.

All the same, Bergson moved the philosophical discussion of the comic beyond the point reached before him. The figure of Don Quixote fascinated him, and it embodies well the qualities of the comic as Bergson saw them. Don Quixote moves through the world in a sustained abstraction from the reality of everyday life (which, of course, is the world of Sancho Panza). He is a kind of somnambulist, inspired by what Bergson calls a "strange kind of logic." His actions are dreamlike, always border on absurdity (as seen from the standpoint of ordinary reality), but they also have a unique quality of freedom. Specifically, they are free of empirical tests: no evidence can persuade Don Quixote that the noble knights and distressed damsels of his world of chivalry are actually simple denizens of the ordinary Spanish countryside. Precisely this freedom is what makes Don Quixote a hero of the comic.

Bergson, unlike many of his profession, fully understood the limits of philosophical analysis. At the conclusion of his book he evokes the image of a child playing on the beach on which the receding waves have left behind a residue of foam:

> The child . . . picks up a handful, and, the next moment, is astonished to find that nothing remains in his grasp but a few drops of water. . . . Laughter comes into being in the self-same fashion. It indicates a slight revolt on the surface of social life. . . . It, also, is a froth with a saline base. Like froth, it sparkles. It is gaiety itself. But the philosopher who gathers a handful to taste may find that the substance is scanty, and the aftertaste bitter.[30]

In conclusion three more recent philosophers will be briefly looked at—one German, one French, and one American. Each one carried the discussion a bit farther.

Joachim Ritter, whose essay on laughter first appeared in 1940, is sometimes cited as having demolished the whole notion of the comic as incongruity.[31] He emphasizes the great variety of laughter, from the

gentle smile to the loud guffaw, and the equally great variety of phenomena deemed to be laughable. The comic does indeed involve incongruity, but what is perceived as incongruous is highly relative and
depending on how reality as such is perceived. Put differently, the
comic always depends on the specific life-world within which it occurs.
Thus one cannot laugh at jokes coming out of life-worlds that one does
not understand. This is why, for example, it is difficult for a modern
reader to find humor in the allegedly comic episodes narrated by Cicero.
The best Jewish jokes fall flat in China. And what seems uproariously
funny to a group of construction workers fails to amuse members of the
English department at Harvard, and vice versa.

Ritter is, of course, quite right about the historical and sociological
relativity of the comic incongruity. But this undeniable fact does not in
itself invalidate the notion that the comic consists of an underlying perception of incongruity that transcends the relativities of time and space.
By analogy, it is possible (for philosophers and others) to inquire into
the underlying structures of language and the manner in which it symbolizes reality, while being fully cognizant of the fact that there are many
different human languages and that reality is symbolized differently,
say, in Chinese than in Hebrew. Ritter himself seems to return to a sort
of incongruity theory at the end of his essay. Humor, he says, is a kind
of game. Yet it is also a kind of philosophy, showing up the limits of
reason in the face of the vastness of reality. The game then becomes
serious, indeed dangerous. Indeed it does. But if this is a perception that
unites a Thracian handmaid with a modern German philosopher, in
essence a perception of incongruity, then one should not be overly
fixated on the relativities enumerated by Ritter.

Francis Jeanson's work on laughter appeared in 1950.[32] His is a phenomenological and existential approach—that is, an approach that does
not reduce the phenomenon of the comical to the result of some unconscious, mechanical process (there is a critical edge here against psychoanalysis), but rather treats it in humanly meaningful (or, as Jeanson
says, "moral") terms. Laughter is an intentional act, in the phenomenological sense of intentionality—that is, laughter always reaches out
toward an object. But it does so in a very distinct manner. It is similar to
dreaming, in that it has a "spontaneous reflection" by which its reality is
justified in the same act in which it is produced. This formulation recalls
Bergson's term of somnambulism used to describe the comic peregrina-
tions of Don Quixote. But the most important aspect of Jeanson's analysis is his description of the liberating power of laughter. Jeanson agrees
with Hobbes that one laughs out of a sense of superiority. But the latter
does not necessarily arise from contempt, as Hobbes believed. One does
not always laugh at the expense of someone else, with the aim of putting

someone else down. Laughter can come out of the sovereign knowledge of being free. The smile, therefore, is the supreme form of laughter, because in it a subject expresses his freedom and his mastery of himself. In this connection it is useful to look at the date of Jeanson's publication—shortly after the liberation of France, when the imagery of the Resistance was very much alive in French minds.[33]

One of the best formulations of the philosophical problem of the comic is found in a work published in 1961 by Marie Collins Swabey.[34] She emphasizes the importance of differentiating the physical, psychological, and social *circumstances* that stimulate laughter from *what it is about*. In other words, she refuses to give up the philosophical inquiry into the essence of laughter because of the relativities of its location in time and space. Like Bergson, she insists that laughter is not simply an emotional expression that affords no satisfaction to the intellect. Rather, she insists on the cognitive character of the comic, on its capacity to enhance understanding. To make this point clear, Swabey distinguishes what she calls "comic laughter" from other types of laughter. Thus one may laugh because one is being tickled, or out of joy, or in embarrassment. Those forms of laughter are of no interest to Swabey. She wishes to explore the distinctive laughter brought on by the perception that something is funny—comic laughter as distinct from any other kind. The question is just what this intellectual or cognitive contribution of the comic is.

Swabey notes that since about the eighteenth century there has been widespread agreement that the essence of the comic lies in incongruity. But there have been different views as to how to define this incongruity (that is, between *what* and *what* is the incongruity supposed to lie), and more importantly as to whether the incongruity is only perceived subjectively or has an objective referent. Swabey strongly comes out for the latter point of view. The perception that a particular item of reality is comic makes sense against the background of a general view of reality. This particular event is perceived as comic against a general background of, implicitly, noncomic reality. One could put it this way (hopefully without going against Swabey's intentions): The perception of the comic is the perception of something that *falls out of* an overall order of things. Or again, to say that something is *incongruous* implies a notion of *congruity*. Thus the perception of the comic depends upon (if you will, is parasitical upon) the basic human urge to order reality. Comic laughter is, so to speak, the philosophical instinct in a lower key.

The cognitive element of the comic excludes utter silliness or nonsense (though, of course, these may occasion laughter—but not comic laughter in Swabey's sense). Swabey discusses this cognitive capacity of the comic through different forms in which it is expressed—irony and satire, wit and humor (the various definitions of these need not be of concern for the moment). In all of these, though, the perception of the comic is more than a purely subjective expression of emotions or of unconscious drives. This is probably at its most sophisticated in those expressions that are primarily in language and where (as, say, in the telling of witty stories of a political sort) there is the deliberate purpose of throwing light on reality. Swabey also rejects the notion that the comic experience is primarily hedonic, rooted in a quest for pleasure. Of course laughter can give pleasure, but this is not what it is finally about:

> The lover of the comic is directed to a goal with imputed objectivity, to something beyond the subjectivity of the experience itself. . . . The search for the comic is not directed simply at the experience of the comic; the object of laughter is not merely the enjoyment of laughter.[35]

Comic laughter can be a weapon, as particularly in irony and satire, but over and beyond these social functions there is the comic intuition of an order of things within which human life can make sense:

There is yet another recent philosopher whose work on laughter will have to be taken into account. This is Helmut Plessner, one of the influential figures in what on the continent of Europe is known as philosophical anthropology. But Plessner's work falls on the boundary between philosophy and human biology, and it will more profitably be examined after this chapter. At the conclusion of this one, it is time to ask whether this jet-propelled journey through the history of Western philosophy has yielded any results.

In classical and medieval philosophy, discussions of the comic are few and far between, and where they occur they tend to deal with the moral issue of laughter (usually in a pejorative mode). Modern philosophers, especially over the last two hundred years, have paid much more attention, yet it is safe to say that the results are not overwhelming. There is also a good deal of repetition. Perhaps this should not surprise us. Philosophers are only surpassed by theologians in the propensity to take their own theories very seriously, and the comic perspective fundamentally puts all seriousness in question. But there is probably a deeper reason for this gingerly treatment of the topic than the self-aggrandizing tendency of philosophers. The philosophical enterprise as such makes for awkwardness in dealing with the phenomenon of the comic, and this may help to explain the reluctance of so many philosophers to deal with it. Philosophy, after all, is the awesome attempt to embrace all of reality in an order of reason. The comic, by its very nature, escapes this embrace. If it is to be intellectually grasped at all, it probably has to be by way of some form of Pascal's reason of the heart. That is why a number of modern philosophers have placed this topic under the rubric of esthetics, even though esthetic experience is notably different from the experience of the comic. As the philosopher tries to hold the comic in his hands it turns to froth and seems to evaporate, as in Bergson's parable of the child playing on the beach.

Nevertheless, at least two significant insights may be drawn from this survey: The experience of the comic is the perception of something objectively *out there* in the world, and not simply (though it is also that) a subjective experience determined by the relativities of history and sociology. In other words, there is a *cognitive component* to the experience. If so, what is it that is known here? And that is the second insight, carried over with considerable consistency from one philosopher to another: the incongruity between order and disorder, by the same token between man, who always seeks order, and the disorderly realities of the empirical world. In other words, the incongruity perceived here discloses a central truth about the human condition: *Man is in a state of comic discrepancy with respect to the order of the universe.* That is why Don Quixote is such a powerful and enduring embodiment of the comic spirit, far beyond the particular circumstances of Spain at the end of the feudal period, which Cervantes intended to satirize.

This insight is succinctly expressed by Baudelaire, not a philosopher but a poet, who was moved to philosophize in a notable essay on the comic in art published in 1855:

> Since (laughter) is essentially human, it is also contradictory, that is to say it is at once a sign of infinite grandeur and of infinite wretchedness: of infinite wretchedness by comparison with the absolute Being who exists as an idea in Man's mind; of an infinite grandeur by comparison with the animals. It is from the perpetual shock produced by these two infinities that laughter proceeds.[36]

Baudelaire also calls laughter "satanic." This word had special meaning for Baudelaire's poetry, but it also points to the demonic, the sinister quality of the comic spirit that already revealed itself in the Dionysian frenzy at the origins of Greek comedy. But Dionysus and Apollo are profoundly linked. The disorder of the former bears implicit witness to the order of the latter, as Apollo's priests at Delphi appeared to have understood. The comic is *au fond* a quest for order in a disordered world. This theme runs through all the forms in which the comic has expressed itself, be it in actions, visual representation, or language.

The comic experience provides a distinctive diagnosis of the world. It sees through the facades of ideational and social order, and discloses other realities lurking behind the superficial ones. The image of the jack-in-the-box, evoked by Bergson, says more than he proposed. One first sees an ordinary box, familiar and unthreatening. Then, suddenly, something or someone not ordinary at all pops out of the box. But it then becomes clear at once that this *other* something or someone was present in the box all long. The jack-in-the box reveals that things are not what they seem. There is an untranslatable German word for this: *Doppelboedigkeit*. It is derived from the theater, where it denotes a stage that contains more than one level. While the actors go through their motions on one level, very different and putatively sinister actions take place on the other level, which lies below the surface. The dividing structure is fragile. All sorts of unexpected things may pop up from "downstairs," just as holes may suddenly open up and make things and people disappear from "upstairs" into the alien world below. The comic discloses that everything that is taken for granted in ordinary life possesses this character of *Doppelboedigkeit*. For this reason, the comic is always potentially dangerous. As Kierkegaard saw very clearly, this makes for its affinity with religious experience.

The philosopher looks at the sky and falls into a hole. The accident reveals the philosopher as a comic figure. But his pratfall is a metaphor for the human condition as such. The comic experience refers to the mind thrown into a seemingly mindless world. At the same time it suggests that perhaps the world is not mindless after all.

## Notes

1.  In B. Jowett's English edition (1892), quoted in Karl-Josef Kuschel, *Laughter: A Theological Essay* (New York: Continuum, 1994), I1. An exhaustive history of this anecdote from classical antiquity to modern times may be found in Hans Blumenberg, *"Der Sturz des Protophilosophen,"* in Wolfgang Preisendanz and Rainer Warning, eds., *Das Komische* (Munich: Fink, 1976), IIff. (I have *not* made up these references!)

2.  Bernhard Greiner, *Die Komoedie* (Tuebingen: Francke, 1992), 25ff.

3.  Walter Burkett, *Greek Religion* (Cambridge, Mass.: Harvard University Press, 1985), 224.

4.  Plato, *Philebus,* trans. J. C. B. Gosling (Oxford: Clarendon, 1975).

5.  Aristotle, *Poetics,* in *The Basic Works of Aristotle,* ed. Richard McKeon (New York: Random House, 1941), 1459.

6.  Cicero, *De Oratore,* trans. J. S. Watson (Carbondale, Ill.: Southern Illinois University Press, 1970), 150.

7.  Cf. Kuschel, *Laughter,* 43ff.

8.  The following is excerpted from an as yet unpublished (perhaps even unwritten) review of the present book by Dorothy Hartmund, the late distinguished professor of classical studies at Southern Illinois A&M University):

> Berger's offhand remarks about medieval thought are as irresponsible as his absurdly inadequate treatment of classical antiquity, reinforcing one's considered opinion that social scientists with a smattering of humanistic education should leave

such topics to those with the proper credentials in the humanities. It is, of course, possible that Berger has never heard of Duns Scotus's work *De ridenda gentium* or of Abelard's elegantly slim essay *Sic et fortasse*. But even he should have come across Thomas Aquinas' massive *Risibilia*, available in my own English translation *(Risibilities*, Centralia, Ill., 1957). 1 would also refer him to the authoritative analysis of this work by Dominic O'Malley, S.J., in the latter's *Scholastic Humor* (Notre Dame, Ind., 1985), p. 2033 ff. It is clear that Berger cannot read Latin (not to mention Greek), but, if one is to judge by his footnotes, he can claim at least some reading knowledge of German and French. He might, then, profitably turn to the lively scholarly debate unleashed by Edith O'Malley, O.S.B., who tried to show in her brilliant article "The Woman Behind Thomas" *(Journal of Feminist History, III:* 1990, p. 68 ff.) that the Risibilia, among other works by the great scholastic, was plagiarized from the writings of sister Placida, the learned abbess of Rimini. Vide Dorothy Hartmund, *"Die lachende Nonne aus Rimini" (Zeitschriftfuer die Wissenschaften des Altertums,* CX: 1991, p. 65 ff.); Jean-Jacques Abukassim, *"Le mythe de l'abesse Placidam" (Annales medievales,* LI: 1992, p. 2 ff.); and my own response to Abukassim (in the following issue of the *Annales).*

9.    Desiderius Erasmus, *The Praise of Folly,* trans. Clarence Miller (New Haven: Yale University Press, 1979).

10.    Ibid., 85f.

11.    From *Les Passions de l'âme,* art. 124, quoted in Francis Jeanson, *Signification humaine du rire* (Paris: Editions du Seuil, 1950), 22. [My translation.]

12.    Cf. Paul Haberland, *The Development of Comic Theory in Germany During the Eighteenth Century* (Goeppingen: Kuemmerie, 1971).

13.    On the relation of comedy as a performing art and theories of the comic during this period, cf. Greiner, *Die Komoedie,* 47ff.

14.    Cited in Haberland, *Comic Theory,* 70f. [My translation.]

15.    Immanuel Kant, *Kritik der Urteilskraft* (Frankfurt: Suhrkamp, 1977), 124.

16.    Ibid., 272ff.

17.    Haberland, *Comic Theory,* 80ff.

18.    Georg Wilhelm Friedrich Hegel, *Vorlesungen ueber die Aesthetik* (Frankfurt: Suhrkamp, 1970), 520ff.

19.    Lest I be accused of being obscurantist, here is Hegel's own phrasing: *"eine Welt, deren Zwecke sich deshalb durch ihre eigene Wesenslosigkeit zerstoeren"* (ibid., p. 527). [Okay, Hartmund, how about translating *that* into Latin?!]

20.    Ibid., 529. [My translation.]

21.    These elephantine observations of mine are taken from my essay "A Lutheran View of the Elephant," first published (where else?) in *InterLutheran Forum* (Advent 1978), then republished in an expanded edition of my *A Rumor of Angels* (New York: Anchor, 1990), 109ff. As Rabbi Meir of Vilna, Talmudist, put it so well: "If an author cannot borrow from himself, from whom can he borrow?" [*That,* Hartmund, was written in Lithuanian Yiddish. I'd like to see *you* take a stab at it!]

22.    Karl Loewith, *Von Hegel zu Nietzsche* (Frankfurt: Fischer, 1969).

23.    Johannes Climacus, *Concluding Unscientific Postscript,* trans. David Swenson (Princeton, N.J.: Princeton University Press, 1941).

24.    Ibid., 82f.

25.    Ibid., 459.

26.   An English translation of the full text is in Wylie Sypher, ed., *Comedy* (Garden City, N.Y.: Doubleday, 1956).

27.   Ibid., 64.

28.   Ibid., 79.

29.   Ibid., 189f.

30.   Joachim Ritter, *"Ueber das Lachen,"* in *Subjektivitaet* (Frankfurt: Suhrkamp, 1974), 62ff.

31.   Jeanson, *Signification humaine*.

32.   Shortly after World War II, David Rousset, who had been in the French Resistance, published a book on his experiences in Nazi concentration camps. I cannot locate this work now, but I recall one interesting passage, in which Rousset asked himself whether he had learned anything from this experience. He answered by saying that he had learned very little that he had not known before. But among the few things he *had* learned was the insight that the comic is an objective constituent of reality, regardless of the circumstances, however wretched, in which it is encountered.

33.   Marie Collins Swabey, *Comic Laughter: A Philosophical Essay* (New Haven: Yale University Press, 1961).

34.   Ibid., 162.

35.   Ibid., 247.

36.   Charles Baudelaire, *The Essence of Laughter*, transl. Gerard Hopkins (New York: Meridian, 1956), 117.

# 3
## Laughing Monks
### *A Very Brief Sinitic Interlude*

All the authors discussed in the preceding chapter are taken from the history of Western philosophy. It would be a grave mistake to gather from this that reflection about the comic is an exclusively Western preoccupation. The phenomenon of the comic as such is universal. Not only do all human beings laugh (and presumably have been laughing ever since *homo sapiens* mutated away from his simian relatives), but no human culture has been studied that does not have a concept of the comic. In other words, not only laughter but comic laughter is universal. In all likelihood this cannot be said with regard to systematic reflection about the comic, be it by philosophers or other theorists. It is all the more important to recognize that there are cases of this outside Western civilization. One clear case is Sinitic civilization.

Travelers in East Asia—China, Japan, Korea—quickly note that people in the region laugh on occasions where Westerners or other foreigners would not. Interpreters of the region have given many explanations for this phenomenon. People laugh to get over moments of social awkwardness, to indicate deference, or to give evidence that the situation is amicable. These facts are of no particular interest here. Travelers also quickly observe that people in these countries find things amusing that they themselves would not, and vice versa. Any American or European who has tried to spice a lecture with jokes in Tokyo or Hong Kong will have discovered this to his dismay. This set of facts belongs to the comparative sociology of the comic and will have to be considered a little later on. But Sinitic civilization has also produced highly intriguing instances of comic philosophy and indeed philosophers who are hard to distinguish from comedians. Probably most important in this matter is the Taoist tradition and movements influenced by it.

A colleague with extensive experience with the dialogue between world religions has remarked that the most difficult partners in this type of exercise are the Taoists.[1] This is not at all because they are intolerant or dogmatic. On the contrary, it is because they keep laughing, treating those solemn ceremonies of interfaith communication as a huge joke. Scholars of Taoism will have to decide whether this comic propensity is intrinsic to this tradition or only characterizes some of its protagonists. Probably the foremost example is Chuang Tzu, or Master Chuang.[2] He died about 280 B.C.E., and the book under his name probably contains chapters of which he is the authentic author and chapters written by imitators belonging to his school (this sort of amiable, indeed reverent plagiarism was, of course, by no means peculiar to China, as biblical scholars among others know all too well). The book actually begins with what can only be called a joke. It is, to be sure, a very Chinese joke, and a foreign-devil reader must make something of an effort to get it. But a joke it is, of sorts, and it may properly be called a philosophical joke:

> In the Northern Ocean there is a fish, its name the *Kun*, its size I know not how many *li*. [One *li* is about one-third of a mile.] By metamorphosis it becomes a bird called the *P'eng*, with a back I know not how many *li* in extent. When it rouses itself and flies, its wings darken the sky like clouds. With the sea in motion this bird transports itself to the Southern Ocean, the Lake of Heaven. In the words of Ch'i Hsieh, a recorder of marvels, "When the *P'eng* transports itself to the Southern Ocean, it thrashes the water for three thousand *li*, and mounts in a whirlwind to the height of ninety thousand *li*, and flies continuously for six months before it comes to rest! . . . "A cicada and a young dove giggled together over the *P'eng*. The cicada said, "When we exert ourselves to fly up onto the tall elms, we sometimes fail to get there and are pulled back to the ground, and that is that. Why then should any one mount up ninety thousand *li* in order to go south?!"[3]

May a non-Sinologist venture an interpretation? One must ask: Why do the cicada and the dove giggle over this cosmic bird? One is then reminded of Hegel's characterization of the comic effect in a discrepancy between effort and result. What is the point of this enormous effort, the cicada implies, when all it accomplishes is moving the bird from one place to another? The experience cannot be very different from that of moving from the ground to the top of an elm tree, and even that is hardly worth it. There is a truly Hegelian *komische Aufloesung* here: The mythological fish-bird performs marvels of metamorphosis and aviation, and the result of all this monumental exertion is negligible. One may as well stay where one is (a classically Taoist piece of advice). The cicada and the dove giggle, and thereby are saying: Come off it, P'eng— we refuse to be impressed!

The best-known passage from Master Chuang is the following:

Once Chuang Chou [that was his full name] dreamt he was a butterfly, fluttering here and there just as if he was a butterfly, conscious of following its inclinations. It did not know that it was Chuang Chou. Suddenly he awoke; and then demonstrably he was Chuang Chou. But he does not know now whether he is Chuang Chou who dreamt he was a butterfly or a butterfly dreaming he is Chuang Chou.[4]

This passage well illustrates Master Chuang's method, according to Kuang-ming Wu, who has been instrumental in interpreting this author to English-speaking readers. Master Chuang himself claimed that his method was "no method" (*wu fang*), but that may be understood as an ironic comment, just as the butterfly story is both irony and an example of the "no method" method. And that method is essentially comic. It demolishes taken-for-granted reality, disclosing its fragility, and thus liberates the mind to take a fresh look at the world. The second chapter of Master Chuang's book, which is often regarded as unintelligible, according to Wu is actually a parody of different schools of philosophy, including the Confucian ones. Here is how Wu characterizes this philosophy of the comic:

The comic lies in a juxtaposition of incongruous elements, such as big nose and small hat, small pants and big shoes, and the like. Since life seems to us a juxtaposition of the incongruous, an appropriate mode by which to approach life may well be the comical.

Humor and irony induce self-recognition to liberate us from our prison of self-content.[5]

Another example of Master Chuang's comic "no method" will have to suffice:

A man of Sung who traded in ceremonial caps traveled to the state of Viet. But the people of Viet cut off their hair and tattooed their bodies, so the caps were of no use. Yao brought order to all the people under heaven and brought peace to all within the four seas. He went to distant Mount Kuyeh to visit the Four Masters. Upon returning to his capital on the north bank of the Fen River, he fell into a doze and forgot all about his empire.[6]

Taoism, undoubtedly because of its very nature, never became a world religion. But its spirit penetrated many areas of Chinese culture and through it other parts of East Asia. Probably its most important consequence was its influence on the Chinese reception of Buddhism. When that Indian faith was first brought to China, Chinese intellectuals thought that it was a variant of Taoism. Despite some similarities, this was, of course, a misunderstanding. But Buddhism underwent a profound change as it was absorbed into Sinitic civilization. The Ch'an school of Buddhism, which became Zen in Japan, exemplifies this Sini-fication. A number of scholars, Kuang-ming Wu among them, have argued that Ch'an/Zen is precisely a modification of Buddhism in the spirit of Taoism. And its monks are famous for their raucous laughter.

The most characteristic exercise in Zen monasteries is what in Japan is called the *koan*. A *koan* is a parable or riddle exchanged between a master and his disciples, but the solution is never a straightforward or rational one. Identically worded solutions may be deemed correct or false, depending on the master's assessment of a disciple's spiritual state. Or the solution may be a violent act or an obscene gesture. The *koan* is a perfect development of the Taoist "no method." Many instances of the *koan* can be described as jokes. The purpose is always to deconstruct reality and thereby to attain liberating enlightenment.

Probably the most famous *koan* is ascribed to Hakuin Ekaku, a Zen monk who lived from 1685 to 1768. He instructed his disciples to listen to the sound of one hand clapping (*sekishu no onjo*), which has been taught ever since as the essence of the Zen view of reality.[7] Here is a typical *koan*, this one attributed to Master Yunmen:

Question:  *What is your statement about going beyond buddhas and sur-passing the ancestors?*
Answer:   *A sesame rice-cake.*[8]

Or take the following:

> Butei, Emperor of Ryo, sent for Fu-daishi to explain the Diamond Sutra. On the appointed day Fu-daishi came to the palace, mounted a platform, rapped the table before him, then descended and, still not speaking, left. Butei sat motionless for some minutes, whereupon Shiku, who had seen all that happened, went up to him and said, "May I be so bold, sir, as to ask whether you understood?"
> The Emperor sadly shook his head.
> "What a pity!" Shiko exclaimed. "Fu-daishi has never been more eloquent."[9]

The liberating result intended by this method allows a good deal of self-mockery. The ability not to take oneself seriously is a good test of whether true enlightenment has taken place:

> A monk asked Master Busshin, "Do heaven and hell exist?"
> "No," the master said without hesitation.
> Some samurai happened to be within earshot and, amazed at Busshin's answer, asked him the same question. The time, again without hesitation, the master said, "Yes."

When accused by the samurai of being contradictory, Busshin said, "Well, if I tell *you* there's neither heaven nor hell, where would the alms come from?"[10]

Hakuin, the master of clapping with one hand, was not only a Zen teacher but also a painter, calligrapher, and poet (often in slang). At the age of seventy-one he added the following verse to a highly unflattering self-portrait:

Loathed by a thousand buddhas in the realm of a thousand buddhas, hated by demons among the troops of demons, this foul-smelling blind bald-head appears again on someone's piece of paper. Damn![11]

Between Taoism and Zen there are all the components of a comic philosophy: The diagnosis of the world as a mass of incongruences. The radical debunking of all pretensions of grandeur and wisdom. A spirit of mocking irreverence. And, in the end result, a profound discovery of freedom. Erasmus's Stultitia, wrapped in saffron robes, has been wandering around East Asia for many centuries.

### Notes

1.  I owe this observation to John Berthrong, who also introduced me to Master Chuang. I express my gratitude amid spasms of Taoist laughter.
2.  Cf. E. R. Hughes, ed., *Chinese Philosophy in Classical Times* (London: Dent, 1942), 165ff.; Kuang-ming Wu, *Chuang Tzu: World Philosopher at Play* (New York: Crossroad, 1982), and *The Butterfly As Companion* (Albany: SUNY Press, 1990).
3.  Hughes, *Chinese Philosophy*.
4.  Ibid., 184.
5.  Wu, *Butterfly*, 264, 374.
6.  Victor Mair, ed./trans., *Wandering on the Way: Early Taoist Tales and Parables of Chuang Tzu* (New York: Bantam, 1994), 7.
7.  Cf. Kazuaki Tanahashi, *Penetrating Laughter: Hakuin's Zen and Art* (Woodstock, N.Y.: Overlook, 1982).
8.  Ibid., 84.
9.  Lucien Stryk and Takashi Ikemoto, eds., *Zen* (Chicago: Swallow, 1981), xxxii.
10.  Tanahashi, *Penetrating Laughter*, 121.
11.  Ibid., 19.

# 4

## Homo Ridens
### Physiology and Psychology

If one fully understood the phenomenon of laughter, one would have understood the central mystery of human nature. That mystery is how human nature is constituted by a body that is part and parcel of biological evolution, and by that elusive entity variously called mind, soul, or spirit.

There can be no doubt that, whatever else it is and by whatever it is provoked, laughter is a physiological process:

> As a muscular phenomenon, laughter is easy to describe. It consists of spasmodic contractions of the large and small zygomatic (facial) muscles and sudden relaxations of the diaphragm accompanied by contractions of the larynx and epiglottis. Laughter differs from smiling simply in that the smile does not interrupt breathing.[1]

It is a reflexoid process controlled by the "old brain" (thalamus and hypothalamus), which governs other reflex activity and purely emotional behavior, and not by the pallial cortex, which governs cognitive faculties. Konrad Lorenz called laughter a "reflex of capitulation": A tension is built up and is then suddenly released, at which point the organism collapses into or, so to speak, capitulates to laughter. This physiological process can be provoked by purely physical stimuli, of which tickling is the best known. There are also the effects of nitrous oxide ("laughing gas") and the symptoms of a number of diseases (such as Alzheimer's and multiple sclerosis).

Even a moment's reflection will point to a profoundly puzzling paradox: How can the same physiological process resulting from tickling also be triggered by a sophisticated political joke? And what business does the "old brain" have to get involved with the highly cognitive faculty that makes it possible for an individual to grasp the political joke? As asserted above, a full answer to these questions will have to await the final solution of the mystery of human nature, more precisely the solution of what many philosophers have called the mind/body problem. In the meantime, however, a more modest step is necessary. One will have to accept the difference insisted upon by Marie Collins Swabey, one of the philosophers looked at earlier in this book—namely, the difference between comic laughter and all other forms of laughter.[2]

Human beings laugh when tickled, when spontaneously happy, when suddenly freed from fear or tension—or when comprehending a subtle exercise of wit. Within the argument of this book, of course, only the last occasion for laughter is of real interest. But precisely because of its proximity to some central questions about human nature, comic laughter must also be compared with these other forms of laughter. Needless to say, such comparison will not end the age-old philosophical enterprise of defining man, but it will place the case of comic laughter within a wider anthropological context. *Homo ridens* puzzles because he stands at the intersection of what is most and what is least animal about human beings.

Do animals laugh? Apparently this is a question about which there is some disagreement. Apes grin, and the physiology of this is similar to the human one just described. Apes grin when engaged in rituals of greeting and of appeasement, the latter signaling that there is no real danger or that the appeaser *hopes* that there is no real danger. The similarities and dissimilarities between these behavior patterns with comparable human ones are certainly interesting, but little would be gained for the present argument if these were further pursued. One thing is quite certain: No ape has ever grinned after being told a political joke (or, for that matter, any other sort of joke). With a good conscience, then, the question of whether animals laugh can be left to the zoologists and other interested parties. The distinctive character of human laughter, though, will have to be considered further.

Laughter clearly is a phenomenon that involves both body and mind. It thus points to the curious relationship of human subjectivity and its embodiment. The same goes for weeping, its twin phenomenon. The most significant treatment of both phenomena in the framework of a philosophical anthropology has been that by Helmuth Plessner.[3]

Plessner's work stands in a tradition of continental-European philosophical reflection about the nature of man of which Max Scheler was probably the most outstanding twentieth-century representative.[4] Scheler, while insisting on the unity of human nature against any version of mind/body dualism, characterized man as being different from animals (or, if one prefers, *other* animals) by both *being* and *having* a body. An animal *is* its body, which it has in common with man, but man also *has* his body as something from which he can subjectively distance himself and that he can consciously *make use of* for this or that purpose. Plessner takes up this characterization, and emphasizes that this peculiar relationship to the body must always be kept going in a precarious balance. Both in laughing and in weeping this balance comes unhinged. The control that the individual normally has over his body collapses, indeed the individual collapses *into* laughing or weeping. At least for a moment, he no longer *has* but *is* his body (in Scheler's terminology). Yet it is not his body but *he* that laughs or weeps, and he laughs or weeps *about something*. In other words, even in the midst of this collapse into an involuntary and uncontrolled bodily condition, the individual retains intentionality: If asked, he can say why—that is, about what—he is laughing or weeping. The very collapse reveals man as a "double being," both embodied and yet somehow existing also beyond this embodiment (though it should be noted that Plessner, like Scheler, carefully distances himself from a dualistic anthropology that would posit mind or soul over against the body).

Plessner's key category to describe this peculiar feature of human nature is man's "eccentric position" (*exzentrische Position*). Man is "eccentric" (*decentered* would perhaps be the better term in English) because his body is experienced both as a *condition* and an *object*. Normally, an individual controls his body, and uses it both as a physical instrument and as a vehicle of expression. Thus the hands, for example, can be used both to operate a tool or a weapon and to engage in gestures signaling anger, desire, appeasement, or what have you. Both kinds of usage presuppose consciousness: The individual, in either use of his hands, knows what he is doing. That very knowledge creates distance between himself and his bodily actions. This distance constitutes his eccentricity. An animal lacks the consciousness and thus lacks the distance; compared to man, it is centered. In laughing and weeping, man's habitual control over the uses of his body is lost. He "falls into" laughing or weeping. But this is still very different from an animal, which cannot fall into a bodily state because it has never been outside it in the first place. And, unlike an animal, a human individual knows that he is laughing or weeping, and what is more he can tell why he is doing so.

An important distinction made by Plessner is between true laughter and purely reactive laughter (as when a person is being tickled or given laughing gas). True laughter is *about* something; reactive laughter is not. Also, true laughter is very close to playing, indeed always has about it an air of playfulness. Plessner's true laughter, however, is not identical with Swabey's comic laughter. Thus one may laugh simply out of joy or relief, and this will be true laughing in that one can clearly tell why one is laughing ("Because I'm so relieved by the diagnosis just given me by my doctor"). Neither explanation relates to the comic. Yet comic laughter is one very important form of true laughter and of course it is the one most relevant here.

Plessner agrees with Bergson that the comic always has a human referent. If we laugh at animals or inanimate objects, it is because they remind us of human beings. Plessner also agrees with what, as was shown earlier, has been a persistent motif in the writings of modern philosophers about the comic—namely, that the comic is essentially about incongruity. Plessner adds the insight that man's eccentricity is the quality that enables him both to perceive the comic and to be an object of comic perception. Only man belongs to different levels of being, and this multiple experience of reality is the basis of comic perception. This is a fundamental anthropological fact that cannot be reduced to this or that historical situation. Therefore, the comic as such is not a social phenomenon, though of course the contents and occasions of comic perception vary socially to an enormous degree: What is funny on one side of the Pyrenees is not at all funny on the other side (to paraphrase Pascal tongue-in-cheek, literally). Put differently, what is laughed at and when one may appropriately laugh are socially relative, but the underlying incongruity of the comic experience is grounded in an anthropological reality that transcends all social variations. As such, of course, it is universal (or, of one prefers, is a cross-cultural constant).

Man's eccentric position allows man to perceive the world as both constrained and open, as familiar and strange, as meaningful and meaningless. One could say that Plessner adds the comic to what Scheler called man's distinctive "world-openness". But further, both laughter and weeping place an individual in marginal or border situations (*Grenzlagen*), where the habitual balance of his existence is disturbed. (Yet these situations are by no means rare or extraordinary. The common, ordinary occurrence of these phenomena reveals man as essentially a marginal being.

Plessner has written a short, elegant essay on the smile in addition to the larger work on laughter and weeping.[5] He emphasizes the difference between smiling and laughter, despite the fact that in several languages (though not in English) the two are etymologically related (*subridere* in Latin and *sourire* in French, with cognate terms in other Romance languages, all denoting "sublaughter"; *laecheln* in German, meaning "little laughter"). If Plessner is right, this etymology is misleading: The smile is not a subcategory of laughter, though related to it, and as with laughter one could distinguish the comic smile from other forms of the phenomenon. The essential difference is that, unlike laughter, the smile is a *controlled* expression; there is no "collapse": "In laughing and weeping man is the victim of his spirit, in smiling he gives expression to it"[6] The smile, even in the midst of shame or grief, indicates that an individual somehow stands above these circumstances, "as if he carried the kiss of a goddess on his forehead." Thus, albeit in very different if not opposite ways, both laughter and the smile disclose essential features of humanity. And, of course, both can be responses to the experience of the comic.

In the course of evolution, when did man first laugh or smile? We may assume that this was the moment when man first emerged as man. One is tempted to linger on it in fantasy: This still rather simian-looking creature giggling uncontrollably, perhaps on the occasion of one of his fellows suffering a spectacular pratfall. The moment, alas, is not retrievable. But perhaps it can be adumbrated, on the theory that evolution is somehow replicated in the development of each individual. The moment when an infant first smiles or laughs is, of course, very commonly experienced—typically to the immense delight of the infant's parents. The laughter of children has been studied in some detail by psychologists, and it is of some interest for understanding the topic of this book.[7]

The smile of an infant is an essential sign of social interaction. It is a trigger (a Lorenzian *Ausloeser*) for parental response, the first form of dialogue between the infant and the adults in charge of him. At first it does not differentiate between the individuals to whom it is directed, signaling contentment just as the infantile yell signals discomfort. Very soon, though, the smile indicates recognition of specific individuals, most commonly, of course, of the mother. Normally it is an optical response, though infants born blind smile upon hearing a familiar voice. The development of laughter comes later and is rather different in meaning. It is a symptom of relief, of tension or fear overcome. In the psychological development of the child, there is a step-by-step progression from the primal smile to the smile of embarrassment, joyful laughter, laughter at a comic situation, laughter in a group, aggressive laughter at an outsider, and finally (a somewhat depressing climax) the laughter of *Schadenfreude*. The chronology of this progression has been studied exhaustively by psychologists and need not be of concern here. What is significant, though, is that at each step laughter signifies an experience of relief (*Entlastung*), both physically and psychologically.

There is widespread consensus among child psychologists that such an experience of relief is the primary cause of comic laughter. Cross-culturally, it appears, young children react with laughter to two games that adults play with them almost instinctively: the games of peekaboo and of jack-in-the-box (the latter actually being an enhancement of the former by means of a mechanical device). The peekaboo effect is primal. The adult looks at the child, typically smiling, then hides for a few moments, then reappears. The jack-in-the-box mimics the same sequence. The child is distressed by the disappearance of the familiar face, relieved by its reappearance. The response is laughter. The timing is important. If the disappearance takes too long, the child will be anxious and start to cry, and the reappearance will not trigger laughter in that case; the child must be comforted, reassured. In other words, the disappearing act must remain within the confines of a game; the ludic character is lost if the act is stretched out too much; it then ceases to be comic, becomes serious. The formula goes something like this: pleasure/an interruption of pleasure/mounting anxiety/cathartic relief. One psychologist writing in the 1920s, perhaps in the first flush of Freudian excitement, has even compared this primal comic experience with an orgasm.[8]

Be this as it may, the peekaboo game is only the beginning, though it suggests much about the psychology of what comes later. A true sense of the comic in the child depends upon his internalization of the adults' reality. The Schutzian categories employed earlier in this book can be helpful again. In the world of an adult there is a clear demarcation between what Schutz calls the paramount reality—the reality of wide-awake, everyday life that one shares with most people most of the time—and the finite provinces of meaning (which include dreams and fantasy worlds) into which one escapes periodically. In the world of the young child these demarcation lines are much more fluid. Dreams and fantasies merge into the real world, weave in and out of it. Put differently, the young child cannot as yet differentiate between various levels of being and therefore cannot grasp the incongruity between them— that incongruity which is constitutive of the comic experience. As the child comes to experience these levels, true comic experience becomes possible. The puppet theater, much beloved among children where that institution exists, is a good illustration of this. In a physically obvious way the events depicted there are separated from real life. What happens there would be very terrifying indeed if it occurred in real life—the puppets knock each other on the head, say terrible things to each other, even disappear into oblivion. This fantasy world does have a certain reality (precisely the fugitive reality of a finite province of meaning), and the child who watches does experience a *frisson* of anxiety. But the puppet reality is indeed finite, the anxiety is limited by this knowledge, and there is relief from real anxiety by the very fact of this limitation. The transition from one level of being to another is perceived as incongruous and ipso facto comic. It can easily be observed that some children are too young for this: They do not understand that the events of the puppet theater are not to be taken seriously, they are *really* terrified, and instead of laughing they cry. Very probably individual children differ as to the chronology of this development. Most psychologists appear to agree that, in most children, a fully formed sense of the comic is established by the age of five or six, when children can themselves make jokes and

derive enjoyment from this.[9] While this development occurs spontaneously, it also seems that children can be educated in comic understanding. Parents with a strongly formed sense of humor can obviously
encourage their children to acquire it. Sometimes this encouragement
can be annoying to outsiders trapped in such a family of determined
comedians. One can easily recall situations in which one had to sit
through the performance of, say, a six-year-old endlessly telling a series
of infantile jokes, to the unrestrained applause of his admiring parents.

One psychologist has made the distinction between what he calls
"sociopositive" and "socionegative" laughter.[10] There is harmless or innocent laughter, which enhances the solidarity of a group, and malicious laughter, which is at the expense of someone who is thereby, at
least momentarily, excluded from the group. The child progresses from
the first to the second type. Perhaps the early inability of children to
engage in malicious humor is one of the reasons why childhood has
been called innocent. In any case, for better or for worse, comic laughter
can be of either kind. The same psychologist has suggested that there is
the possibility of retaining the capacity for innocent laughter in adult life
and that this can be a great help in meeting the exigencies of life. Folk
wisdom has long held the view that this capacity (more or less what is
commonly meant by a sense of humor) is conducive to good health. As
will be discussed shortly, there is some evidence in support of this view.

Leaving aside the physiology of laughter and the biographical development of the sense of the comic, the principal psychological question is
that of the *uses* of the comic experience. Put differently, the question is
about the psychological *functions* of the comic experience. In what follows, the categorization employed is the one suggested by Avner Ziv,
an Israeli psychologist who has managed to write about this topic in a
lucid and indeed witty manner that avoids the esoteric style to which
many of his fellow psychologists are addicted.[11]

Ziv begins his list with the aggressive function (thus paying respect to
a tradition of interpreting the comic that goes from Plato to Hobbes in
Western philosophy, as was indicated earlier). Modern psychology suggests that this dour view is not altogether false.[12] Ziv cites Stephen
Leacock: "The savage who cracked his enemy over the head with a
tomahawk and shouted, 'Ha, ha' was the first humorist." Experiments
trying to establish what people laugh at do indeed show that a common
occasion for comic laughter has to do with belittling, humiliating, or
debunking an individual or an entire group of people. This, of course, is
mostly the case with irony and satire, the most aggressive forms of
humor, but aggression is also present in other forms of the comic experience. Put simply, humor can be used as a weapon. Ziv mentions an old
Arab institution, the *hidja*. It dates from tribal times and refers to the

practice of reciting satirical poetry belittling the enemy on the eve of battle. But this form of humor is not peculiar to warring Bedouins.

The aggressive use of humor can range from comically defined physical assaults (pranks, practical jokes), through visual representations (such as cartoons), to verbal acts running on a scale from an ad hoc sarcastic remark to a play by Aristophanes. The verbal prototype is the put-down joke. The aim can be to put down a group, an institution, a belief system. A classical (if morally reprehensible) version of this is what in America has been called the Polish joke, belittling this ethnic group as being allegedly stupid. It has cross-cultural variants—Frisian jokes in Germany, Belgian jokes in France, Irish jokes in England, Newfie jokes in Canada (referring to inhabitants of Newfoundland), Portuguese jokes in Brazil, *Van der Merwe* jokes told by English-speaking South Africans (referring to their Afrikaans-speaking compatriots). This is not a complete list. The capacity for ethnocentric malice is clearly universal. Other types of jokes belittle a group for alleged traits other than stupidity—greed, laziness, sexual promiscuity, sexual frigidity, and so on. Cases in point would be, respectively, jokes directed against Jews, African-Americans, Puerto Ricans, WASPs. A point to note is that, however deplorable the sentiments expressed in these jokes may be from a moral standpoint, they may nevertheless be perceived as funny; indeed, the very fact that such jokes may be deemed morally offensive may enhance their attractiveness as a forbidden pleasure. No useful purpose would be served by giving examples of this variety of aggressive humor here (readers will have no difficulty, alas, remembering examples from their own experience). Instead, jokes expressing aggression of a nonethnic sort may serve by way of illustration.

Professional groups with high status—such as lawyers and psychiatrists in America—are preferred targets of comic aggression:

> It has been announced by the National Institute of Health that in future lawyers rather than rats will be used in experiments conducted under NIH auspices. This has three advantages. One: There are more of them. Two: There is no danger that one will get fond of them. And three: There are some things that rats won't do.[13]

> In a building containing a number of psychiatrists' offices two of them frequently find themselves using the same elevator coming in or leaving. One evening they go down together and one of them turns to the other: I have been meaning to ask you about this for a long time. There is something I don't understand. At the end of the day I'm completely exhausted, disheveled; I can barely make it out of the office. You on the other hand look as fresh and chipper as when you come in the morning. I don't get it. In our profession, when one has to listen all day to these awful stories. . . . To which the other psychiatrist responds: Who listens?!

Aggression against institutions (this one is from Italy where, possibly by dint of long familiarity, respect for the Roman Catholic church and its dignitaries has not been very high for a long time):

> This happened around the turn of the century, when moral standards were still quite intact. An unmarried young woman, just before going into labor, said to the attending physician, "Please, you must help me. If I come home to my village with this baby, my father will kill me."
>
> The doctor told her not to worry. It so happened that in the same hospital the Archbishop of Bologna was undergoing an appendectomy. When he came out of anesthesia the doctor sat at his bedside and told him, "Your eminence, a miracle has occurred. You have given birth to a son." The archbishop is appalled, denies the possibility. The doctor keeps insisting, says that the archbishop, as a prince of the church, cannot deny the possibility of miracles. Finally the archbishop gives in and accepts the baby.
>
> The baby grows up in the archiepiscopal palace, turns out to be a sturdy lad. On his eighteenth birthday the archbishop calls him in and addresses him as follows: "My son, today you come of age and it is time that you know about your origins. You grew up in the belief that I am your father. That belief is mistaken. I am your mother. Your father is the Archbishop of Pisa."

Aggression against a belief system: For example, in the Soviet Union a genre of jokes called "Questions to Radio Yerevan" circulated, supposedly reporting on questions addressed to a mythic radio station in Soviet Armenia. The jokes cleverly attacked the bases of Communist ideology.

Question:  *What is capitalism?*
 Answer:  *The exploitation of man by man.*
Question:  *What is Communism?*
 Answer:  *The reverse.*
Question:  *We know that the tsarist regime was very bad. How is it that it was more popular than the Soviet government?*
 Answer:  *It governed less.*

Or take this American assault on a very American religious belief system:

> A Catholic priest, a rabbi, and a Christian Science practitioner meet in hell. They ask each other how they got there. The Catholic priest says, "Well, it was late on a cold winter evening. My housekeeper brought me a cup of tea and a snack. I could not resist the temptation, I grabbed her lustily— and then there was a clap of thunder, and here I am." The rabbi said, "I

was at a reception. On the buffet table I saw some delicious ham sandwiches. I could not resist the temptation. I picked up one of the sandwiches, there was a clap of thunder, and here I am." The Christian Science
practitioner says, "I am not here."

Depending on who tells these jokes, there may be feelings of inferi-
ority or resentment that are given vent by putting down people and
institutions held responsible for these feelings. But no matter who tells
the jokes, there is the Hobbesian effect of feeling superior to those
targeted by the jokes, the savoring of a moment of triumph. But there is
also a circumvention (in Freudian language, a sublimation) of the taboo
against aggressive actions, a taboo that in one way or another necessarily exists in every human society. In other words, one deals a verbal
blow rather than a physical one. This is almost always the less risky
course, And not only under repressive regimes.

If the taboo against aggression is one of the pillars of any social order,
then the tabu against illicit sexuality is another, equally important one.
And if humor is used to subliminally circumvent the former, it is equally
functional in circumventing the latter.[14] It is, of course, in terms of
sexuality that Freud invented the concept of sublimation in the first
place. It occupies an important place in what one may call the hydraulic
model of the psyche that Freud designed—an invisible system of
pumps, repressed libidinal urges being pushed down, coming up again
in strangely distorted forms. Needless to say, one does not have to
accept this psychological model in its entirety in order to find useful
some of Freud's brilliant insights. His work most relevant to the present
topic is the long essay "Wit and Its Relation to the Unconscious," which
was first published in 1905.[15]

There is actually very little about sexuality in this work, unless one
knows the larger Freudian context. (There is, if you will, little redeeming
prurient interest.) The main point of the work is an elaboration of
Freud's at first startling discovery of the similarity between jokes and
dreams. It came a few years after he had published his *The Interpretation
of Dreams*, one of the seminal works in the emerging conceptualization of
psychoanalysis. Freud's theory of wit is essentially an extension of his
theory of dreams.

Wit is seen by Freud as a subcategory of the comic (about which he
has few original things to say). It is characterized by a playful approach
to reality, by the discovery of hidden similarities and connections, by
linking up what is normally separate, and by giving sense to what is
normally perceived as nonsense. Except for the element of playfulness,
all these qualities are as characteristic of dreams as of the exercises of
wit. And both dreams and jokes are also marked by a great economy of

effort, by contraction and brevity. In this connection Freud cites a famous line by Shakespeare's Polonius (*Hamlet,* II:2): "Brevity is the soul of wit." Both in dreams and in jokes, these shared qualities all serve a basic psychological function: Repressed thoughts are pushed into the unconscious, out of which they reemerge wearing various disguises. This disguised reemergence is, of course, what the concept of sublimation refers to. Applied to wit, one might aptly call it an extended psychology of the game of jack-in-the-box. Its root technique Freud calls "condensation with substitutive formation." There is typically ambiguity, double meaning, and play on words. One of Freud's examples refers to the then-recent Dreyfus affair in France: "This girl reminds me of Dreyfus. The army does not believe in her innocence." (This joke certainly exemplifies both "condensation" and "substitutive formation." It is less clear just what was repressed here.) There is a preponderance of Jewish jokes among Freud's examples. This can readily be attributed to Freud's social situation. It has also led to speculations about Freud's ambivalent relation to Judaism and Jewishness, but that is a topic that cannot be pursued here.[16]

In the Freudian view, the underlying psychological mechanism in both dreams and jokes is substitute gratification or wish-fulfillment: "Wit affords us the means of surmounting restrictions and of opening up otherwise inaccessible pleasure sources."[17] Again without necessarily buying into the entire Freudian scheme, this is clearly correct with regard to many if not all sexual jokes. Sexuality has a dark, threatening side. In the sexual joke, this threat is neutralized, rendered harmless. Take the twin fears of impotence and frigidity (the first two jokes are told by Ziv):

> A man to the woman he has just made love to: Do you ever wonder what it is like to experience this as a man?
> The woman: Do you?
>
> A man in the same circumstance: Have I hurt you?
> The woman: Why do you ask?
> The man: You moved.

Or take the fear of homosexuality:

> A bear is charging this hunter in the woods. The hunter fires, and misses. The bear breaks his rifle in two, sodomizes the hunter, then walks away. The hunter is furious. The next day be is back in the woods, with a new rifle. Again the bear charges, again the hunter misses, again he is sodomized. The hunter is now beside himself. He is going to get that bear, if it's the last thing he does. He gets himself an AK-47 assault rifle, goes back into the woods. Again the bear charges and, believe it or not, again

the hunter misses. The bear breaks the assault rifle, gently puts his paws around the hunter and says "Okay, come clean now. This isn't really about hunting, is it?"

Or take the fear of diminishing sexual powers with aging:

> This old man is on a walk when he comes upon a frog. The frog addresses him: "This is your lucky day. I'm a talking frog and I've been sent here specially for you. If you just say the word, I'll turn into a beautiful woman and I'll do anything you want."
> The man picks up the frog, puts it in his pocket, and resumes his walk.
> After a while the frog gets restless: "Hey, you up there. Didn't you hear what I said?"
> The old man says, "Yeah, I heard you. But I figure, at my age, rather than a beautiful woman, I'd prefer to have a talking frog."

Wit can be employed as a form of rebellion against authority. Most political jokes have this function. But Freud argues that there is a deeper rebellion; that against reason. This implies a kind of infantilization, a return to what Freud calls the "old homestead" of childhood in which wishes come magically true and in which playing (including the play with words) makes up much of life. Joking is, in a way, becoming a child again for a few moments, and that in itself is a source of pleasure.

For his own theoretical reasons, Freud makes a sharp distinction between the comic (which one "finds") and wit (which one "makes"). This is a useful distinction. But Freud also asserts that "Wit is . . . the contribution to the comic from the sphere of the unconscious."[18] That is a much more dubious formulation. All the same, Freud contributes to an understanding of the comic. His discovery of the parallels between dreams and jokes can quite easily be detached from his hydraulic model and indeed from his theory of the unconscious. It fits neatly into Schutz's understanding of both dreams and humor as finite provinces of meaning. Wit creates a separate reality, luminous with magical power, with its own distinct rules, some of which Freud correctly identified. And even if one is not persuaded that all jokes (or dreams, for that matter) express wish-fulfillment, many do indeed sublimate desires, including sexual desires, that are normally frustrated by society.

Then there is what Avner Ziv calls the social function of the comic.[19] This involves many issues of macrosocial institutionalization (such as comedy, the carnival, court jesters, circus clowns). These will be dealt with in the next chapter and can be put aside for now. But psychologists have mainly studied the microsocial dynamics of humor—that is, the way humor functions in small groups—and this should be looked at here.

As already mentioned, the smile and laughter play a crucial role in early socialization. They continue to play an important role in adult social relations, typically signaling friendliness, relaxation, solidarity. More specifically, the evocation of comic laughter is a common means by which individuals seek acceptance by others. Most individuals do this at one time or another. There is also the specific role of the group clown or comedian, an individual to whom the task of making everyone laugh has been explicitly or tacitly assigned. Sometimes this assignment is deliberately sought, sometimes it is inflicted without or even against the individual's desires. This role is near universal, in the most varied groupings and in different cultures. Humor functions sociopositively by enhancing group cohesion. The formula here goes something like this: Those who laugh together, belong together. A newcomer to just about any group is well-advised to find out quickly what people in this group laugh about—and, just as important, which topics are considered to be inappropriate for humorous treatment. Almost inevitably, though, humor also has socionegative aspects. It draws the boundaries of the group and ipso facto defines the outsider.

The boundary-marking function of humor becomes very clear in the case of so-called in-group jokes. Take the following two variants of a recent genre of American intellectual jokes:

What happens if you cross a Unitarian with a Jehovah's Witness?
A person who goes from house to house, and doesn't know why.

What happens if you cross a Mafioso with a deconstructionist?
Someone who makes you an offer that you cannot understand.

Try telling the first joke to someone with no knowledge of American religion, the second to someone unacquainted with postmodern literary theory. For another example:

This Jewish fellow was on vacation out west, met this Native-American girl, fell in love, married her, and took her back to New York. After a year she goes home for a visit.
"Are you happy?" her folks ask her. "Oh, yes, very happy."
"Is he treating you right?"
"Oh yes, he is just great."
"And what about his family? We've been told that Jews don't much like it if their children marry outsiders. How does his family feel about their son marrying an Indian girl?"
"Oh fine. They've been wonderful to me. They've even given me a new name. They call me Sitting Shive."

To find this joke funny one has to know the Jewish practice of mourning, sitting *shiva* (or *shive*) and, in a leap of arcane Americana, associate this with the historic warrior-chief, Sitting Bull. Try telling this joke to some visiting German, even one who speaks very good English.

Humor can also be used to soften hierarchical relationships. Ziv tells the story of how a supervisor responded to an employee who has yet again missed a day of work: "Don't forget that your grandmother has already died twice." Such jocular maneuvers are nowadays recommended very earnestly as "management tools." But also humor can be used (socionegatively) as an instrument of social control within a group. Here the individual who dissents from or does not measure up to the norms of the group is punished by ridicule. This less user-friendly utilization of the comic is commonly used in Japanese executive training workshops, part and parcel of the sadistic initiation for which this institution has become notorious.

There is also what Ziv calls the defensive function of humor.[20] This is not really a separate category. It is another variety of sublimation, already discussed in terms of reducing the anxiety incurred by aggression and sexuality. But more generally, humor can help manage fears associated with any threat, no matter what the case. Ziv reports on an experiment he conducted with young children. They were shown two short videos, one a very harmless, cuddly one, the other a rather frightening one. This was followed by a play period, after which the children were told that, before leaving for home, they could watch one of the two videos again. A large majority of the children chose the second, the frightening video. This experiment, Ziv argues persuasively, exemplifies the pleasure that both children and adults derive from horror movies, roller coaster rides, and other experiences that provide a *frisson* of terror without being *really* threatening. The pleasure comes from the relief from fear, a relief that, given the situation, can be confidently anticipated. However, humor also functions to contain terror deriving from events that are threatening in actual fact. Humor in war, in hospitals, and in other circumstances in which death or serious injury is a real possibility, is a well-known fact. There may be no atheists in foxholes, as Cardinal Spellman observed during World War II, but there are plenty of humorists.

A genre of jokes that illustrates this defense function is the one variously called black humor, gallows humor, or sick jokes. Some of these jokes refer to specific terrors, others relate more generally to the terror of mortality, as respectively in the following two examples:

A doctor has just received two laboratory reports on two of his patients, one of whom was found to have AIDS, the other Alzheimer's. Unfortunately, the lab has failed to put names on the reports, so that the doctor doesn't know which is which. Just then the wives of one of the patients calls. She is very worried about her husband, wants to know the test results. The doctor thinks for a moment, then says, "Here is what I suggest. Send him out for a walk. If he comes back, don't make love to him."

A child: May I play with grandmother?
The mother: No, I'm not going to unscrew the coffin a third time.

People whose professions regularly confront them with death or acute physical dangers are particularly given to macabre humor. Funeral directors are a case in point:

> A funeral director has finished laying out the corpse for viewing. He calls in the widow and asks her whether her husband looks all right to her.
> "Yes, fine," she says. "Only one thing: I think my husband should wear his blue suit for this occasion, the one I gave you."
> "No problem," says the funeral director. "It'll only take one minute." And really, it only takes one minute before the funeral director calls the widow back into the viewing room.
> "Is this all right now?" he asks.
> "Yes, indeed," says the widow. "But tell me, how come you could make the change so quickly?"
> "Oh, that was easy. Just switched heads."

The relief provided by defensive humor is psychological. But there is also evidence to the effect that humor is related to physical health and that it helps individuals recover from physical illness, as Kant indicated in his discussion of the comic.[21] Not all humor does. There is unhealthy laughter, presumably associated with socionegative humor. But positive, essentially harmless laughter appears to be health-inducing. Thus it was found that hospital patients recover faster if they can look at their situation with humor. An appreciation of the comic appears to be positively related to the will to live and the capacity to cope with illness. Also, humor facilitates the interaction between patients and hospital personnel, as well as relations between different echelons of the latter. Beyond that, humor has been deliberately used as a therapeutic tool, especially by psychotherapists.[22] This may involve various forms of kidding, but also irony or satire. The latter, it has been argued, can be conducive to insight: the patient laughs and ipso facto gains new insight into his condition:
A psychotherapist told the following story:

> One of his patients kept complaining about his wife's blatant unfaithfulness. She regularly invited her lover home, they made love on the sofa in the living room no matter whether the husband was home or not, they even left the door open when they were doing it. The therapist had

been suggesting to this man that he should begin to assert himself. Then one day the man came in for his session, looking very satisfied with himself. "Well, today I really followed your advice. I really asserted myself."

"What did you do?"

"I insisted that they close the door!"

At that point the therapist lost his professional cool and started to laugh uncontrollably. The patient was at first offended, then started to laugh too. This, according to the therapist who told the story, marked a positive turn in the course of the therapy.

In this story, seeing the point of the humor (in fact, a joke culled from real life) had a cognitive impact. This leads to what, in the context of the present argument, is the most interesting of the functions listed by Ziv, which he calls the intellectual one.[23]

At about four months of age, children laugh when tickled. At about eight months, they laugh at the game of peekaboo. At about one year of age they laugh at inappropriate behavior by an adult, such as the adult drinking from the child's bottle, walking on all fours, or making funny faces. Each step in this development involves an expansion of cognitive capacity, even the first. For while tickling is, as previously stated, a trigger for a physiological reflex, it is noteworthy that, not only must the tickling be performed by another person (one cannot tickle oneself), but for most children this person must be familiar. What is more, the tickler must, by his behavior, indicate that it is a game that is being played, that he has no aggressive intent; if the child is truly afraid, the same tickling movements will fail to produce laughter. At about two years of age, children will themselves engage in elaborate games of pretend, including word play and complicated structures of incongruity, often accompanying these activities with smiles or laughter.[24] At each step of this comic evolution there must exist, at whatever different levels of sophistication, the cognitive act of distinguishing what is pretend from what is for real. After the previous discussion of how philosophers have dealt with the comic experience, it will come as no surprise that psychologists have pointed out that this cognitive act involves the perception of incongruity: "One of the first indications of amusement [is] founded on incongruity. Incongruity is the basis for understanding the intellectual aspects of humor."[25]

The comic experience, already in young children, offers a release from the tyranny of the reality principle, a release from reason into a peculiar zone of liberty. Freud saw this very correctly. But because of his preoccupation with the mechanisms of what he thought of as the unconscious (an irrational entity par excellence), he failed to appreciate that the comic experience has a crucially important cognitive or intellectual function. This function is dependent on the ability to think in more than one dimension. It is, of course, most visible in wit, the most intellectual form of humor, but it is always present, at least potentially, in all manifestations of the comic. The psychological findings on this fully support the philosophical thesis of Marie Collins Swabey.

The most interesting contribution to the cognitive psychology of humor was made by a nonpsychologist. Arthur Koestler, best known for his brilliant novels on the ideological madnesses of the twentieth century, became increasingly interested in his later years in the processes of scientific discovery and thus in the psychology of creative thinking. The entire first part of his major work on the latter subject is devoted to humor.[26] He claims that three creative activities are closely related, embodied respectively in the jester, the sage, and the artist: the acts of creation in humor, in scientific discovery, and in the innovative art. He further claims that the boundaries between these three forms of creativity are fluid. The quality common to all three is "the perceiving of a situation or idea . . . in two self-consistent but habitually incompatible frames of reference."[27] This is exemplified in two jokes he tells (they are reworded here). The first is also told by Freud in his essay on wit:

> The marquis finds his wife in bed with a bishop. He doesn't say a word, but goes to the window and blesses the people walking under it. When his wife asks him what he thinks he is doing, he replies, "He is performing my function; I will perform his."[28]

The other joke in turn makes fun of Freudian psychoanalysis:

> Two Jewish ladies are talking.
> "My son is in psychoanalysis," says the first. "It seems that he has an Oedipus complex."
> To which the other lady replies: "Ach, Oedipus, Shmoedipus. Main thing, he loves his mother."

Both jokes juxtapose normally incompatible frames of reference, in the first case the logic of marital honor with that of the division of labor, in the second the conceptual edifice of psychoanalysis with the commonsensical world of Jewish motherhood.

The term coined by Koestler for the distinctive cognitive act involved here is "bisituation." It is the capacity to associate, to draw together two (or more) previously nonassociated aspects of reality. In German there are two verbal constructions that aptly express this feat: *mitdenken* (to think with), and *zusammendenken* (to think together). When this act is successfully accomplished, it brings with it a catharsis—the experience of "eureka!" or if one prefers, the "*aha!* experience." This is the structure of any creative act, but especially that of intellectual innovation—be it by the humorist, the scientist, or the creative artist. Koestler here adumbrates what Thomas Kuhn in his work on scientific revolutions has called a "paradigm shift": Science does indeed progress through the bit-by-bit accumulation of empirical data, as has been conventionally argued, but the big steps forward in science then come suddenly, with a jump from one theoretical framework into a new one. Koestler's central thesis is that getting the point of a joke is very much the same act as solving a scientific problem (or, for that matter, any kind of intellectual problem). This is a cathartic event. But the emotional catharsis is dependent on a cognitive perception. In the case of satire, the comic perception shades off into social science.

Further differentiations are possible—between voluntary and involuntary humor, between formal and informal humor. There are some, not terribly illuminating data on what kind of people laugh at what sorts of humor. But directly connected with the intellectual function of humor is the distinction between creative and receptive humor, which leads to the question: Who are the comedians? [29] Both amateur and professional comedians tend to be creative people—in Ziv's wording, people with "the ability to look beyond the obvious." Data indicate that such people tend to be men rather than women (who in turn are better at receptive humor—that is, they more readily laugh at the antics of comedians). This almost certainly tells nothing about the creative abilities of the two sexes, being rather rooted in socially defined gender roles. American data show a preponderance of Jews in the ranks of professional comedians, which fact can be easily related to what Thorstein Veblen called the "intellectual preeminence" of the Jews. Both forms of preeminence can be explained by the twin causes of an age-old Jewish culture of learning, honed in the subtleties of Talmudic argumentation, and the social marginality of Jews in Christian societies, which favored the skeptical, potentially sardonic perspective of the outsider. The somewhat sparse findings on professional comedians also indicate a poor family background marked by parental conflict. Wit in these circumstances is cultivated early as a defense mechanism. Very probably the question, Who are the comedians? is more usefully answered in sociological rather than psychological terms. The question then becomes, How is the comic institutionalized? This, precisely, is the next topic to be taken up.

### Notes

1. Norman Holland, *Laughing: A Psychology of Humor* (Ithaca, N.Y.: Cornell University Press, 1982), p. 76.

2. Marie Collins Swabey, *Comic Laughter*.

3. Helmuth Plessner, *"Lachen und Weinen,"* in *Philosophische Anthropologie* (Frankfurt: Fischer, [1941] 1970), 13ff.

4.  Max Scheler, *Die Stellung des Menschen im Kosmos* (Munich: Nymphen-burger Verlagshandlung, [1928] 1949).

5.  Helmuth Plessner, *"Das Laecheln,"* in Plessner, *Philosophische Anthro-pologie,* 175ff.

6.  Ibid., 185. My translation.

7.  J. Y. T. Greig, *The Psychology of Laughter and Comedy* (New York: Cooper Square, [1923] 1969), pass.; Paul McGhee, "Human Development: Toward a Life Span Approach," in Paul McGhee and Jeffrey Goldstein, eds., *Handbook of Humor Research,* vol. 1 (New York: Springer, 1983), 109ff.; Reinhard Lempp, *"Das Lachen des Kindes,"* in Thomas Vogel, ed., *Vom Lachen* (Tuebingen: Attempto, 1992), 79ff.

8.  The aforementioned J. Y. T. Greig. This author (whose gender is left undefined) was registrar of Armstrong College in the University of Durham. It is tempting to imagine how his (or her) hypothesis was received in a provincial British university in the 1920s.

9.  1 feel constrained, however, to report the following (although it seems appropriate that such grandfatherly bragging should be kept out of the text and be modestly confined to a footnote): When my granddaughter Diya was three years old, she made her first fully authenticated joke. She was coming down the stairs, proudly exhibiting a new dress. Her father said to her, "Hello, my beau-ty!" She smiled (she knew what she was doing) and replied, "Hello, my beast!"

10. Lempp, *"Das Lachen des Kindes."*

11. Avner Ziv, *Personality and Sense of Humor* (New York: Springer, 1984). In what follows, I make extensive use of Ziv's argument. If I may once more cite the legendary Rabbi Meir of Vilna, "If you find something good, don't be embar-rassed to enjoy it!"

12. Ibid., 4ff; C. R. Gruner, *Understanding Laughter* (Chicago: Nelson Hall, 1978); Lawrence La Fave et al., "Superiority, Enhanced Self-Esteem, and Per-ceived Incongruity," in Antony Chapman and Hugh Foot, eds., *Humor and Laughter: Theory, Research and Applications* (London: Wiley, 1976), 63ff.; Dolf Zill-man, "Disparagement Humor," in McGhee and Goldstein, *Handbook,* vol. 1, 85ff.

13. Washington gossip had it that this was one of President Ronald Rea-gan's favorite jokes.

14. Ziv, *Personality,* 15ff.

15. Sigmund Freud, "Wit and Its Relation to the Unconscious," in A. A. Brill, trans./ed., *The Basic Writings of Sigmund Freud* (New York: Modern Library, [1905] 1938), 633ff. *Wit* is Brill's translation of the German *Witz.* The German word can mean either wit or joke. Other English translators have given the title of Freud's work as "Jokes and Their Relation to the Unconscious." Either transla-tion does justice to Freud's intention. The joke is the most succinct form of wit.

16. Cf. John Murray Cuddihy, *The Ordeal of Civility* (New York: Basic Books, 1974). Cuddihy argues that what Freud was really talking about (and repressed!) was the conflict between modern civility and unassimilated Yiddishkeit or Jew-ishness, summed up in the lapidary formula "the id is the yid." Maybe so. *Se non e vero . . .*

17. Freud, "Wit and Its Relation," 698.

18.    Ibid., 782.

19.    Ziv, *Personality*, 26ff; Antony Chapman, "Social Aspects of Humorous Laughter," in Chapman and Foot, *Humor and Laughter*, 155ff.; Antony Chapman, "Humor and Laughter in Social Interaction," in McGhee and Goldstein, *Handbook*, vol. 1, 135ff.

20.    Ziv, *Personality*, 44ff.

21.    Vera Robinson, "Humor and Health," in McGhee and Goldstein, *Handbook*, vol. 11, 109ff.

22.    Harvey Mindess, "The Use and Abuse of Humor in Psychotherapy," in Chapman and Foot, *Humor and Laughter*, 331ff.

23.    Ziv, *Personality*, 70ff.; Thomas Shultz, "A Cognitive-Developmental Analysis of Humor," in Chapman and Foot, *Humor and Laughter*, IIff.; Jerry Sals, "Cognitive Processes in Humor Appreciation," in McGhee and Goldstein, *Handbook*, vol. 1, 39ff.

24.    Jean Piaget, *Play, Dreams and Imitation in Childhood* (London: Macmillan, 1951), pass.

25.    Ziv, *Personality*, 71f.

26.    Arthur Koestler, *The Act of Creation* (New York: Macmillan, 1964), 27.

27.    Ibid., 35.

28.    This is an anecdote told by Chamfort about the court of Louis XIV. Jokes do travel!

29.    Ziv, *Personality*, 130ff.; Howard Pollio and John Edgerly, "Comedians and Comic Style," in Chapman and Foot, *Handbook*, 215ff.; Maurice Charney, "Comic Creativity in Plays, Films and Jokes," in McGhee and Goldstein, *Handbook*, vol. 11, 33ff.

# 5

## *Homo Ridiculus*
## *Social Constructions of the Comic*

The clue to an understanding of the place of the comic in society is its profound affinity with religion and magic.

Social order, when it functions well, envelops the individual in a web of habits and meanings that are experienced as self-evidently real. This, as discussed earlier, is what Alfred Schutz called the paramount reality of everyday life. Despite this semblance of solidity, social order is always vulnerable to disruptions. These disruptions are caused, among other things, by the intrusions of *other* realities. The sacred is one such intrusion. The comic is another. The two have a lot in common, which is why saints and fools have often had an uncomfortable similarity. Any sociological treatment of the comic must take cognizance of this initially strange-seeming affinity. This has been adumbrated by Anton Zijderveld, one of the very small number of sociologists who have dealt systematically with the comic phenomenon.[1] In discussing the nature of the comic. Zijderveld uses the term *fascinans*, which Rudolf Otto, in the classic work *The Idea of the Holy*, employed to describe the strange ambiguity of attraction and dread that typically accompanies religious experiences. The comic, when it manifests itself in full force, engenders a similarly ambivalent fascination. So, of course, does magic (which differs from religion in that it is typically done by individual practitioners rather than social groups).

Both the sacred and the comic constitute what Schutz called finite provinces of meaning—islands, as it were, within the fabric of ordinary, everyday reality. They are simultaneously alluring and anxiety-provoking. If allowed to take over, they threaten normal reality. The person who lacks a sense of humor, or at any rate fails to see what is funny about a particular joke or humorous observation, feels irritated, perhaps even angry. He has been had, as the English phrase goes, and this fact discloses the vulnerability of his taken-for-granted normality. But the person who *does* get the point and who accordingly laughs at a humorous story or action also cannot sustain the laughter for too long a period before a certain anxiety develops. A few jokes can be very pleasant; a barrage of jokes, going on and on, will cease to be pleasant. The ominous dimension of the comic will then come to the fore. As with the sacred, the comic must be contained, domesticated, if its potential threat to social order is to be prevented from realization.

In the case of the comic, one may observe a gradation of threat, from harmless or innocent humor to the grotesque inversion of all accepted norms. The gradation runs from a mild joke to biting satire. If one wants to visualize the gradation, one could trace it from, say, the gentle fun of a Norman Rockwell picture to the savage humor of a Goya or Daumier. There is finally what has traditionally been called folly, in which the entire world is turned upside down. This is why Zijderveld uses the metaphor of the looking-glass in his analysis of traditional folly. In its mirror-effect the normal social world is both distorted and sharply illuminated.

Both the sacred and the comic can be contained in space, or in time, or in both. There are sacred places and sacred seasons. In the case of the comic, however, containment in time is much more important than containment in space. There may indeed be places that have been designated as the proper locales for comic performances. Most obviously, a building may be called a cabaret or even named the Opéra Comique. Other places, while also serving different functions, may have come to be defined as locales in which one may expect to hear jokes or witty conversation, such as the salons of eighteenth-century Paris or the coffeehouses of Central Europe in more recent times. Yet the coffeehouse is not like a cathedral. The latter is itself sacred space, the former is space that is not in itself comic but that offers an occasion for the comic. The difference is interesting, and not too easily explained. Perhaps an explanation may be sought in the exceedingly fugitive character of the comic experience. Time flattens all experiences, including that of the sacred. This is the process that Max Weber called routinization: The extraordinary becomes ordinary with repetition, indeed becomes a routine. The comic is peculiarly subject to this process. This is why one cannot effectively keep telling the same jokes to the same people:

> A recently incarcerated individual has his first exercise period in the prison yard. One prisoner calls out, "Thirty-four!" Everyone laughs. Another prisoner calls out, "Twenty!" Again everyone laughs. This goes on for a while. Then the new prisoner asks an older convict what is going on here. "You see," says the old convict, "most of us have been here a long time. We all know each other's jokes. So we have given them numbers and instead of telling the jokes, we just call out the numbers." The new prisoner thinks that this is an excellent idea. He wants to try it too. So he

calls out, "Forty-one!" Nobody laughs. "Fifteen!" Nobody laughs. And so on. "What did I do wrong?" asks the prisoner. "Was I not telling numbered jokes?" "Yes," says the old convict, "but it's a matter of *how* you tell them."

As was discussed in an earlier chapter, the comic most commonly appears in frequent though brief intrusions into ordinary social interaction. So that these intrusions can be perceived as indeed being comic, there is a need for what sociologists call a definition of the situation. These definitions not only determine the proper times for comic intermissions; they also draw the parameters of what may be treated comically. Put differently, there will always be conventionally understood signals announcing the appearance of the comic. These may be verbal. A joke may be introduced by the phrase, Have you heard this one?, a sardonic remark by a somewhat disarming preface such as, I hope you will not be offended if I say. . . . But more commonly the signal will be nonverbal: A shift in intonation. A conspiratorial smile. A sort of anticipatory laugh. Or a wink. Needless to say, these signals will vary as between social groups and settings. A wink in one group may signal a joke, in another an attempt at seduction. In a gathering of salesmen the phrase, Have you heard this one? may announce a joke; in an assembly of politicians it may be the preface to the latest gossip about the governor or some inner circle of power. The parameters of acceptable humor will vary as between salesmen, business executives, construction workers, or cloistered nuns. There is, as it were, a microsociology of the comic here, much of it already discussed in the preceding chapter.[2] But such signals are also institutionalized across entire societies, allowing at least in principle a macrosociology of humor. Thus there is something like a national sense of humor, which will usually be further differentiated by region, ethnicity, and class. In line with what has been said earlier on the need to contain or domesticate the potentially explosive power of the comic, one may add that there are differences in degree of this in different social settings. Thus, for example, one may compare the restrained, understated humor of upper-class American WASPs with the wit and surrealism of American Jewish humor. Perhaps Jews are more ready than WASPs to face up to the intrinsic vulnerability of social order; they certainly have the historical experience for it.

As the comic typically intrudes into ordinary social life in brief, even spasmodic moments, it is all the more important that people understand just when to laugh and what to laugh at. Every sociology student in America has learned the famous statement by W. I. Thomas, "If people define a situation as real, it is real in its consequences." Thomas would not disagree with a paraphrase: If people define a situation as comic, it will be comic in its effects. As the comic situation is socially defined, it is at the same time contained. Now one is permitted, even expected to laugh; when the comic moment has passed, one can (perhaps with some relief) revert to "for serious" interaction. Again, there will signals for this transition. They may be verbal: "And now, seriously . . . " More often they will be nonverbal. The intonation shifts again, the smile disappears, no more winking. But these signals are not just ad hoc, invented anew by the participants in a particular interaction. Rather, the signals are diffused through entire social groups or societies, and people learn them in the course of socialization along with the rest of the socially constructed symbol system. The term "laughing culture" has been used to denote this phenomenon.[3] The term "comic culture" is probably preferable.

A comic culture can be described quite simply as the definitions of comic situations, roles, and acceptable contents in any social group or society. Once again, it is possible to differentiate micro- and macro-sociological aspects of the phenomenon. There are comic cultures *en miniature,* within families, groups of friends, or other people in ongoing face-to-face interaction with each other. And then there are the comic cultures of regions, miscellaneous subcultures (such as ethnic, religious, or professional ones), and entire societies.

The comic culture of families is frequently created by young children. Little Johnny or little Jeannie said something very cute at age three, and ever since the whole family falls into maniacal laughter every time this historic dictum is quoted or alluded to. Anyone outside the family may have difficulty in seeing the humor, but this is just the point: the outsider is precisely identified as such by his failure to understand the comic culture of the in-group. In this, comic culture performs the same important social function of all symbol systems: it draws the boundary between insiders and outsiders. Comic culture is inclusive and exclusive at the same time. The same goes for all intimate groups other than families. There will be a common stock of experiences to which insiders refer or allude in a code that the outsider does not know. If the outsider is to be eventually included in the group, he will have to learn this code. This can be a difficult and lengthy learning process. Knowing when and at what to laugh is an important part of the process by which the outsider is, so to speak, naturalized within the in-group and vicariously internalizes its history. As in the joke about the convicts in the prison yard, it is not enough to call out the numbers; one must know *how* to tell the funny stories. An interesting case in point is what happens upon marriage, at least in modern societies. The marriage partners come not only from different families but very often from widely different social backgrounds. They begin to construct a common world of meaning in what can be called the ongoing marital conversation.[4] In the course of this they internalize, often in a somewhat modified or reinterpreted form, each other's premarital histories. This includes the allegedly amusing episodes. After some years of this, each spouse can tell the funny stories of the other's past as well or even better than the one to whom they originally happened. Old married couples, like the convicts in the prison yard, can chuckle away as they give each other coded shorthand signals that are completely incomprehensible to anyone else.

One could go on endlessly about macrosociological comic cultures, and indeed there are many books about such cultures—books on the humor of the American South or the different regions of Germany, of Irish-Americans or African-Americans, of doctors or lawyers, or indeed of entire nations.[5] While it might be entertaining to provide samples of these here, it would do little to advance the argument of the book. It should be pointed out, though, that there is often considerable divergence between an empirically observable comic culture and popular myths about it. Thus it is probably correct that the comic cultures of large, cosmopolitan cities (such as New York, Paris, or pre-Nazi Berlin) are sharper and more witty than the comic cultures of their respective provincial hinterlands. But there are also comic stereotypes that probably have little empirical basis. Thus in Iranian folklore three cities have been associated with different comic figures: Rasht with loose women and their stupid cuckolded husbands, Tabriz with bucolic fools, and Isfahan with practitioners of witty repartee.[6] It is very doubtful if these stereotypes have much to do with the real comic cultures of these localities. Another point should be made here: There has always been a distinction between the comic culture of the streets and that of formal comedy—say, between what ordinary Parisians laughed at while taking a break at Les Halles and what their highly educated compatriots laughed at while watching a performance at the Opéra Comique. The distinction is that between the comic in the life world and that in fiction.[7] In most cases, the latter must be rooted in the former, or it will be either not funny or downright incomprehensible. The exception would be esoteric esthetic elites who cultivate an idiosyncratic sense of humor that deliberately eschews what other people find amusing.

Leaving aside the aforementioned imperative of containing the threat that the comic potentially holds for social order, the social uses or functions of the comic are basically the psychological functions writ large. They can be conveniently subsumed under Avner Ziv's typology discussed in the previous chapter. There is the aforementioned boundary-drawing function: A comic culture delineates the boundaries of the group and ipso facto identifies those who are excluded from it. A classical Jewish joke makes this point with elegant succinctness:

A Jew, commenting on someone or other: *"Nebbich!"*
A Gentile listening to this: "Just what does *nebbich* mean?"
The Jew: "You don't know what *nebbich* means? *Nebbich!"*

Then there is aggression and the sublimation of taboos. Closely related to this is the rebellion against oppression. Examples of these given
in the previous chapter would do equally well here. What should be
strongly emphasized is what Ziv calls the intellectual function of the
comic. As we argued in several earlier passages of this book, the comic
faculty in human beings, whatever else it may be, is also a cognitive one.
It brings about distinctive, objective perceptions of reality. If this is true
philosophically and psychologically, it is certainly also true sociologically. Comic perceptions of society often give brilliant insights into the
latter. A good cartoon or a good joke can often be more revealing of a
particular social reality than any number of social-scientific treatises.
Thus the comic can often be understood as a sort of popular sociology.
Take the phenomenon of American capitalism and its effect on American culture—the ubiquity of competition, the excesses of consumerism,
business success as a dominant value. These have been dissected and
criticized from different angles, not only from the ideological left. Complex theories and unreadable tomes could be cited. Alternatively, one
could tell the following three jokes:

> Two businessmen are on safari. Suddenly they hear drums in the distance.
> Their native guide calls out "A lion is heading this way!" and promptly
> disappears into the bush. One of the two businessmen sits down and puts
> on running shoes. "What are you doing?" says the other businessman,
> "You can't outrun a lion." "I don't have to outrun the lion," says the first
> businessman. "I only have to outrun you."
>
> An American businessman is in India. An Indian colleague wants to
> sell him an elephant: "Special price for you: One thousand dollars, that's
> all."
> "Look, I live in Chicago, in a one-bedroom studio apartment on the
> thirtieth floor of an apartment building. What would I do with an
> elephant?"
> "Okay, okay. Eight hundred dollars."
> "No, as I told you."
> "Okay, okay. Seven hundred dollars."
> "Look, let me tell you again. I live in a one-bedroom apartment, on the
> thirtieth floor . . . "
> "Ah, you are a hard bargainer? Let me make my last offer: *Two* ele-
> phants for eight-hundred-and-fifty."
> "Good. Now you're talking!"

Two partners in New York's garment district are facing bankruptcy. They decide that one will commit suicide, the other will collect the insurance and save the business. They draw straws. The loser cries a bit, writes a note to his wife, then goes up to the roof and jumps off. His partner watches from the window. As the suicide falls, he looks into the windows of the competitors on the higher floors. As he falls by his partner's window, he calls out his last words on earth: "Cut velours!"

The experience of the comic is a human universal. Comic cultures can differ greatly. Some social scientists, especially anthropologists, have tried to generalize on the cross-cultural character of some manifestations of the comic. Among them, in two different generations, have been two distinguished British scholars: A. R. Radcliffe-Brown and Mary Douglas.

Although he did not coin this phrase, Radcliffe-Brown popularized the concept of "joking relationship."[8] This is defined as follows: "A relation between two persons in which one is by custom permitted, and in some instances required, to tease or make fun of the other, who in turn is required to take no offense."[9] There are two versions of this, symmetrical and asymmetrical. In a symmetrical joking relationship the two persons can make fun of each other, be it at the same time or on different occasions. In an asymmetrical joking relationship one person is the comedian, the other must always be the straight man. Radcliffe-Brown gives examples from Africa (his original field), Asia, Oceania, and North America. Joking relationships are found, for example, between in-laws and between grandparents and grandchildren. A few cases involve entire tribes or clans. Always, the relationships evince what Radcliffe-Brown calls a "peculiar combination of friendliness and antagonism." His theory of the function of these relationships is summarized as follows: "Both the joking relationship which constitutes an alliance between clans or tribes, and that between relatives by marriage, are modes of organizing a definite and stable system of social behavior in which conjunctive and disjunctive components . . . are maintained and combined."[10] Or, if one prefers: "If you can no longer hit them with a machete, hit them with a joke!"

Radcliffe-Brown belonged to the so-called functionalist school of British social anthropology (which later bloomed into so-called structural-functionalism in American sociology), and his discussion of joking relationship suffers from the limitations of this school. The main limitation is brought out by a concept often used by Talcott Parsons, the most influential American sociologist who carried on where Radcliffe-Brown and his associates left off—the concept of "system maintenance." Social phenomena are analyzed in terms of their contribution to the stability of the social order, to maintaining the system. This approach has been rightly criticized as overemphasizing the rational, systemic character of human societies. Mary Douglas, in her essay on the comic, criticizes Radcliffe-Brown as being both too abstract and too obsessed with systemic order.[11]

Douglas also uses miscellaneous ethnographic materials, though most of them are from Africa. Using both Bergson's and Freud's theories of the comic, she sees joking as "an attack on control," with "a subversive effect on the dominant structure of ideas." The scatological aspects of humor provide a good illustration of this. Yet there is no intention here of actually overthrowing the controlling structures. Rather, the comic is a "play upon form," a momentary relativization that is pleasurable in itself as well as permitting the sublimation of forbidden desires. In order to preserve this harmless character of humor, comic situations must be signaled as such: Have you heard this one? and the like. There is a paradox here: Jokes are antiritual, yet joking is itself established in rites. One could say that joking ritualizes antirites. As Douglas puts it, "The message of a standard rite is that the ordained patterns of social life are inescapable. The message of a joke is that they are escapable. A joke is by nature an anti-rite."[12]

Douglas comes close here to the dimension of containment that has been emphasized in this chapter, though she does not quite get there. In any case, joking provides a relief from social classifications and hierarchies, a softening of the boundaries, "a temporary suspension of the social structure." It can also be a form of ritual purification, as in cases where joking is used to cleanse an offender from certain sexual offenses, Douglas's discussion of the comic phenomenon is most profound when she describes the joker as a great relativizer, indeed as "a kind of minor mystic." One could also say that the joker is a kind of minor magician. He waves his magic wand and, at least for a moment, the harsh contours of social reality melt away and imagination can fill the resulting empty space. Douglas enumerates a number of joker-gods—the Greek Proteus, the Hindu Ganesh, the Yoruba Legba (who continues in sinister forms in Haitian Voudun). She then claims that it is "not too bold to suggest" that some African cultures, through their joking rites, have developed their own philosophy of the absurd. These rites attempt to express the unfathomable, often in highly poetic forms. In this context Douglas refers to Victor Turner's work on the cult of Chihamba among the Ndembu of Zambia.[13] If Douglas is right (and she very probably is), cults like that of Chihamba represent the universalization of Erasmus's vision of the rule of Lady Folly.

Thomas Luckmann, in his book *The Invisible Religion*, which has become a classic in the sociology of religion, makes a very useful distinction.[14] He distinguishes between institutionally diffuse and institutionally specific religion. Through much of history, religion was not relegated to specialized institutions; rather, it was diffused through all social institutions—kinship, the polity, the economy. Only in some societies have there been institutions defined specifically as dealing with religion; the Christian church has been such an institution (enormously important, of course, in the development of Western civilization). A similar distinction can be made with regard to the comic. Much of the time it is diffused throughout the whole spectrum of social institutions, popping up virtually everywhere, without a specific institutionalization of its own. There are loose cases of institutionalization, which might be called intermediate stages. Such a case would be the "appointment," by tacit consent, of an individual to be the comedian in a small group (this case was discussed previously as an example of the microsociology of the comic). But also there have been specifically institutionalized roles and aggregates of roles with the assignment of representing the comic. The most important of these roles has been that of the fool; aggregations of the role, sometimes in highly organized form, can be found in different versions ranging from elegantly stylized comedy to the chaotic world of the carnival.[15]

In modern usage the terms *fool* and *folly* refer either to stupidity or to madness. Traditionally, in European languages, the terms had a wider meaning. Traditional folly, in Anton Zijderveld's description, was "beyond sanity and insanity." Looking at the accounts of folly in the Middle Ages and the Renaissance, we would clearly classify some of its practitioners today as mentally retarded or psychotic. Even then, it was recognized that some fools were slow or crazy. But an interesting distinction was made, that between "natural" and "artificial" fools. The former were destined to play the fool by some congenital defect; the latter *chose* to play the fool as a result of what today would be called a career decision. In France there was a wonderful phrase defining the latter case: such an individual was a *fou en titre d'office*—an officially accredited fool, if you will—a fool ex officio. Some of these individuals were clearly not crazy and anything but stupid. They were performing an institutionally defined *social role*. If some of them happened to be mentally retarded or psychotic, that fact was, strictly speaking, irrelevant to the role performance. The role represented and indeed reproduced a specific perspective on reality—precisely that of folly. It was a surreal, an upside-down perspective. It embodied quite clearly the central features of the comic analyzed by philosophers and psychologists—incongruity on the one hand, sublimation and a strange kind of liberation on the other.

In Western civilization, the roots of the fool go back to classical antiquity, especially to the Dionysian cult and its later Roman adaptation, the festival of the Saturnalia. The more proximate roots are in the Middle

Ages, specifically the various types of "wandering folk" (called *fahrendes Volk* in German), which crowded the roads of Europe for centuries. They were a motley band—pilgrims, preachers, scholars, minstrels, brigands—but also every kind of entertainer—musicians, jugglers, acrobats. The medieval fool was an amalgam of all of these, often appearing in the garb of any of them, recognizable as distinctive only by the role he performed. The wandering fools were frequently of monastic origin, individuals (usually men, though there were some cases of renegade nuns) driven from their monasteries in punishment for their own misdeeds, by a desire to be free of monastic discipline, or by economic circumstances. A French term for these monastic escapees was *goliards*. They constituted a bizarre mixture of vagabondage, crime, scholarship, and entertainment, living by their wits, relegated to the margins of society, always on the move. In a slightly ironic way one might apply to them the label a "free-floating intelligentsia," which Karl Mannheim coined for a much more recent phenomenon (Mannheim applied the term to modern intellectuals, who are very rarely free-floating; the *goliards* fit his idea much better).

A good deal of *goliard* literature has survived, as well as other accounts of medieval and Renaissance folly. Zijderveld described it as "a brimful and coarsely joyous reality" and as "a world of freedom outside the confines of church and society."[16] In this marginal world, the fool enjoyed a strange freedom (the German *Narrenfreiheit*). In word, song, and action he was allowed to debunk both religious and secular authorities (though, obviously, there were occasions when some of the authorities lost their tolerance and suppressed the folly). A key theme in folly was inversion. It was expressed literally in language and ritual—Latin sentences pronounced backwards, Catholic ceremonies performed in inverted order. But more generally everything was turned upside down in the enactments of folly—all social differentiations (including gender) and hierarchies (including those of the church) were obliterated, parodied, or turned upside down. In the late Middle Ages, in a curious synthesis, folly merged with death, as expressed in the carnivallike "death dance" (*Totentanz*). Zijderveld observed that folly and death appeared here as the "twin revelers." Folly, which relativized and subverted all social order, finally foreshadowed death, which obliterates all social order once and for all.

Folly as a general cultural phenomenon began to decline in the early modern period. Zijderveld explains this fact in terms of what Max Weber called rationalization. He is very probably correct in this explanation. If so, the principal culprit is the rising bourgeoisie, that most rational and serious class. But as folly began to disappear from the streets, it was immortalized in literature.[17] In 1494 Sebastian Brant's book *The Ship of*

*Fools (Das Narren Schyff)* was published. Here, following a long ecclesiastical tradition, folly was perceived and condemned as sinful. But not long after, in 1515, came the publication in High German of a collection of stories about the great fool and prankster Till Eugenspiegel, "a kind of peg on which all kinds of funny stories about pranks, tricks and jests could be conveniently hung."[18] Erasmus's *Praise of Folly*, published in 1511, was probably the first *positive* treatment of folly in European literature (even if, as was mentioned earlier, Erasmus kept saying that he did not really mean it, that it was not "for serious"—one should not believe him). One might say, though, that in this Erasmus is more representative of a medieval perspective than (as is usually maintained) of a modern worldview.[19]

At the same time, folly became professionalized. Both as literature and as profession, folly moved off the streets. In this move it lost both its rootage in popular culture and its marginality. The most important institutionalization of this move was the role of the court fool.[20] Folly was now confined in the courts of the *ancien regime*, this last bastion of an earlier nonbourgeois culture. Here too there were "natural" fools (among them dwarfs, for whom the aristocracy, especially its ladies, had a bizarre and frequently lascivious affection). But mostly the court fools performed their role *en titre d'office*. Some of them were highly sophisticated professionals, periodically exercising considerable power. They were known not only for their wit (which, of course, was the defining precondition for their profession), but also for their political cunning and personal malice. Having no outside base of support, the court fool was totally dependent on the good will of the monarch who kept him, and it was undoubtedly this dependence and the resultant complete loyalty that endeared the role to the monarch. Needless to say, the good will of the monarch was something that one could not rely upon. Thus the role of the court fool was a very precarious one. But even while he could bask in the monarch's favor, the court fool's existence was not very enviable. He had to march around in an absurd costume and, while exercising his wit, keep alert at all times to the shifting moods and prejudices of his master. In a real sense he was a sort of pet. Indeed, at some courts the fools had to sleep in the dogs' kennel. European courts contained fools from the sixteenth through the eighteenth centuries, but the decline in the institution began around 1700.

Zijderveld sums up this final period as follows: "First absolutist monarchs could do without their parasitical fools, then the society which they themselves lived off as true parasites could do without these monarchs. In this sense, the decline of the court fool was the prologue to the decline of absolutism and thus the prologue to the Revolution of 1789."[21] This, of course, was the moment when the Goddess of Reason usurped the throne of Lady Folly. Or so it seemed. Looking back on the two centuries since this usurpation one may well conclude that the new rational divinity has produced more destructive folly than was ever dreamed of when Stultitia roamed the streets and strutted in the palaces of Europe.

Zijderveld's view is that folly died with the triumph of modern rationality and that any attempts to revive it are futile. He may be too pessimistic about this. Again, the analogy with religion is useful. One reason why Thomas Luckmann made the distinction between institutionally diffuse and institutionally specific religion was to run against the widespread view of sociologists at that time (in the 1960s) that decline of churches was to be equated to decline of religion. Against this Luckmann insisted on the continuing importance of an "invisible religion," diffused through many sectors of society and not confined to specifically religious institutions. The same may well be the case with folly. Institutional embodiments of folly, such as the *goliards* or the court fools, may have disappeared. But folly almost certainly continues in institutionally diffuse ways and it may pop up in the most unexpected places. But there have even been institutional continuities. Leave aside for the moment the development of the comic theater and its professional comedians, which we will look at briefly a little later. Also leave aside the popular theater, such as vaudeville and burlesque in America, in which many elements of traditional folly reappear in unexpected guises. One may focus instead on one distinctly modern institution—the circus and its clowns.[22]

The circus as an institution originated in the late eighteenth century, thus coinciding more or less with the demise of the court fool. It was an emphatically nonaristocratic institution, at first patronized by the bourgeoisie and then commanding much broader popular appeal. It began with an arena for equestrian exhibitions started by one Philip Astley on the outskirts of London in 1768. In a circular riding ring he staged feats of horsemanship, acrobatics on horseback, and he interspersed these with comic skits. The last of these, of course, became the domain of the clown, a figure in direct apostolic succession from the medieval fool via the Harlequins and Pierrots of the formal theater of the early modern period. Within twenty-five years, now under the name of circus, Astley's invention was introduced throughout Europe and North America. It has survived every since.

Here is a description of the circus clown dating from 1802: "rustic appearance, vacant or gazing eyes, arms dangling, yet the shoulders raised, the toes turned inwards, a shambling gait with a heavy step, great slowness of conception, and apparent stupidity of mind and manner."[23] The figure has hardly changed since then. Neither has the bulk of his repertoire, with its stylized pratfalls, games of peekaboo, and feats of magic invulnerability. A prototypical clowning scene involves the clown's antagonist, a serious figure, going after him with a hammer or some other weapon. The clown eludes the antagonist, executing versatile evasive maneuvers despite his seeming awkwardness, and when he is finally caught and hit over the head and thrown to the ground, he always jumps up again, unhurt and invincible. Like the fool, the clown is a magician. And, like the world of folly, the world of the circus creates an oasis of enchantment within the reality of modern rationality. Most modern adults, at least those with a measure of "higher" education, are not easily amused by the antics of the circus clown. Children invariably are. This is revealing. For even if, as Max Weber believed, the modern world is one of radical disenchantment, every generation of children recreates the enchanted garden from which the Goddess of Reason was supposed to liberate mankind. Children immediately identify with the clown and his world. One might put forth the thesis that they know something that their elders have forgotten.

In the history of the circus, as in other manifestations of comic culture, one can observe a dialectic between popular and high cultural forms. The circus clown as such is rarely an object of attention by serious cultural critics, though some of the great virtuosi of circus clowning have been—such as Grock (1880–1959), a Swiss clown who dominated European circuses for many years, and Oleg Popov, the star of the Moscow Circus beginning in the 1950s. It is only a short step from these circus figures to comic actors and mimes such as Charlie Chaplin, Marcel Marceau, and Jean-Louis Barrault. The career of Chaplin in the development of motion pictures suggests, all by itself, that the announcement of the final demise of the fool has been premature.

Nor is the fool a role limited to Western civilization.[24] There are reports of official jesters at the courts of the Incas and the Tokugawa *shogun.* Clowns (*vidusaka*) appear in ancient Indian plays, and this theatrical convention continues in contemporary Japanese drama.[25] Ceremonial clowns have been studied in certain African cultures.[26] Possibly the most interesting cases of ritual folly outside Western civilization come from several Native American cultures. Here one finds ceremonial fools, who are supposed to engage in what is nicely called contrary behavior. This includes transvestism, backward speech, mockery of sacred rituals, and revolting acts (such as drinking urine). The similarity to the medieval European practices described earlier is striking. The fool also occupies a place in Native American mythology. The best-known description of one such case is Paul Radin's account of the so-called trickster cycle of the Winnebago Indians.[27] The mythical trickster is Wakdjunkara, a fool of classical form, whose exploits are

strongly reminiscent of Till Eugenspiegel and the latter's probably antecedents in the Middle East.

These cross-cultural appearances of the role of the fool are especially
interesting because it is unlikely that all of them can be explained by
cultural borrowings. Cultural diffusionists might hypothesize that the
fool was invented in, say, India, and then wandered off in all directions.
To be sure, there very probably was some such diffusion (certainly in the
case of Till Eugenspiegel). However, it is stretching the explanatory
power of diffusionist theory to assume that it can account for phenomena stretching from medieval Europe to Tokugawa, Japan from East Africa to the plains of North America—all before the development of
modern communications. A more functionalist interpretation suggests
itself. It seems plausible that folly and fools, like religion and magic,
meet some deeply rooted needs in human society. The cross-culturally
common features of the phenomenon suggest what these needs might
be: the violation of taboos, the mockery of sacred and profane authorities and symbols, reversals of language and action, and a ubiquitous
obscenity. All of these are nicely subsumed under the Native American
term contrary behavior. What could be the *social* function of this? Clearly, there are psychological functions writ large, as was observed earlier.
Zijderveld uses the phrase "safety-valve hypothesis" to describe these:
Society allows the carefully circumscribed expression of prohibited impulses and, by doing so, prevents their disrupting the social order "for
serious." There is certainly something to that. Beyond this, however,
social order is enhanced by allowing a place within it of counterthemes,
counterworlds. Zijderveld quotes the Dutch sociologist W. F. Wertheim,
who described the phenomenon of folly as a "counter-point to the leading melody," thus finally contributing to the integration of society.[28]
This is probably as far as functionalist explanations can carry one. As
Mary Douglas criticized A. R. Radcliffe-Brown, it does not go far
enough. Zijderveld understands this. He sees in folly the element of
magic, the numinous quality of a counterworld that is haunting the
world of ordinary life and thereby putting it in danger. This quasi-
magical, quasi-religious character of the comic is intrinsic to its very
nature and as such universal. It haunts all societies, and all societies
must find ways of protecting themselves against it. Given this, it should
not be surprising that the fool appears in so many places.

Formal comedy has been, ever since Aristophanes, an important
manifestation of high culture in Western civilization.[29] Yet comedy, as
performed for the aristocracy or the bourgeoisie, ever again derived
inspiration from the comic culture of the general populace and in turn
influenced the latter (especially, of course, since the advent of modern
media of mass communication). Medieval fools reappear in new forms

in Shakespeare's plays (and not only in those categorized as comedies), in Cervantes's *Don Quixote* and, probably in the most elegant transformation, in the *commedia dell'arte,* especially those of Harlequin and Pierrot, who in turn helped shape the character of the circus clown. Its dirty old man with the baggy trousers, Pantalone or Pantaloon, experienced an American incarnation in the comedian of burlesque theater and country fair. Busy literary scholars, if they try hard enough, could probably trace some of the obscene jokes that have titillated audiences in these American locales of emphatically low culture all the way back to the verbal orgies of the *goliards.*

The theater, as a physical structure and as a social organization, is the setting for formal comedy. It contains both actors and audience in an ongoing interaction. The audience is an essential part of the event, creating an antiphony of performance and laughing response. Thus comedy, true to its cultic origins, constitutes a sort of ceremony, even in its most modern versions. The same is true of the cabaret and the performances of stand-up comedians. The ceremonial element, of course, is lost when a solitary reader immerses himself in the written text of a comedy, as it is lost when comedy is transmitted through the modern media of radio, film or television. There can be little doubt, though, that the comic experience is diluted as a result. By the same token, the task for the creator of comedy (the comic author or actor) becomes more difficult in the absence of a live audience. It is instructive that the producers of television comedies have found it useful to invite live audiences to the studio during filming and to broadcast canned laughter when the comedy goes on the air.

The theater has always been a magical place. This quality has repeatedly been noted. This is a place where anything might happen, a place of mystery and fascination. The magic of the theater, of course, expresses itself in tragedy as well as comedy, and it is intrinsic to the Aristotelian catharsis that ideally is engendered by either. The catharsis of comedy, as was noted earlier, is different from that of tragedy. Albeit sometimes in very muted tones, it reiterates the primeval catharsis of the Dionysian orgy. The theater as an institution rigorously contains this chaotic element—in space, in time, and through the constraints of artistic form. The modern theater is a building: What is plausible inside the building is not plausible outside it. The comic performance is scheduled at certain hours on certain days: at other times its fantastic reality can be put aside. Comedy as played in the theater follows very specific rules and conventions: This ensures that not quite "anything might happen." When the performance is over, one leaves the building and, somehow refreshed, returns to the "standard time" (Alfred Schutz's term) and the routine activities of ordinary social life.

Bernhard Greiner, a historian of comedy, has proposed that comedy is constituted by an act of "doubling" (*Dopplung*). That is, comedy establishes a counterworld to the world of ordinary life. Tragedy, of course, does the same. It could be argued, though, that the doubling of comedy is more radical. Tragedy, after all, is always based on the actual realities of the human condition.

Consequently, the necessary suspension of doubt (what phenomenologists call the *epoché*) must be more radical in the case of comedy. The tragic hero incurs guilt, his efforts to avert destiny are doomed to fail, the consequences of his actions are ironically perverse, and in the end he typically dies. The tragic drama compresses and stylizes these events in a manner that requires a certain *epoché*, yet all these components of the tragic trajectory are in fact present in the empirical realities of human life. By contrast, the comic hero is eternally innocent, he triumphs over all adversities, the ironic consequences of his actions actually turn out to be to his advantage, and in the end he typically marries or triumphs in love. To enter into *this* counterworld surely requires a more radical *epoché*. The comic author and the comic actor must seduce the audience into this *epoché*, a task that is arguably more difficult than that of their colleagues in the business of producing tragedies. The distinctively comic suspension of doubt or disbelief is necessitated by the most accomplished works of Shakespeare or Molière, as it is by the flimsiest operetta or the crudest episodes told by a vaudeville comedian.

The *commedia dell'arte* was the fullest reappropriation of the Dionysian element and its magic in modern theater.[30] It is virtually impossible to appreciate this by reading its texts. There is a very close linkage between word and action, which the written text cannot reproduce. One can attempt an approximation of the experience by looking at pictures, such as the famous ones by Antoine Watteau. The *commedia dell'arte* was drama cast in quite rigid forms, almost liturgical in character. There were fixed characters, costumes and masks, stereotyped movements, and schematic plots. Yet within these forms there was great variability through improvisations, both spoken and acted out. What was presented to the audience was the magic of a rich, densely populated counterworld. The principal characters present themselves as timeless, mythopoetic figures, headed by Harlequin (originally Arlechino), the prototypical fool who began his career as a stumbling rustic bumpkin and who was transformed in France into Pierrot, a witty philosopher. Ever since, fools and clowns have alternated between these two prototypical characters. Then there was Columbina/Columbine, Harlequin's saucy girlfriend (the two were immortalized in music as Papageno and Papagena in Mozart's *Magic Flute*); the aforementioned Pantalone; followed by Dottore, the timeless embodiment of the fraudulent expert;

Capitano, a strutting, *macho* man of action whose efforts are invariably frustrated (he was originally depicted as a Spaniard); and the wily servants (*zanni*), to whom Arlechino originally belonged (he reappears in this character in Cervantes's Sancho Panza and as Leporello in Mozart's *Don Giovanni*). If one were a Jungian (a possibility not recommended here), one would say that these figures are archetypes surfacing from the deepest levels of the collective unconscious of Western civilization; the non-Jungian can still marvel at their enduring fascination.

The *commedia dell'arte* had three sources: the *commedia erudita* (formal comedy) of the Renaissance, popular dramas, and the traditions of the carnival. The dialectic between high and popular comic culture can be clearly observed here. And as with the more popular forms of comedy, the *commedia dell'arte,* in its improvisations, provided occasions for sharp satire directed against every kind of authority. This repeatedly led to political difficulties, as when the *Theatre Italien* in Paris was temporarily closed in 1697. Many years later, during the post-Napoleonic period of political repression, the Viennese comic actor and author Johannn Nestroy gave elegant form to this tradition of satire. He was only temporarily restrained from practicing it by the prohibition of all improvisations by the censorship office. All police states must worry about improvisation. Yet the alternation of formal stylization and spontaneous improvisation is one of the very essences of comedy. Greiner's characterization of the *commedia dell'arte* could be applied to comedy in general: "Nothing in this world is certain, everything could be revealed as illusion from moment to the next. Such a world is only tolerable if only the moment counts. Earlier events must not have been congealed into depressing 'treasury of experience,' future events must not be anticipated as possible threats. Thus this form of theater liberates from the heaviness of life."[31]

Finally, a different social construction of the comic must be looked at here. Here there is containment in time only. It is spatially unbounded, with relatively loose forms of behavior and speech, and with no dividing barrier between performers and audience. Here, even in modern times, one is closest to the Dionysian *komos*. The generic term for this institution is *carnival*.[32] It is originally a European construction, but it has absorbed into itself very different cultural elements (as in the carnivals of Brazil and the Caribbean). There are also analogs in non-Western cultures.

Originally, of course, the term *carnival* (literally, goodbye to the flesh) refers to the festivities on the Tuesday before Ash Wednesday, the last expression of *joie de vivre* before the fasting period of Lent. The scheduling of the event within the Christian church year is instructive. The wild celebration of all the joys of the flesh is already overshadowed by the impending gloom of Lent, life is celebrated in the shadow of death. The generic use of the term was employed by the Russian scholar Mikhail Bakhtin (of whom more in a moment). It is useful, since the carnival spirit has not been limited to Mardi Gras. A whole series of festivals has been characterized by the same eruption of folly. There was notably the Feast of Fools, celebrated in Western Europe at the New Year and organized by the lower clergy (the same resentful population from whom the *goliards* were recruited). There were other celebrations, mostly observed in the period between Christmas and Epiphany. All of these events were planned and conducted by organizations that constituted, as it were, committees or fraternities of fools. This form of social organization has survived to the present day, as for instance in New Orleans, where these groups are closely related to the overall status system in both the white and black communities.

To get a sense of these events the following description is useful. It is taken from a statement by the Theological Faculty of Paris in 1444. The statement, describing the Feast of Fools, was intended to put a stop to these practices (it failed to do so):

> Priests and clerks may be seen wearing masks and monstrous visages at the hours of the office. They dance in the choir dressed as women, panders or minstrels. They sing wanton songs. They eat black puddings at the horn of the altar, while the celebrant is saying mass. They play at dice there. They cense with stinking smoke from the soles of old shoes. They run and leap through the church, without a blush at their own shame. Finally they drive about the town and its theaters in shabby traps and cars; and rouse the laughter of their fellows and the bystanders in infamous performances, with indecent gestures and verses scurrilous and unchaste.[33]

One of the most influential interpretations of the carnival is that of the aforementioned Mikhail Bakhtin, in a book written in 1940.[34] The aim of the book is to place Rabelais within the history of the "folk culture of humor." The most important expressions of the latter, according to Bakhtin, were in the ritual events generically subsumed under the term *carnival*, in verbal compositions of various sorts (including parodies) and in an assortment of popular curses, oaths, and ditties. In all of these Bakhtin detects a common idiom, which evolved over centuries going all the way back to the comic rituals of classical antiquity. This is the idiom of "carnival laughter." It was, and is, characterized by a profound egalitarianism (official hierarchies ignored or turned upside-down). It was festive; not individual but "laughter of all the people"; universal in scope, perceiving the entire world as folly; ambivalent, in that it was both deprecating and triumphant. Bakhtin also uses the phrase "grotesque realism" to describe this idiom. It debunked all idealistic preten-

sions and emphasized the grossest bodily functions: "Laughter de-
grades and materializes."[35]

Some of this reads as if the carnival spirit was a sort of precocious
dialectical materialism. Leaving aside the question of whether Bakhtin
really believed this or whether these Marxist tones provided protective
coloring against the Stalinist censors of the time, this quasi-revolutionary
interpretation of the carnival is highly unpersuasive. As Zijderveld points
out in his discussion of the same phenomena, there was hardly ever the
intent here of overthrowing either secular or ecclesiastical authorities.
This, however, does not touch upon the accuracy of Bakhtin's descriptions, nor on the profoundly subversive force of the Dionysian comic,
though this subversion must be understood in a metapolitical sense. This
indeed is well-expressed in Bakhtin's formulation of the Renaissance
conception of laughter:

> Laughter has a deep philosophical meaning, it is one of the essential forms
> of the truth concerning the world as a whole, concerning history and man,
> it is a peculiar point of view relative to the world; the world is seen anew,
> no less (and perhaps more) profoundly than when seen from the serious
> standpoint. Therefore, laughter is just as admissible in great literature,
> posing universal problems, as seriousness. Certain essentials aspects of
> the world are accessible only to laughter.[36]

Such laughter is indeed subversive, but in a sense far removed from any
Marxist theory of revolutionary consciousness.

Bakhtin also emphasizes what has repeatedly been pointed out in the
preceding discussions here—that the laughing culture of the Middle
Ages and the Renaissance created a counterworld:

> It [medieval laughter] builds its own world versus the official world, its
> own church versus the official church, its own state versus the official
> state. Laughter celebrates its masses, professes its faith, celebrates mar-
> riages and funerals, writes its epitaphs, elects kings and bishops. Even the
> smallest medieval parody is always built as part of the whole comic
> world.[37]

One might add that this doubling is characteristic of all creations of the
comic spirit, though rarely with the force or completeness of the traditional carnival. This kind of laughter liberates (the aforementioned *Narrenfreiheit*). It allows at least temporary victories over fear, including the
fear of death (note again how the late medieval dance of death incorporated the symbols and gestures of the carnival). The grotesque, obscene,
and scatological treatment of the body is an intrinsic part of this overcoming of fear—the most vulnerable, least spiritual aspects of human

existence are magically rendered harmless in these parodies. In this context it is not irrelevant to note that Rabelais studied and later taught medicine at the Montepellier Medical School, where there was much discussion of the therapeutic power of laughter. It is from there that Rabelais derived his concept of the "joyous physician." Perhaps one might also fantasize about the possibility of a joyous sociologist, one who has incorporated a Rabelaisian comic vision into his understanding of the precariousness of society.

The carnival may be seen as the final stage in the progression of the comic from brief interruption of social order to the full-blown construction of a counterworld. These comic intrusions are temporary, but they are always there as haunting possibilities, simultaneously liberating individuals and making the guardians of order very nervous. The institutions that contain and channel the comic intrusions are available for sociological analysis, even though it has only been possible to look at a few of them, and then only cursorily, in this chapter. Still, the basic character of these institutions should by now have been somewhat clarified.

Contrary to Zijderveld's pessimism, folly has not disappeared from the modern world, just as religion and magic have not disappeared. Specific institutional forms appear and disappear, but the comic experience is grounded in anthropological necessity and it will invent new forms of expression whenever earlier ones have become obsolete. The procession of all the figures of folly continues, literally in contemporary carnivals (Venice, Cologne, New Orleans, most richly in Rio de Janeiro), but also in the perennial comic imagination. The procession of fools marches down the centuries, on all continents. Here is a consoling thought: The procession will not end while the human story lasts.

### Notes

1.   Cf. Anton Zijderveld, *Reality in a Looking-Glass: Rationality through an Analysis of Traditional Folly* (London: Routledge and Kegan Paul, 1982), 39f. This chapter is strongly dependent on this uniquely useful book. Also cf. Zijderveld's earlier work *Humor und Gesellschaft: Eine Soziologie des Humors und des Lachens* (Graz: Styria, 1976), and the annotated bibliography on the sociology of humor edited by him, in *Current Sociology*, 31:3 (winter 1983). There is mythopoetic plausibility to the fact that Zijderveld teaches sociology in Rotterdam in the university named after Erasmus.

2.   On the microsociology of humor, cf. Zijderveld, *Humor*, 67ff.

3.   Cf. Hermann Bausinger, *"Lachkultur,"* in Thomas Vogel, ed., *Vom Lachen* (Tuebingen: Attempto, 1992), 9ff. Bausinger did not coin this term. It is a German translation of the Russian of Mikhail Bakhtin, whose interpretation of the carnival will be discussed presently.

4.   Cf. Peter Berger and Hansfried Kellner, "Marriage and the Construction of Reality," in Peter Berger, ed., *Facing Up to Modernity* (New York: Basic Books, 1977), 5ff.

5.   Just as an example of this genre, cf. Herbert Schoeffler, *Kleine Geographie des deutschen Witzes* (Goettingen: Vandenhoeck & Ruprecht, 1955). Edited and with a commentary by none less than the philosopher Helmuth Plessner (whose work on laughing and weeping was discussed earlier), this book covers the major German-speaking regions and gives examples of the allegedly distinctive humor of each. There are similar works on, at any rate, most if not all Western countries.

6.   I'm indebted to Ali Banuazizi for this example.

7.   Cf. the collection of short papers under the heading *"Das lebensweltliche und das fiktionale Komische,"* in Wolfgang Preisendanz and Rainer Warning, eds., *Das Komische* (Munich: Fink, 1976), 362ff.

8.   A. R. Radcliffe-Brown, *Structure and Meaning in Primitive Society* (New York: Free Press, 1968), 90ff. These are essays originally published in the 1940s.

9.   Ibid., 90.

10.   Ibid., 95.

11.   Mary Douglas, *Implicit Meanings* (London: Routledge and Kegan Paul, 1975), 90ff.

12.   Ibid., 103.

13.   Cf. Victor Turner, *Chihamba, the White Spirit* (Manchester: Manchester University Press, 1962.)

14.   Thomas Luckmann, *The Invisible Religion* (New York: Macmillan, 1967).

15.   The definitive sociological work on the fool is Anton Zijderveld's previously cited *Reality in a Looking-Glass.* For very useful historical works, cf. Barbara Swain, *Fools and Folly* (New York: Columbia University Press, 1932); Enid Welsford, *The Fool: His Social and Literary History* (Gloucester, Mass.: Peter Smith, [1935] 1966); William Willeford, *The Fool and His Scepter* (Evanston, Ill.: Northwestern University Press, 1969). Less useful for the present purposes, but with some interesting data, is a work by another sociologist, Orrin Klapp, *Heroes, Villains and Fools* (Englewood Cliffs, N.J.: Prentice-Hall, 1962).

16.   Zijderveld, *Reality,* 52.

17.   Cf. Barbara Koenneker, *Wesen und Wandlung der Narrenidee im Zeitalter des Humanismus* (Wiesbaden: Franz Steiner, 1966).

18.   Zijderveld, *Reality,* 83. The antecedents of *Till Eugenspiegel* have preoccupied generations of literary scholars. Many of the stories can be traced to the Middle East, from where they came to Europe in the figure whom the Turks called Nasreddin Hodja. Some may ultimately go back to Persia and India. Once again, the fool reveals himself as a broadly cross-cultural if not universal figure.

19.   On the place of Erasmus's book in the evolution of the *Narrenidee,* cf. Koenneker, *Wesen und Wandlung,* 248ff.

20.   Zijderveld, *Reality,* 92ff.

21.   Ibid., 126.

22.   Cf. John Towsen, *Clowns* (New York: Hawthorn, 1976).

23.   Ibid., 88f.

24. Cf. Zijderveld, *Reality*, 131ff.

25. Clifford Geertz discussed this in various works on Japanese culture, but for a recent vivid description of comic theater in Bali cf. Ron Jenkins, *Subversive Laughter* (New York: Free Press, 1994), 13ff. Jenkins, who teaches at Emerson College, has the distinction of also being a graduate of the Ringling Brothers Clown College in Florida. His book testifies to the fact that this has helped him achieve empathy with comedians in Bali and everywhere else.

26. Cf. Geoffrey Gorer, *Africa Dances* (London: John Lehmann, 1949), 125.

27. Paul Radin, *The Trickster: A Study in American Indian Mythology* (New York: Philosophical Library, 1956).

28. Cf. Zijderveld, *Reality*, 146ff.

29. Cf. Greiner, *Komoedie*.

30. Cf. ibid., 69ff.

31. Ibid., 73. My translation.

32. Cf. Zijderveld, *Reality*, 60ff.

33. Ibid., 61f.

34. Mikhail Bakhtin, *Rabelais and His World,* trans. Helen Iswolsky (Cambridge, Mass.: MIT Press, 1968). Bakhtin has recently been rediscovered as an alleged precursor of contemporary literary theory. Be this as it may, there was a "Bakhtin school" in Russia in the 1920s, in line with the so-called discourse analysis of Ferdinand de Saussure and Roman Jakobson. All of this is only marginally relevant to the argument of this chapter (though it puts in a broader framework Bakhtin's analysis of comic idiom). The cited book, though written in 1940, did not become available until the 1960s because of the author's political difficulties. It is not hard to understand why the Stalinist authorities were less than happy with Bakhtin's view of the rebellious nature of the carnival and of comic laughter in general.

35. Ibid., 20.

36. Ibid., 66.

37. Ibid., 88.

# 6

## Interlude
### *Brief Reflections on Jewish Humor*

It is no accident (as Marxists used to say) that many of the jokes cited in the preceding chapters have been Jewish. The best jokes are Jewish jokes. This is a well-known fact among, at any rate, college-educated Americans of whatever ethnic or religious background. The college education is relevant only insofar as Jewish humor tends toward a high level of sophistication; whatever else a college education may be useful for today (this is a very controversial issue that cannot be pursued here), it does lead to the acquisition of a measure of sophistication. At least since the 1950s Jewish humor, both in its explicit form and in what might call a certain covert infiltration (the tone is Jewish even if the content is not), has become a central ingredient of American comic culture. It is not only that so many entertaining writers and professional comedians have been Jewish. More significant is the fact that a distinctively Jewish comic sensibility has become established in the culture at large. Thus, for example, midwestern or southern college students of undiluted gentile antecedents will learn to use Yiddish phrases or even affect a Yiddish intonation when they want to appear witty. Humor has been an important element in the cultural ascendancy of Jews in America.

This development is interesting in itself. And, of course, there have been a number of works exploring the historical evolution of Jewish humor. It cannot be the present purpose to look into these works or to analyze the manner in which Jewish influences have shaped recent American culture. However, the case of Jewish humor is important also in that it helps to clarify the dynamics by which a comic culture is socially constructed, and these brief reflections are intended to contribute to this clarification.

Whatever may have been the earlier roots of Jewish humor, such as in the Talmudic literature, the more proximate origins are to be found in the Yiddish culture of eastern Europe, both in its folklore and in its higher literary expressions. The latter is represented by such classic

Yiddish authors as Sholem Aleichem or Yitzchak Leibush Peretz, but this literature derived its inspiration from the pulsating vitality of Yiddish culture as lived by ordinary people. It flourished within the confines of the *shtetl* and remained impenetrable to the gentile world outside (not that many gentiles had an interest in penetrating it). But with the coming of emancipation in the nineteenth century this culture burst out of its centuries-old confines and transmuted itself into a much more complicated synthesis. To some extent this occurred in a number of metropolitan centers to which large numbers of Jews migrated, both in Eastern and Western Europe. It was especially in the cities of the erstwhile Austro-Hungarian monarchy that a distinctive comic culture developed, a comic culture that could not be divorced from its Jewish components. The coffeehouse, as it emerged as a strategic urban institution in this region, was a central locale of this comic culture. It flourished with particular splendor in the three great capitals of Vienna, Budapest, and Prague, but it was to be found as well in such lesser urban centers as Zagreb, Brno, and Czernowitz. There, in the peculiar late-evening atmosphere permeated by the aroma of too much coffee and too many cigarettes, was cultivated a form of wit as impenetrable to the outsider as had been the comic culture of the *shtetl*. Now, however, insiders and outsiders were no longer identified only in terms of ethnicity and religion, for many non-Jews fully participated in these esoteric exchanges. In a heartbreaking way, and in the virtual absence of living Jewish interlocutors, faint echoes of this distinctive comic culture can still be heard in this region today. It is a sign of the invincible survival power of the Jewish people that—even as Nazi barbarism had destroyed most of Jewish culture in Europe—it found new incarnations in America and in Israel. The comic culture of Israel, by its very nature, is an intra-Jewish affair. It is in America that large numbers of gentiles have been drawn into the magic world of Jewish humor.

The distinctiveness of Jewish humor is not explained by its subject matter. To be sure, there are some notable deficits. Thus Jewish humor contains almost no scatology and remarkably little sexuality (even the jokes about sexual situations are usually about something else, such as money or the complexity of family relations). One can say that Jewish humor is at a great distance from the raucous carnival laughter that Mikhail Bakhtin goes on about. But that is also true of other comic cultures (for example, that of the Irish). The compilers of an anthology of Jewish humor describe its subject matter as follows: "Food (noshing is sacred), family, business, anti-Semitism, wealth and its absence, health and survival."[1] With the obvious exception of anti-Semitism, however, these topics occur in other comic cultures as well. There is a matter of form. Modern Jewish humor, in Europe as well as in America, has refined the form of the joke. While the comic, as has been strenuously argued throughout this book, is a universal human phenomenon, the joke as a form of comic creativity is not. There are cultures with rich comic traditions where people rarely if ever tell jokes (this seems to be the case, for instance, in Eastern Asia). For the present purpose, the joke can be described simply as a very short story with a comic twist at the end (the punch line). Jewish humor, for a very long time, has brought forth a cornucopia of jokes. Undoubtedly this has deep roots in Jewish cultural history, going back to Talmudic times and the rabbinical propensity to make a point by telling a story, usually a short one. Again, though, the joke is not a uniquely Jewish form of comic expression. It has roots in medieval and Renaissance comic culture; its origins are probably in the Middle East (as in the tales of Nazreddin Hodja), possibly in India.

The distinctiveness of Jewish humor lies not so much in either its subject matter nor in its expressive form. Rather it lies in its peculiar sensibility, its tone. *C'est le ton qui fait la musique.* It is a sharp, cutting tone. It is strongly intellectual, which makes for its association with urbanity and sophistication. It also has a surreal dimension, which one is tempted to call religious in origin. One example will have to serve here. Business has been listed as one frequent topic for Jewish humor. More specifically, a common theme in Jewish jokes is the superior acumen of the Jewish businessman (ironically, the same theme that occurs in a pejorative mode in gentile jokes is an occasion for self-congratulation when it is treated in Jewish jokes—it is not just a question of *how* jokes are told, but *by whom* and *when*!). This theme is not unique either. It was common in American humor, long before it was infiltrated by Jewish sensibilities. There was the comic figure of the Yankee peddler, a smart city-slicker who always outsmarted country bumpkins and other people with inferior business sense. Here is a story about this character dating from before 1800:

> A Yankee captain is drinking in a London tavern when some locals try, unsuccessfully, to lure him into a card game. He refuses, and they leave. The landlord asks him to pay for everyone's drinks, as is supposedly the London custom when someone turns down an invitation to play cards. The Yankee puts on a stricken expression, draws out some silver coins, then asks for another bottle. As the landlord goes to fetch it, the Yankee scrawls the sum allegedly owed on the mantelpiece, and underneath it writes "I leave you a Yankee handle for your London Blades," then runs out the door.[2]

There is wit here, of a certain intellectual quality (the word *blade* in the English of that period meant a smart character as well as the edge of a knife). It hardly compares, though, with the sharpness of Jewish jokes on the same theme. One may recall here the joke told in the preceding chapter of the businessman in New York's garment district who commits suicide so that his partner can collect the insurance and whose last words, as he falls by his partner's window, consist of the recommendation to cut velours. Or take the following joke:

> Two partners in the garment business face a crisis. They have a huge number of madras shirts on supply and no buyers. Then, wonderfully, a buyer from out of town comes in and orders a thousand shirts. There is just one thing, he says: He must get confirmation from the home office; but, unless he sends a telegram by the end of the week to cancel, the order stands. The partners are very anxious. The days go by. On Friday, just before closing time, a Western Union boy delivers a telegram, The partners blanch. With an effort of will one of them tears open the envelope, then calls out to his partner, "Abe, wonderful news! Your sister has died!"[3]

Is there any way of explaining this very distinctive comic style? An exhaustive explanation may remain out of reach, but some suggestions are possible. Two can be made with some assurance, based on the two historical factors of Jewish marginality and Jewish intellectuality. More cautiously, one may point to some features of Judaism as a religious tradition.

In Western civilization Jews were a marginal group for many centuries. This in all likelihood made for a certain clear-eyed perspective on society in and of itself. When emancipation came, this marginality did not altogether cease, but it became more nuanced. In a very curious way, Jews were both inside and outside the European societies that had given them citizenship. One may hypothesize that it is precisely this ambivalence of being simultaneously an insider and an outsider that makes for a disillusioned, skeptical view of society. The classical American sociologist Thorstein Veblen has accounted in this way for the extraordinarily large contribution that Jews have made to Western intellectual life since emancipation. He characterizes the modern Jewish intellectual as "a skeptic by force of circumstances."[4] However, in twentieth-century sociology the two writings that most accurately make this point are two essays that, though both were authored by Jews, do not deal with the Jewish situation as such. These are the essays on the social role of the stranger by Georg Simmel and Alfred Schutz.[5] Simmel does indeed mention what he calls the classical example of Jewish history in Europe, but his aim was to delineate the social type of the stranger in a general, cross-cultural manner. The stranger embodies a peculiar "unity of nearness and remoteness" and this condition leads to a distinctive posture of detachment and objectivity. Thus the stranger sees many things that the native, who takes them for granted, fails to see or sees much less sharply. Schutz consciously wrote his essay on the stranger as an addendum to Simmel's text. He particularly emphasizes that the stranger's taken-for-granted world is much more precarious than that of the native. He too mentions the objectivity that comes from having to learn, as an outsider, the rules of the game dictated by the in-group. In addition, though, as Schutz poignantly puts it, there is "his own [the stranger's] bitter experience of the limits of "thinking as usual," which has taught him that a man may lose his status, his rules of guidance, and even his history and that the normal way of life is always far less guaranteed than it seems."[6]

The pilgrimage of Jews through Western history as outsiders/insiders goes a long way to explaining their intellectual preeminence (to use Veblen's phrase) in modern culture. It also helps to explain the distinctive character of modern Jewish comic culture, spanning its flowering in Yiddish to its amazing resurgence in America. As has been argued earlier, the comic invades and subverts the taken-for-granted structures of social life. It reveals their incongruities and their fundamental vulnerability. This is a perspective that comes more readily to the stranger. It is a deeply disturbing, indeed dangerous perspective. This is at least one reason why modern Jewish consciousness has been a perennially troubled one. The Yiddish saying that it is *shver tsu zein a yid* (difficult to be a Jew) has been verified even in some of the most rarified products of the modern Jewish mind. Unfortunately, the same skeptical, implicitly dangerous perspective on society and all its works has also fueled the anti-Semitic mentality. In any case, one encounters here once more the doubling (*Dopplung*) of vision that Bernhard Greiner has proposed as the essence of comedy.

Jews have had to survive in this ambivalent situation and much Jewish with has been put at the service of this survival. This has produced a distinctively Jewish version of gallows humor or black humor. The following jokes may provide illustrations:

Three Jews have inadvertently strayed close to the sultan's harem and have caught a glimpse of its beautiful denizens in skimpy dress lounging in the garden. The Jews are caught and brought before the sultan. He orders that they be punished by having large quantities of fruits stuffed into their behinds. However, since they strayed into the forbidden area inadvertently, the sultan, as a gesture of mercy, will let them choose the fruits. The first chooses grapes, the second bananas. The sultan's henchmen begin the very painful process of pushing huge quantities of these fruits into the respective behinds. Suddenly the first man begins to laugh. "What is there to laugh?" asks the second. "Look," says the first, "here comes Moshe with his melons!"[7]

Under some tyrannical regime or other three Jews are about to be shot. The officer in charge of the execution offers them a last cigarette. The first accepts, so does the second. The third refuses. Whereupon the second turns to him and says, "Moishe, don't make trouble!"

And the following recent American joke has no explicit Jewish reference. Yet, arguably, it has a definite Jewish flavor—precisely the tone that was mentioned earlier:

A doctor is talking to his patient: "I have good news and bad news. Which do you want to hear first?"
"Give me the bad news first."
"Well, the bad news is that the X-rays clearly show a tumor."
"So what's the good news?"
"The good news is that I'm making out with the X-ray technician."

Even if marginality is a causal factor in the genesis of Jewish humor, it cannot be the only factor. There have been other marginal groups, in Europe and elsewhere, who did not develop anything remotely resembling Jewish comic culture—the Gypsies, say, or the Tinkers. Another important factor, almost certainly, was the distinctive Jewish intellectual tradition, especially as it has developed since the Talmudic period. This tradition, of course, is grounded in the very character of rabbinical Judaism and the centrality of law in the latter. Other religious traditions, of course, have been much concerned with law—Roman Catholicism with its development of casuistry, or Islam with its different legal schools interpreting the *shari'ah*. But it is probably fair to say that Judaism is unmatched among the world religions in the central place it has given to legal reasoning, to the endless intellectual efforts to understand and refine the requirements of *halacha*. Christian writers have often misinterpreted this as an arid legalism, thus overlooking the fervent religious passion that vibrates through all these disputations, a passion grounded in the commitment to discern and follow the will of God in all areas of human life. All the same, rabbinical Judaism is above everything a religion of law, a law that must be ongoingly studied, argued over, and applied to new situations. No other religious tradition has called its place of worship a *shul*, or made study and scholarship *the* essential religious vocation. An anecdote tells of a famous rabbi being asked by one of his disciples how God occupies himself in eternity. "He studies," replied the rabbi. The reply, one may assume, was only half-facetious.

Talmudic study developed a specific intellectual method, that of *pilpul*, a form of dialectical reasoning. Teachers and students interact in a process of questions and answers, defining and redefining a legal problem, citing authorities from the past, trying to arrive at solutions that do justice to new situations. There can be little doubt that this unique cognitive style (to use another Schutzian term) carried over into the period when Jewish minds turned to secular problems. It is a cognitive style of making fine distinctions, putting things together and taking them apart again—a cognitive style that turned out to have a very good fit with the requirements of modernity.[8] The same cognitive style can be detected in Jewish wit. The question of whether some Talmudic passages were intentionally comic must be left to the experts. But it is difficult to avoid the impression that some of these ancient rabbis were chuckling as they debated what one recent author has called "strange and bizarre problems" in the Talmud—for instance, the problem of the number of crumbs brought by a mouse or a rat into a house cleaned for Passover that would nullify the cleansing, or the question of whether a *golem* (an artificial being created by magic) is entitled to participate in communal prayer.[9] Be this as it may, one may propose that minds honed by this methodology were made ready for Jewish humor. The habits of *pilpul* may still be detected in modern Jewish jokes. The following is a perfect example:

> A Jewish man is sitting in a railway carriage in the old country. A considerably younger man, evidently also Jewish, joins him after a while and sits across from him after a perfunctory greeting. As the train begins to move, the younger man says: "Excuse me, could you tell me what time it is?"
> The older man does not reply.
> "Excuse me again, but could you tell me what time it is?" The older man looks out the window. The younger man is quite irritated by this: "Look here, I asked you a perfectly civil question. Why don't you answer me?"
> The older man says: "All right, I will tell you. If I tell you what time it is, we will start a conversation. You will find out things about me. You will find out that I am a rabbi in the town of X, that I have two daughters, one of them unmarried. You will want to see pictures of my family. You will find out that my unmarried daughter is very beautiful. You will come to visit us. You will fall in love with my daughter. You will marry her . . . "
> "Well, would this be so terrible? I am a perfectly respectable Jewish man."
> "Perhaps," says the older man. "But I don't want a son-in-law who cannot afford a watch."[10]

There is, finally, another feature of Judaism that may have had a part in shaping Jewish comic culture—a distinctively Jewish conception of the relation between God and man. More than people of any other religious tradition, Jews have *argued* with God. There are already adumbrations of this in the Hebrew Bible: Jacob wrestling with God, Job questioning God's dealings with him. Later Jewish texts have much more of this, for example in the literature of Hasidism. It would be another misinterpretation to see this as a lack of reverence. Rather, it is more plausible to understand this as a profoundly religious conviction of God's moral perfection: If God is morally perfect, He cannot be inferior to man in His accessibility to moral argument. But be this as it may, this curious proximity of the Jewish God raises the casuistic propensities of the Talmudic mind to cosmic dimensions. The entire cosmos, as it were, becomes the subject of argument. It would seem that this makes for a surreal vision, a view of reality as full of immense incongruities reaching all the way to the divine Throne—a vision that is very close to the essential comic perspective. One final Jewish joke may be allowed here to make this (admittedly questionable) point:

> Three Hasidim are bragging about their respective rabbis. The first says, "My rabbi is so pious that he thinks about God all the time, and so he trembles all the time." The second says, "My rabbi is so pious that *God* thinks about *him* all the time, and so God trembles all the time." The third Hasid says, "My rabbi has been through both these stages. And so last week he said to God: Is it really necessary that both of us should tremble all the time?"[11]

## Notes

1. William Novak and Moshe Waldoks, eds., *The Big Book of Jewish Humor* (New York: Harper Perennial, 1990), xx. This is a very fine book, mixing literary texts with a rich selection of jokes and humorous dicta. When it comes to the jokes, of course, anyone with a modicum of comic education will keep on meeting old friends; like the new convict in the prison yard, he will be tempted to call out the numbers. But, here as there, it is a question of *how* one tells the jokes; Novak and Waldoks do it very well.

2. Cf. Constance Rourke, *American Humor* (Garden City, N.Y.: Doubleday-Anchor, 1953), 17. In fidelity to the venerable tradition of joke-telling, I have retold the episode in my own words.

3. This joke is recorded in Novak and Waldoks, *Jewish Humor*, 188. I have told it here in my own version.

4. In the essay "The Intellectual Pre-Eminence of Jews in Modern Europe," in Max Lerner, ed., *The Portable Veblen* (New York: Viking, 1948), 467ff. [the essay was first published in 1919]. Veblen knew what he was talking about when it came to marginality. Raised in a Norwegian ethnic enclave in the Middle West, he did not speak English until he went to school. In a very basic way he remained both insider and outsider in American society all his life.

5. Kurt Wolff, transl./ed., *The Sociology of Georg Simmel* (Glencoe, Ill.: Free Press, 1950), 402ff.; Alfred Schutz, *Collected Papers*, vol. II (The Hague: Nijhoff, 1964), 91ff.

6. Alfred Schutz, *Collected Papers*, vol. II, 194. Simmel wrote long before

World War II. Schutz wrote on the stranger after having come to America as a refugee from Nazism; the "bitter experience" was his own.

7.   I have no idea when or where I heard this joke. Given its context, my "joke-nose" suggests that it might be of Sephardic origin. Come to think of it, the concept of joke-nose (*Witznase?*) merits further development. Not here, not now . . .

8.   Cf. Peter Berger, Brigitte Berger, and Hansfried Kellner, *The Homeless Mind: Modernization and Consciousness* (New York: Random House, 1973), especially the discussion of abstraction and "componentiality." As modernization proceeds and increasing numbers of people become "homeless" in their consciousness, they become ipso facto more open to Jewish cultural sensibilities. In that sense, one might paraphrase the statement of Pope Pius XI, "We have all become Jews." This fact may go a long way toward explaining the ascendancy of Jews and Jewish themes in contemporary American culture.

9.   Adin Steinsaltz, *The Essential Talmud* (New York: Basic Books, 1976), 235. One might also mention the problem that recently got an American professor into trouble: If a man falls out of a window, lands on a woman, and has intercourse with her—is he guilty of rape? The feminists who accused the professor of sexual harassment for mentioning this problem in a lecture were definitely *not* chuckling.

10.   For reasons which I do not claim to understand, many European Jewish jokes begin with the line "Two Jews meet on a train." Reportedly, when someone once started to tell a joke with this line, his interlocutor interrupted: "You know, I'm really getting tired of these stories about two Jews meeting on a train. Don't you know any other jokes?" "All right, all right," said the joke-teller. "So, two Hungarians meet on a train . . ."

11.   My *Witznase* tells me that the point may have been reached in this book where a surfeit of jokes may begin to exhaust the comic receptivity of its readers (*vide* the earlier discussion about the negative effect of repetition). I should make a promise here to cut down on jokes from now on. However, I may also quote once more the legendary Rabbi Meir of Vilna: "When a joke-teller tells you that he is no longer joking—don't believe him!"

# II

## Comic Forms of Expression

# 7

## The Comic as Diversion
### *Benign Humor*

The first part of this book has been an attempt to outline the anatomy of the comic with the help of different perspectives, such as those of philosophy, psychology, and the social sciences. It goes without saying that this attempt could only partially succeed. It is salutary to recall Bergson's description of laughter as a foam that disappears as one tries to hold it (salutary, one may add, both for the nervous author and the skeptical reader). As stated at the outset of this arguably Quixotic enterprise, all one can try to do is to keep walking around the phenomenon in the hope of seeing it more clearly as a result. And that is all that this book can continue to do. For most of the rest of it the topic will be different forms of expression of the comic, most of them literary. There is a particular problem here. The relevant material is overwhelmingly vast. The literature of every human culture contains huge accumulations of comic writings. Even the most cursory overview of these would daunt the most unabashed megalomaniac, or alternatively would require the establishment of a large number of scholarly committees with a work schedule measured in decades. All that a solitary author bereft of delusions of grandeur can do is to look at a few clear cases (to use a phrase of Max Weber's)—that is, cases that help to bring into sharp focus these different manifestations of the comic phenomenon.[1]

Benign humor is most easily defined as what it is not. Unlike wit, it does not make excessive intellectual demands, Unlike irony and satire, it is not designed to attack. Unlike the extravagant creations of folly, it does not present a counterworld. Rather, it is harmless, even innocent. It is intended to evoke pleasure, relaxation, and good will. It enhances rather than disrupts the flow of everyday life. It is, so to speak, at the far end of the Dionysian ecstasies in which the comic experience was originally rooted. One might perhaps argue that this darker side is always there, under the surface of the most innocuous jokes, but it is almost completely hidden, present if at all as a mere *soupçon*.

In this incarnation, then, the comic functions as a mild and thoroughly healthy diversion. It is in this form that "humor is the best medicine," as the *Reader's Digest* puts it.

Benign humor is the most common expression of the comic in everyday life. It provides the mellow amusement that makes it easier to get through the day and to manage the minor irritations. It is what is intended when people are criticized for not having a sense of humor, a character flaw (perhaps even a moral flaw) that makes them less capable of coping and harder to live with. Suppose that there is an escalation of minor mishaps in, say, a work situation. The boss has just come in showing all the signs of a brooding bad temper, the computer system is down, the coffee machine has also broken down, and—to top it off—it turns out that the overnight cleaning staff has thrown out a pile of important papers that had been prepared for the boss's perusal. The very accumulation of these mishaps will induce laughter in those who have the putative sense of humor and thus make is easier for them to overcome the difficulties, while those lacking this redeeming quality will stew in their frustration. Humor, the *Reader's Digest* could go on to say, is the best management tool. (It may be observed in passing that just this has been suggested seriously, and often very humorlessly, by business experts.)

Benign humor in such instances manifests itself in momentary interruptions of the sober activities of living. It is a spontaneous reaction to the incongruities of an ordinary situation. It is not planned or staged by anyone. There may also be entire episodes, by design or happening accidentally, that evoke a humorous response. Take a very common episode of family life: A little girl is dressing up in her mother's clothes. She puts on a dress or a blouse, far too big for her, so that she virtually disappears in it. She slips on a pair of high-heeled shoes, perhaps tops the costume with a hat that slips down to her nose. In this get-up she stumbles around the room in a perfect parody of her mother. No matter whether she has staged this performance before or whether this is the first time, it may be safely assumed that the family (including the parodied mother) will find the entire episode hugely amusing. But even an outsider, innocently trapped in this little comedy, may find it quite funny and respond accordingly. The little girl may conclude her performance to unanimous laughter and applause (which, one may further assume, will encourage her to repeat it frequently and may even give her the idea, held onto into adulthood, that she is a natural-born comedian).

Unlike other forms of the comic, this kind of humor does not have to be deliberately produced or explicitly articulated. It can just happen. Also, it can be enjoyed by oneself, in a solitary chuckle as it were. By contrast, wit, jokes, or satire are always conscious products, and their production depends on a social situation in which the comic producer has an audience. Yet, obviously, benign humor can also be deliberately produced or staged, be it by amateurs like the aforementioned little girl or by people who make a profession out of this. Only when benign humor is deliberately produced can it create a finite province of meaning, though of a very distinctive sort. It is quite close to everyday life, though it takes out of it whatever is painful or threatening. It brings into transitory being a world of mellow lightness. Its effect is that of a brief, refreshing vacation from the seriousness of existence. Almost any medium of creativity can bring this about. World literature is obviously full of examples, and even Shakespeare, who in other works confronts every conceivable depth of human anguish, wrote comedies from which every trace of pain or sorrow has been removed. The contemporary American in quest of benign humor may find it in the poetry of Edward Lear or Ogden Nash, in the stand-up performances of Bob Hope (still going strong, indeed heroically, at age ninety), by watching an old movie of the Marx Brothers, or by contemplating the pictures of Norman Rockwell. This or that product of benign humor may, of course, be dismissed by some people as too cute, too unsophisticated, or as expressing a comic sensibility that is too foreign to enjoy. Be this as it may, nobody, however sophisticated or ethnocentric, will have reason to complain of a shortage of sources of benign humor to turn to in case of need.

In what follows, three clear cases will be looked at. They are very different from each other, coming from different countries and working in different media, though all three were contemporaries. What they have in common is that each one, in his way, produced an opus of unmistakably benign humor. The three cases are the English novelist P. G. Wodehouse, the American comedian Will Rogers, and Franz Lehár, the twentieth-century master of the Viennese operetta.

P. G. (Pelham Grenville—no kidding) Wodehouse (1881–1975) must be one of the most prolific writers in the history of literature.[2] Depending on how one counts anthologies, he published a little over or a little under one hundred books in his lifetime. On his ninetieth birthday he gave himself a present by finishing yet another novel. And writing is what he did all his life, virtually all the time. The child of colonial civil servants (not at all part of the aristocracy about which he was to write all those novels), he turned to full-time writing early on, and the immense success of his novels gave him a comfortable income. Despite the unambiguously English sensibility of his opus, Wodehouse has had a devoted American readership from early on and he spent a large part of his life in America, where he also played an important part in the development of the Broadway musical and for a while did film scripts in Hollywood. He was happily married, lived in stable circumstances, worked hard and painstakingly at his craft as a writer. By all accounts he was an amiable, well-meaning, and easygoing individual. Indeed, his biography yields just one very distressing episode, worth telling because it suggests an innocence of character that seems to come right out of one of his own novels.[3] Wodehouse and his wife were stranded in France at the time of the German invasion in 1940. Wodehouse was interned as an enemy alien. He was treated very well and did a lot of writing while in custody. When he was visited by an American journalist (this was before the United States entered the war) he agreed to do some broadcasts to his American readers, telling some funny stories about his imprisonment. It did not occur to him that the Germans, who allowed him to use their radio facilities, could look on these broadcasts as a propaganda coup. The broadcasts were naturally much resented in Britain and after the liberation of France Wodehouse was briefly arrested and investigated on suspicion of treason. He was lucky in that the first British intelligence officer to interview him was no other than Malcolm Muggeridge, who was completely captivated by Wodehouse and exonerated him in his report of any fault other than political stupidity.[4]

Though they constitute only a part of Wodehouse's entire opus, his most famous and enduringly successful novels are those that deal with the adventures of Bertie Wooster, an endearingly imbecile young aristocrat, and Jeeves, his omniscient "gentleman's gentleman" (the term *butler* is somewhat below the latter's dignity). One may say that these two figures have by now attained almost mythological status. Two stories will have to suffice here to explicate the inspired idiocy surrounding them.

The first is entitled "Jeeves in the Springtime."[5] Bertie feels the onset of spring and the following dialogue ensues with Jeeves:

"In the spring, Jeeves, a livelier iris gleams upon the burnished dove."
"So I have been informed, sir."
"Right-o! Then bring me my whangee, my yellowest shoes, and the old green Homburg. I'm going into the park to do pastoral dances."
"Very good, sir."

Never mind what a "burnished dove" may be, let alone a *whangee*. It is hard to imagine a more idiotic exchange. It is typical of the interaction between the two characters, Bertie charging ahead with mindless energy, Jeeves standing by with ironic detachment yet ever ready to get his master out of the scrapes he invariably ends up in. The interaction follows a more or less fixed formula. The amazing thing is that Wodehouse's comic genius makes it seem fresh every time around.

Here is how Bertie experiences spring: "Kind of uplifted feeling. Romantic, if you know what I mean." But just in case anyone imagines an
eruption of vernal eroticism, he adds: "I'm not much of a ladies' man,
but on this particular morning it seemed to me that what I really wanted
was some charming girl to buzz up and ask me to save her from assas-
sins or something." This is again very typical of Bertie's relations with
the other sex. When it is not a matter of trying to escape from the
demands of terrifying aunts and marriage-minded viragos, Bertie's notions of romance are romantic in a basically prepubescent style. Jeeves
indeed appears to have liaisons of one kind or another, usually with
female members of the domestic staffs of Bertie's circle of friends and
relatives, but no prurient details are ever revealed or even hinted at. A
not unimportant point: Wodehouse's world is singularly devoid of any
sort of sexuality, is thus innocent in the most literal sense.[6]

What happens in the park is a bit of an anticlimax. Bertie runs into
young Bingo Little, a young gentleman of an intellect about equal to his.
Bingo drags him off to a somewhat seedy restaurant and introduces him
to Mabel, a waitress there and "the most wonderful girl you ever saw."
Bingo is in love with Mabel and wants to marry her. The problem is his
uncle, old Mortimer Little, on whom he is financially dependent and
who might cut off his allowance if he enters into this kind of més-
alliance. This financial circumstance is once again typical of Bertie's circle and indeed of Bertie himself (who is dependent on his ferocious
Aunt Agatha). These people have neither work nor money, but they
manage to support a lavish life-style on the basis of obscure and precarious subsidizations. One is reminded here of the way someone once
described the characters in Dostoyevsky's novels, as unemployed and
unemployable. But none of Wodehouse's characters are greatly affected
by this economic situation beyond a peevish annoyance, and they are
certainly not driven by any remotely Dostoyevskyan passions.

The story unfolds in a sequence of events that could not ever be
plausible except in a Wodehouse novel. Bingo implores Bertie to ask
Jeeves's advice (who is "by way of being the brains of the family").
Jeeves, it turns out, is well-placed to be of help, since he is "on terms of
some intimacy," practically amounting to an engagement, with old Mortimer's cook, a Miss Watson. Jeeves knows that the frightful uncle is
suffering through a painful episode of gout and likes to be read to in bed
by his valet. Jeeves suggests that Bingo should volunteer to take over
this chore and to read from the works of one Rosie M. Banks, an author
who specializes in romances between individuals of divergent class
backgrounds. It is not long before Bertie is invited to lunch in the Little
household. He discovers, to his chagrin, that Bingo has told his uncle
that Bertie is the real author of the Banks novels. When Bertie brings up

the matter of Bingo's class-defying marriage plans, old Mortimer is not in the least disturbed. Indeed, inspired by the Banks ideology, he himself is about to take a similar step by marrying Miss Watson. When Bertie recounts all this to Jeeves, the latter is also quite untroubled. He had concluded some time ago that he and Miss Watson were not really suited, and he now has a new understanding—with Mabel, the waitress who so beguiled poor Bingo! Once again Jeeves stands revealed as a mini-Macchiavelli in the miniworld of Bertie Wooster.

The other story (picked more or less at random—almost any one would do) is called "Without the Option."[7] The title refers to a sentence of imprisonment without the option of paying a fine. Bertie and his friend Sippy (Oliver Randolph Sipperley) have been arrested. They had been in a state of advanced inebriation on the night of the Oxford/Cambridge boat race, and Bertie had suggested that Sippy (who was depressed because of demands made on him by his Aunt Vera—yes indeed, a lady on whom he is financially dependent) cheer himself up by snatching off a policeman's helmet. Bertie is only fined, but Sippy, the actual assailant, is sentenced to thirty days "without the option." This would not be so bad, except that Aunt Vera had ordered Sippy to visit friends of hers, the family of one Professor Pringle in Cambridge. If he does not go, she will find out about his shameful brush with the law, and (yes indeed) she might cut off his allowance. As usual, Jeeves is called upon for advice. He suggests the only possible solution: Bertie must go to Cambridge, pretending to be Sippy. Bertie refuses, but when he hears that Aunt Agatha had telephoned, evidently aware of his own legal contretemps, he wants to leave as quickly as possible. As usual, Jeeves has already anticipated this turn of events:

> "Jeeves," I said, "this is a time for deeds, not words. Pack—and that right speedily."
> "I have packed, sir."
> "Find out when there is a train for Cambridge."
> "There is one in forty minutes, sir."
> "Call a taxi."
> "A taxi is at the door, sir."
> "Good!" I said. "Then lead me to it."

The *Maison Pringle* is as forbidding as Bertie had feared. Professor Pringle is "a thinnish, baldish, dyspeptic-looking cove with an eye like a haddock," and Mrs. Pringle gives the appearance of "one who had had bad news about the year 1900 and never really got over it." And then there are "a couple of ancient females with shawls all over them," the mother and an aunt of the professor. The latter remembers Bertie/Sippy as a nasty boy who teased her cat many years ago. But worse is yet to come. Heloise Pringle, the professor's daughter, appears. She closely resembles Honoria Glossop, to whom Battle had been disastrously engaged for three weeks until thrown out by her terrible father, Sir Roderick Glossop (the loony doctor). She even talks like Honoria. No wonder because, as Jeeves knows, the two are cousins. Heloise fixes her attention on Bertie and, with "the look of a tigress that has marked down its prey," immediately decides that he is a promising matrimonial prospect. Bertie, of course, is terrified. This time even Jeeves has no solution. The possibility that Bertie might turn down the formidable Heloise evidently occurs to neither himself nor Jeeves. But the two engage in an almost philosophical exchange about the mystery of Bertie's repeatedly attracting young women as "brainy" as Honoria and Heloise:

> "Jeeves, it is a known scientific fact that there is a particular style of female that does seem strangely attracted to the sort of fellow that I am."
> "Very true, sir."
> "I mean to say, I know perfectly well that I've got, roughly speaking, half the amount of brain a normal bloke ought to possess. And when a girl comes along who has about twice the regular allowance, she too often makes a bee-line for me with the love light in her eyes. I don't know how to account for it, but it is so."
> "It may be Nature's provision for maintaining the balance of the species, sir."

Bertie desperately tries to avoid the frightening Miss Pringle, stays mostly in his room, only leaving it by climbing down the drainpipe (thus reinforcing the aunt's opinion of him as both criminal and mad). The situation is resolved by the appearance of none less than Sir Roderick, who has been invited to dinner. He, of course, recognizes Bertie and, upon being told that Bertie had pretended to be Sippy, confirms the aunt's diagnosis of his being perfectly insane. Bertie escapes in extreme distress, seeking refuge (of course) with Jeeves: "Hell's foundations are quivering and the game is up." To which *cri de coeur* Jeeves can only observe: "The contingency was one always to have been anticipated as a possibility, sir." Only one course of action is possible—to go to Sippy's Aunt Vera and tell her all. This is what Bertie does, precipitately. To his surprise, Aunt Vera is delighted with the news about her nephew's attack on a policeman. Jeeves knows why: She has had a number of unpleasant encounters with the local constable, who has been serving summons on her for speeding and for allowing her dog out without a collar, and she is therefore angry at policemen as a class. How does Jeeves know this? The constable is his cousin.

Throughout his work Wodehouse has moved in a distinctive world of his own creation, both totally unreal if compared with the actual England of the times and tangibly real to any reader willing to suspend doubt in order to enter it. It is a frozen Edwardian world kept going by Wodehouse long after Edwardian England had passed into history, an almost mythical England that, among other things, corresponded to all the stereotypes held in the minds of Americans. It is a world full of carefully depicted individuals, very many of them—among others, fifty-three named members of Bertie's Drones Club and sixty-three butlers (not counting Jeeves). An enormous stylistic genius went into the creation of this (if one may put it paradoxically) profoundly trivial world. Hillaire Belloc called Wodehouse the best living English writer and Auberon Waugh called him the most influential novelist of the time. His biographer put it as follows. "Wodehouse made an infinite number of amusing remarks in his lifetime, invented a teeming population of clowns. The dream he dreamed of the England he preferred to the real one is an amusing dream, a vividly conceived and tightly constructed dream, but *above all it is benign.*"[8]

Thus Wodehouse is an unusually clear case of benign humor. He presents his readers with a world utterly without darkness, without real pain, without any strong passions. One enters it as a sort of enchanted kindergarten. The humor, of course, is in the characters and the plots, but above all in the style (not so much in the dialogue as in the descriptive passages). No one but Wodehouse could have written, for example, of "Aunt calling to Aunt like mastodons bellowing across primeval swamps," or could have summed up a situation by stating that "ice formed on the butler's upper slopes." David Cecil, another admirer, sums up Wodehouse's opus as follows: "We embark on his books assured that we shall find nothing to make us shudder or reflect or shed tears; but only to laugh. And with a laughter that is a laughter of pure happiness."[9]

On the face of it, no two authors could be more different than Will Rogers and P. G. Wodehouse, embodying, respectively, a prototypically American, homespun, folksy approach to life and the fastidious, manneristic understatements of an aristocratic culture in terminal decline. Upon closer inspection, though, one recognizes kindred spirits across all the differences of nationality, class, and creative style. It is not only that both men were enormously productive, had very great success, and lived essentially happy lives (though Rogers's was cut short by a fatal airplane accident at age fifty-six). More relevant to the present considerations, they exuded a compelling benevolence, an invincible innocence, throughout their work and by all accounts in their personalities as well.

Will Rogers (1879–1935) was born in what is now Oklahoma, of partially Cherokee descent, a fact of which he was very proud (as he told his WASP audience, when their folks arrived on the Mayflower, his folks were there to greet them).[10] He learned all the skills of a cowboy on his father's ranch and indeed worked as a cowboy in his early years. He was particularly adept in the use of the lasso, and it was this that first led him into the world of entertainment, or that segment of it where the audience was thrilled by a performer's ability to rein in almost anything by means of the lasso. There is some disagreement as to the exact moment when Rogers first began to speak to the audience in the course of these athletic feats. At first he did so to gloss over incidents when one of his tricks failed, and one of his first funny statements was to the effect that the management would not allow him to utter the vulgarities that he felt like uttering on such an occasion. He graduated from cowboy shows to vaudeville, made a big jump in his career in entertainment when he was employed by the Ziegfeld Follies in New York, and from there branched out into radio, films, and eventually into the writing of a newspaper column (which for a while even appeared in the *New York Times*).[11]

Rogers spoke with a western accent. His humor reflected the stereotypical "cracker-barrel" philosophy of the Old West—robust yet relaxed, animated by common sense and healthy skepticism, yet never hurtful or overly witty. There were individuals who doubted the authenticity of this, but the great majority of witnesses testify that Rogers the man had very much the same benign character as Rogers the performer. Be that as it may, it is as the embodiment of benevolent wisdom that he was loved by millions of Americans and mourned by them upon his premature death. He made no pretense of intellectual superiority ("All I know is what I read in the papers") and he could thus be inspiring without intimidating. His most famous statement, of course, was, "I never met a man I didn't like," which he repeated frequently. It is noteworthy that he first made it with reference to Leon Trotsky! [12] He rarely gave offense, even when he was critical of people, and he was usually willing to scratch an observation if someone claimed to be hurt by it: "I don't think I ever hurt any man's feelings by my little gags. I know I never willfully did it. When I have to do that to make a living I will quit."[13]

Some extracts from Rogers's columns may serve by way of illustration. The first is from a piece entitled "Male Versus Female—Mosquito":

> Just the other day, a fellow in Atlantic City, New Jersey, come through with some statistics that really ought to set us thinking! . . . This guy is a professor and chief "entomologist." That word will stop you ignorant ones. But you got a fifty-fifty break, I don't know what it means either. Well, this professor delivered this address at a convention of the New Jersey Exterminators Association, duly assembled in the very heart of the mosquito belt. So I gather from that, that an entomologist is a man that has devoted his life to a study that must include this New Jersey product. He has either given his life's work for, or against, the mosquito. It's a surprise

that New Jersey had such an organization called "The New Jersey Mosquito Exterminators, Inc." Anyone who has ever visited that state could not
possibly understand how there could be an organization devoted to the
annihilation of those comical little rascals. Or if they have got such a
society, where have they been exterminating, and when? But you see,
what they have been doing is holding dinners. All you do in America
nowadays, is get a name for some kind of organization, then you start
holding dinners. An organization without a dinner is just impossible.
Now the only mosquitoes exterminated was at the dinner. Well, during
the scratching and slapping and singing of the mosquitoes, this guy read
off the following authoritative statistics. "The normal productivity of one
lone female house mosquito in one year is 159,875,000,000 offsprings."[14]

This opening is pure Rogeriana: slow, rambling, in no hurry to make
a point. An immediate disclaimer of superior knowledge—Rogers does-
n't know what the word *entomologist* means, has to figure it out from
the context ("All I know is what I read in the papers"). Then a series of
mild digs, at the state of New Jersey, at American organizations that
have no real purpose. And then a deft sketch of an absurd situation—an
assembly of mosquito fighters being helplessly bitten by hordes of mos-
quitos. There is some satire in this, of course, but it is so mild that it is
hard to imagine anyone being really offended by this, not even professional exterminators or citizens of New Jersey.

Having given the thought-provoking statistic, Rogers goes on to ram-
ble. He figures out that all these zeroes add up to billions of little mos-
quitos. Then he provides the information that only half this number
should really trouble us, because only the females bite human beings.
The males are quite harmless:

> Now women, what have you got to say for yourselves? Get that, the
> males are harmless. They don't bite, buzz or lay eggs! That's great. It
> makes me proud I am a male. That fellow Kipling had it right when he
> wrote (or maybe it was Shakespeare, or Lady Astor or somebody over
> there), "The female of the species is more deadly than the male." Women
> denied it then, and there was a great mess raised about it. But this New
> Jersey entomologist has finally got the dope on 'em.

Would feminists be offended by this? Teachers of English literature?
Perhaps they would be if Rogers had developed these remarks into full-
blown satire. But he does no such thing. Despite the title of the piece,
this is no satirical take-off on male/female relations. (To emphasize this
point, just imagine what James Thurber might have made of this episode.) Rogers goes on to say what the learned professor failed to say in
Atlantic City: The exterminators should concentrate on the females only.
Or, alternatively, they should teach the females birth control: Perhaps

they should be moved from New Jersey to Fifth Avenue in New York, where they would learn that their exuberant fertility is definitely lower-class. And this is how the piece ends:

> Course the whole thing is kinder mysterious to me. I don't see how the female can be the one that lays all the eggs, raises all the young, does all the biting, and still has time to sing. Now when do they find time to raise all these children? There must be times when they can't be singing or biting. Now the way this entomologist has left us now, about the only way we have left open to do, is to watch a mosquito till he bites you, and then destroy him—I mean her. In other words, if he bites you, he is a her, and if he sings, he is a her. Watch him and if he lays an egg, then it's a her. But if he just sits there all day and don't do anything, why, about the only conclusion we can come to is that it is a he. Don't kill him, he does no harm, he just sits and revels in the accomplishments of his wife. So when you find a male, the best thing to do is just to sit there and wait till his wife comes between bites. How does the male live? That's what they are going to take up at the next dinner?

What is, finally, the point of all this? It is safe to say that the question is irrelevant. There is no deeper point here, no satirical intent. It is a play on situations, on words, on absurd incongruities. The point is pure entertainment.

Now, not all of Rogers's writings are that harmless. He commented widely and with definite satirical intent on American mores and politics. But here, too, the tone is mild, conciliatory. The evidence is that most of the individuals actually named in some of these spoofs did not resent this and enjoyed laughing at themselves as portrayed by Rogers (Calvin Coolidge was apparently an exception, but then he was notorious for his lack of humor). The following, from a piece entitled "Investigations, Hearings and Cover-ups," is as timely as it was in Rogers's day. Here is the beginning:

> Say, did you read what this writer just dug up in George Washington's diary? I was so ashamed, I sat up all night reading it. This should be a lesson to presidents to either behave themselves, or not to keep a diary. Can you imagine, 100 years hence, some future writer pouncing on Calvin Coolidge's diary? What would that generation think of us? Calvin, burn them papers!

There is another investigation going on in Congress into slush funds. Rogers comments:

> Imagine a Congress that squanders billions, trying to find out where some candidate spent a few thousand! But these boys in Washington have

had a lot of fun investigating. You see, a senator is never as happy as when he is asking somebody a question without that party being able to ask him one back. But the only trouble about suggesting that somebody, or something, ought to be investigated is that they are liable to suggest that *you* ought to be investigated. And from the record of all previous investigations, it just looks like nobody can emerge with their noses entirely clean. I don't care who you are, you just can't reach middle age without having done and said a whole lot of foolish things. So I tell you, if I saw an investigating committee heading my way, I would just plead guilty and throw myself on the mercy of the court.[15]

Rogers has some suggestions to make this investigating business more efficient. There should be certain days for certain things— Mondays for confessions, Tuesdays for accusations, the other weekdays for denials. But what really troubles Rogers is how dumb people appear on the witness stand: they mumble, they deny the obvious, they claim not to remember anything. The more education people have, the dumber they seem to be as witnesses. This has given Rogers a really good idea: Since public figures in America spend over half their time testifying before investigative committees, he is going to start a school that will teach them how to testify (it will be located in Claremore, Oklahoma, "the hub of everything"). The students will be taught how not to be nervous, not to get rattled, but above all to keep records of everything. Whatever they are asked, they will have a record giving the exact answer. This will greatly expedite these proceedings. Also, the graduates of Rogers's school will not only not fear but positively look forward to being investigated. And here is Rogers's ultimate motive in suggesting this innovation:

> It's really patriotic reasons that make me want to do this, for I am afraid that foreign nations will read some of our papers and find the testimony of some of our men who are in the Cabinet and high in public office. And they will judge them by that testimony. They will think they are no smarter than their testimony. Well, that will leave a bad impression, and if I can change that and get them to make their testimony as smart as the men really are, why, I will have performed a public service.

This is satire, a "modest proposal," if you will. But there is no Swiftian edge here. Rogers is making mild fun of the politicians and their foibles. He is bantering. And all the time he includes himself in the foibles he depicts.

While Wodehouse and Rogers share the benign quality of their humor, their comic strategies are quite different. Wodehouse creates a separate world, self-contained and remote from the empirical realities in which his characters act out their systematic inanities. Rogers did not do this. His humor deals with the real world of America, but in doing so it transforms that world, envelops it in a cloud of basically benevolent commentary. Both authors gently debunk all authorities and all pretensions. If there is one virtue that both teach, it is the virtue of tolerance. However, it is unlikely that either would have admitted such a didactic purpose.

The final clear case of benign humor to be discussed here is of a very different sort indeed from the two preceding cases: Franz Lehár (1870–1947), the master of what has been called the silver age of the Viennese operetta.[16] The operetta as a form of musical theater has a complex set of antecedents, its origins probably in Italy's *opera buffa,* which in turn began with comic insets within the action of *opera seria.* But the real beginnings of the operetta are in the nineteenth century, centered in Paris, Vienna, and London, dominated respectively by Jacques Offenbach, Johann Strauss the Second (that was the golden age of Viennese operetta), and Gilbert and Sullivan. The operetta soon reached America, where it eventually evolved into the Broadway musical. Lehár's opus in general and his masterpiece *The Merry Widow* (first performed in 1905) represent a late flowering of this tradition. It embodies more than any other artistic creation the *joie de vivre* of the twilight period of Habsburg Central Europe. The older tradition of the operetta had elements of satire and parody in it, some of it quite political (one may recall here the attempt of the Austrian censors in an earlier period to prohibit all improvisations on the popular stage). Also, there is a dark, melancholy undertone in all Strauss music. Lehár purged the operetta of both satirical and tragic elements. He allowed a lot of emotion, but it tended always toward sentimentality. At the same time, Lehár was a musical genius, and the glory of his music regularly transcends the rather insipid actions on the stage. Perhaps it is only in retrospect, in the knowledge of what happened to the Habsburg order soon after *The Merry Widow* began its triumphant career, that one detects a sense of resignation in the sentimental hedonism of the Viennese operetta of that period. Be that as it may, to this day Lehár's music represents the spirit of the last great flowering of a now disappeared empire.

Lehár as a person is also very representative of that empire, with its cosmopolitan population. He was born in Hungary and was ethnically Hungarian, but he was also the child of a military bandmaster and he lived in a long list of garrison towns scattered throughout the vast reaches of the Austro-Hungarian monarchy. He himself conducted a military band for the few years of his army service. Like Wodehouse and Rogers, Lehár was enormously successful in his lifetime, both financially and in terms of status. Various cultural critics despised what they thought of as the superficial sentimentality of his work. Thus, for example, Karl Kraus, the great Viennese satirist, wrote that the first performance of a Lehár operetta in the Turkish empire was a clear signal of the coming end of civilization. The larger public, though, loved him. Among his admirers, alas, was Adolf Hitler, as a result of which Lehár's works continued to be performed in the Third Reich despite his Jewish wife and the fact that his two favorite librettists were Jews.

In all operetta (and the same probably goes for opera) there is a degree of tension between the music and the libretto. The comic effect of operetta may well come out of that tension. The music in itself may be light, but it can rarely be described as comic. The action on the stage, as prescribed by the libretto, would most of the time be too insipid to be funny if performed without music as a straight play or if read as a text. Beaumarchais, the author of the play *The Marriage of Figaro* (which Offenbach also turned into an operetta), once observed that one may sing that which is too stupid to be spoken. In what follows, therefore, it will help if one hears the music (inwardly if not actually) as the essential accompaniment of the dramatic action.[17]

The action of *The Merry Widow* takes place "today" (say, 1905) in Paris. The center of the action is the embassy of Pontevedro, a vaguely Balkan state. Originally, incidentally, Lehár named it the embassy of Montenegro, but at that time Montenegro was a real Balkan state (as it has become again) and its embassy in Vienna protested. Thus Montenegro became Pontevedro, and its capital of Cetinje became Letinje (though that is mentioned only once). After the brisk, cheerful overture, the first act opens with a reception in the Pontevedrin embassy in honor of the ruler's birthday. Two plots interweave. Ambassador Mirko Zeta instructs his henchman Njegus (a sort of Leporello figure) to make sure that Count Danilo Danilowitsch marries the rich Pontevedrin widow Madame Glawari, since without her fortune the state is about to go bankrupt. Meanwhile the charming Frenchman Camille Roussillon is ardently wooing Valencienne, the ambassador's wife. Political and erotic intrigue became elaborately mixed. The latter allows Valencienne to sing one of the most melodious arias of the operetta: "I Am a Respectable Woman" (*Ich bin eine anstaend'ge Frau*), she sings, as she fends off the amorous Frenchman. She warns him against the dangers of passion, which must be domesticated—a warning, one may say, that all operetta has always taken to heart.[18] Madame Hanna Glawari arrives, surrounded by admirers. Valencienne would like Camille to become interested in the rich widow, to be rid of the temptation. As for Danilo, he is a diplomat and always ready to do his duty, but he is also not very happy with his matrimonial assignment. He sings yet another famous aria, in which he praises the delights of the cabaret "Maxim" where he intimately knows all the ladies (the easygoing *grisettes* of the Parisian *démi-monde*), who help him to forget his dear fatherland. Yet it is clear that Hanna and Danilo are quite attracted to each other. Danilo sings another aria, quite different in tone, celebrating the stirrings of love, "as the flowers first bloom in spring." As the evening progresses, the time has come for "ladies' choice" (*Damenwahl*) for the dance. Hanna chooses Danilo, who, to spite her, offers to sell *his* dance to anyone paying ten thousand francs. No one offers to pay. Hanna, of course, is furious. As everyone leaves, she is left alone with Danilo and they begin to dance. Hanna: "You horrible man! How wonderfully you dance!" Danilo: "One does what one can!"

Without the music, it hardly needs repeating, this dramatic action is about as stupid as Beaumarchais would have deemed it to be. The characters are paper thin, the setting is as implausible as can be, and the action follows a well-known sequence (which probably derives from the *commedia dell'arte* if not earlier): In the first act boy meets girl; in the second act there are difficulties; in the third act boy gets girl. In other words, a very vigorous suspension of doubt (*epoché*) is called for if one is to be sucked into this little drama. To be sure, good acting and imaginative stage settings can help, but it is above all Lehár's triumphantly joyful music that has led generations of theatergoers to make this leap of faith. Some will always refuse. Those who assent are rewarded by several hours of perfectly mindless entertainment.

Everything becomes complicated in the second act, which takes place at a garden party at Madame Glawari's, who is also Pontevedrin and wishes to celebrate the royal birthday "as at home in Letinje." A vaguely Slavic dance opens the proceedings. Then Hanna sings another famous aria, "Vilja, Oh Vilja," a romantic love song based on an alleged Pontevedrin legend about an affair between a hunter and a forest nymph. Danilo and Hanna engage in elaborate flirtations, and she berates him (this time in a vaguely Hungarian aria) as a stupid cavalryman who cannot see when a woman loves him. All the men join in a chorus bemoaning the difficulty of knowing what women really want (did Lehár read Freud? Did Freud attend Lehár operettas?): "Women, women, women, women!" No theory explains how women will respond. Meanwhile Camille is making headway with the seduction of Valencienne, as the orchestra plays another famous Lehár waltz with the refrain "I love you" (*Ich hab' dich lieb*). Camille sings the insinuating aria "Come into the Small Garden-House, Come to the Sweet Assignation" (*Komm' in den kleinen Pavillon*). Valencienne's respectability collapses and she does indeed follow him into the small garden-house. Unfortunately the ambassador has also made an appointment there, with Danilo, to discuss the great matrimonial plot. He recognizes his wife, erupts into jealous fury. Njegus (a sort of Balkan version of Jeeves, one is tempted to say) quickly acts to save the situation. He lets Valencienne out by the back door, ushers Hanna in, who then emerges to announce her engagement to Camille. The ambassador is reluctantly convinced that he did not see his wife there after all, but he is desperate about the failure of his plan to acquire Hanna's fortune for the Pontevedrin treasury. Danilo, who does not understand that Hanna only acted to save Valencienne's reputation, is deeply hurt but pretends indifference. He and Hanna sing a duet, in which marriage is described as an obsolete point of view, unless it is "in the Parisian manner" in which each spouse does as he or she pleases.

Needless to say, all these complexities are resolved in Act III. The scene is still Hanna Glawari's garden party, later in the evening. She has rigged up a facsimile of the cabaret "Maxim" and all of Danilo's favorite *grisettes* are there to perform, joined by Valencienne, who has disguised herself as one of them (for reasons one is left to guess). The ambassador insists that Danilo must marry Hanna, whatever his personal preferences. Hanna explains the garden-house incident to him, whereupon they confess their mutual love in a duet that repeats the earlier love song ("Love Me!" "I Love You!"). The ambassador finds his wife's fan in the garden-house, realizes that she has been deceiving him after all, declares himself divorced as of this moment. He then proposes to Hanna himself. Hanna explains that, alas, her late husband's will stipulates that, if she remarries, she will have no money at all. The ambassador retracts his proposal. But Danilo, fired by love, asks her to marry him anyway, money or no money. Hanna then finishes her earlier sentence: No money goes to her if she remarries—because her new husband will now administer her fortune. General rejoicing: The state of Pontevedro is saved from financial ruin, Danilo and Hanna get each other, and (one may assume) Valencienne's respectability is restored. The *grisettes* are left to go on with their lives of charming sin.

This chapter has looked at three instances of benign humor. The argument has been that, despite the great differences between them, they have in common an essentially similar expression of the comic. They are far removed from the magic of Dionysian folly. They offer no threat to the social order or to the paramount reality of ordinary life. They provide a vacation from the latter's worries, a harmless diversion from which one can return refreshed to the business of living. Yet there is a kind of magic here too, especially when this form of the comic creates an enchanted world of its own, as Wodehouse does with his writing and Lehár with his music. This enchantment has its own value, perhaps even its own moral status. The many people who have yielded to it (because they were unsophisticated to begin with or because they temporarily put their sophistication away) have understood this. They have been right. And those who have despised these vacations from seriousness have been wrong—one may say, paradoxically, that they have been *profoundly* wrong.

## Notes

1.  The legendary Rabbi Meir of Vilna, after reading this paragraph in his heavenly study, is reputed to have said, "So, enough apologizing already. Go make the knishes." I have given some thought to moving this great sage from the notes to the main text.

2.  Cf. Benny Green, *P. G. Wodehouse: A Literary Biography* (New York: Rutledge, 1981).

3.  Ibid., 181ff.

4.  Muggeridge wrote about this in Thelma Cazalet-Keir, ed., *Homage to P. G. Wodehouse* (London: Barrie and Jenkins, 1973), 87ff. There was another, truly Wodehousian twist to this story. German intelligence, singularly bereft of an English sense of humor, read Wodehouse in the belief that he provided an ethnographically accurate picture of life in his native country. They dropped an agent in England wearing spats. He was immediately spotted and arrested.

5.  P. G. Wodehouse, *The World of Jeeves* (New York: Harper and Row, [1967] 1989), 22ff.

6.  I understand that some critics have suggested that the relationship between Bertie and Jeeves is a homosexual one. This is about as plausible as a theory interpreting Jeeves as a proletarian revolutionary. As he might have put it: "A most injudicious suggestion, sir."

7.  Wodehouse, *World of Jeeves*, 300ff.

8.  Green, *P. G. Wodehouse*, 237. My italics.

9.  Cazalet-Keir, *Homage to P. G. Wodehouse*, 6.

10.  Cf. Ben Yagoda, *Will Rogers* (New York: Knopf, 1993).

11.  Wodehouse, when he was writing for Broadway musicals, also had dealings with Ziegfeld (reputedly a very humorless individual). I have not been able to find out if Wodehouse and Rogers ever met in New York.

12.  Actually, he didn't meet Trotsky. He was prevented from doing so on a visit to the Soviet Union. He regretted this, commenting, "I bet you if I had met him and had a chat with him, I would have found him a very interesting and human fellow, for I have never yet met a man I didn't like" (Yagoda, *Will Rogers*, 234). It seems that Rogers was as perceptive of the Communist as Wodehouse was of the Nazi version of totalitarianism. An intuition that there are hidden connections between all things (Rabbi Meir understands) makes me add that Trotsky also occurs in the aforementioned Wodehouse story "Without the Option": Sippy, upon being arrested, gives his name as Leon Trotsky. The magistrate, when he sentences him to jail, ventures the opinion that this is not his real name.

13.  Yagoda, *Will Rogers*, 190.

14.  Bryan Sterling, ed., *The Will Rogers Scrapbook* (New York: Grosset and Dunlop, 1976), 71.

15.  *Will Rogers Scrapbook,* 113f.

16.  Cf. Richard Traubner, *Operetta: A Theatrical History* (Garden City, N.Y.: Doubleday, 1983).

17.  In my case that was a CD of a 1973 Deutsche Gramophon recording of the Chor der Deutschen Oper Berlin. A libretto came with the CD, containing the German text and a perfectly terrible English translation.

18.  *"Sehr gefaehrlich ist des Feuer's Macht*
*wenn man sie nicht bezaehmt, bewacht!*
*Wer das nicht kennt, sich leicht verbrennt.*
*Nimm vor dem Feuer dich in acht."*

# 8

# The Comic as Consolation
## *Tragicomedy*

It was proposed earlier that the comic should be understood as a form of magic. The comic, like magic, brings about a sudden and rationally inexplicable shift in the sense of reality. But there are different forms of magic. There is little magic and big magic: A rabbit jumping out of a top hat, and a swarm of witches descending from the sky. There is white magic, which miraculously heals, and black magic, which curses and destroys. Benign humor, as discussed in the preceding chapter, usually produces little results and is clearly a manifestation of white magic. But the comic, as already indicated, also comes in more massive and much darker versions. Tragicomedy is a curious in-between case. As such it deserves some attention.

Tragicomedy can be described as that which provokes laughter though tears. It is mellow, forgiving. It does not bring about a profound catharsis, but it is moving nonetheless. Above all, it consoles. This consolation may or may not have religious overtones.

The discerning reader (and what other reader should this book be addressed to?) will already have noted that the categories applied to the experience of the comic will inevitably overlap to a certain extent. There are few absolutely clear cases. Still, no phenomenon can be understood without making some categorical distinctions. Tragicomedy differs from benign humor, which, as far as possible, banishes the tragic from its fragile constructions of an artificial reality (though the world of P. G. Wodehouse demonstrates that some of these constructions can be quite robust). So-called black humor defies the tragic, as its synonym, gallows humor graphically suggests. Then there is grotesque humor, in which the tragic is absorbed into an absurd universe, as in the *danse macabre* of the late Middle Ages. In tragicomedy the tragic is not banished, not defied, not absorbed. It is, as it were, momentarily suspended.

Tragicomedy, like benign humor, often inserts itself in small, fugitive dosages into the flow of everyday life. It does not eradicate whatever sorrow or sadness has obtruded, but it makes these emotions more bearable. Also like benign humor, it is often mediated by children. The vibrant vitality of children is obviously incongruent with whatever may be the tragic situation. The incongruence is comic, but it also reaffirms the power of life in the face of all that darkens the human condition. This was eloquently expressed by Meister Eckhart, the great medieval mystic: "If I were alone and full of dread in a wilderness, and if I had a child with me, all dread would leave me and I would be strengthened. This is how noble and joyful is life."[1]

In the preceding chapter the example was given of a little girl producing a comic effect by dressing up in her mother's clothes. Transpose this performance to the scene of a funeral. It has to be modified, of course, since little girls (if allowed to attend at all) would hardly show up in this sort of disguise. But children do attend funerals and they will be dressed in formal, quasi-adult attire. The tragicomic effect may be produced by this incongruence all by itself. To imagine further such effects, it is not necessary to assume that the children will misbehave. Let it be assumed that they are well brought-up and make every effort to behave appropriately. Yet something could easily happen to interrupt their solemn behavior: they start to giggle about something that strikes them funny in the proceedings, they make faces at each other because they are getting bored, or they make some mistake in the ritual they are supposed to follow. The mourners may, of course, be annoyed by these childish intrusions into the solemnity of the occasion. They may also be amused, however, and the little tragicomic performance may make the occasion less dreadful. Such a tragicomic consolation in the face of death is quite different from other comic responses to the presence of death. Black humor, of course, frequently revolves around death (though it would generally be felt to be inappropriate at a funeral). And there are expressions of the comic on such occasions that confront death in frequently grotesque ways, as can easily happen at an Irish wake (perhaps describable as a late version of the *danse macabre*). Tragicomedy offers much gentler comforts.

There are limits to tragicomedy. If people at a funeral are entertained and consoled by the antics of children, they are most likely to be those not immediately bereaved. There is grief so profound that tragicomedy is excluded. There are horrors before which even the best-intentioned attempts at comic consolation must fail and indeed should not be undertaken. There are occasions when no one either can or should laugh, when the tears are too bitter. It would probably be pointless to try to define or enumerate these occasions with the intention of establishing a moral code for tragicomedy. This is a definition that must be left to the reason of the heart, or to whatever approximations of such of which an individual is capable.

There are tragicomic roles in life as well as in art. Here one meets once again with the role of the fool, though in his mellower incarnations. Sad clowns and mimics reappear. Tragicomedy is also a form of drama; in the history of the film, Charlie Chaplin is probably the paragon of this. But it is in prose literature that tragicomedy in everyday life is best caught. In European literature, Cervantes's Don Quixote is probably the paradigmatic embodiment of the tragicomic hero. There are more recent cases.

The case chosen for the present purpose is Sholem Aleichem (1859–1916), widely considered to be the greatest figure in Yiddish literature. Arguably, though, this entire literature, or much of it, could be used to illustrate the category of the tragicomic. To American ears, a comic quality has come to be attached to certain Yiddish words and intonations that have infiltrated American English, but this is very probably due to their use by popular Jewish comedians and their imitators; there is nothing intrinsically comic or tragicomic about the Yiddish language. The tragicomedy is rooted in the condition of the people who used this language, the Jews of Eastern Europe and especially those living in intolerable circumstances in Russia. Yiddish culture, in consequence, developed a sense of comic incongruity possibly unparalleled anywhere else. The incongruity was between the majestic destiny of the Jewish people as proclaimed by Judaism and the miserable conditions under which Jews lived in the real world of Eastern Europe. Both in everyday speech and in literature (very much so in the case of Sholem Aleichem), Yiddish was used as an ironic commentary on the grandiose pronouncements of Hebrew. A common saying uses this Hebrew/Yiddish antiphony to express a profoundly ironic view of the world: In Hebrew, "You have chosen us from among the nations" (a recurring phrase from the daily prayers), followed by the Yiddish counterpoint, "Why did you have to pick on the Jews."[2] Many of Sholem Aleichem's characters use this Hebrew/Yiddish antiphony to express their sardonic angle on things. Take a concrete instance from the Jewish liturgical year, the Feast of Tabernacles or Sukkot, celebrated in the autumn to commemorate the Exodus from Egypt.[3] Imagine a group of Russian Jews observing this ritual—a group of people barred from even owning land reading texts that refer to a Middle Eastern agricultural festival—people sitting outside their houses in a flimsy hut, shivering, as the Russian winter is not far off, people with barely enough to eat, if that, praising God for the bounties bestowed on them. No wonder that they were moved to ask why, of all nations, He had to pick on them to be His chosen people! But they were still too much embedded in their faith to utter such rebellious thoughts in Hebrew; they were free to do so in Yiddish.

The very nature of Yiddish contains the history of the Jewish diaspora—an underlying structure of medieval German, with overlays of Hebrew and various Slavic languages. This is how another Yiddish writer, I. L. Peretz, put it:

> Yiddish, the language which will ever bear witness to the violence and murder inflicted on us, bears the marks of our expulsions from land to land, the language which absorbed the wails of the fathers, the laments of the generations, the poison and bitterness of history, the language whose precious jewels are . . . Jewish tears.[4]

This notion of the language as a sedimentation of history is well expressed in the Israeli joke of a woman who insists on speaking Yiddish instead of Hebrew with her son and, when asked why, says, "I don't want him to forget that he is a Jew!"[5] Yet, amid all these tears, there was also an irrepressible laughter.

There is another incongruity that should be mentioned here: that between the world of men and the world of women, the former marked by scholarship, the latter by the management of the family's practical affairs. And, of course, the former mainly used Hebrew, the latter Yiddish. The term *mother-tongue* is used in English and in other Western languages, but when Yiddish is referred to as the mother-tongue (*mameh-loshen*), this has a specific sociological significance. Women were usually not taught Hebrew, except the little needed to say certain prayers. Yiddish was thus a women's language *par excellence*, the language in which mothers spoke to their children—the same mothers who often enough worked from morning till evening in some little store, making enough money for the family to live on, so that their husbands could sit in *shul* and carry on the highest vocation for Jewish men—the vocation of study—in Hebrew. The Hebrew/Yiddish antiphony is thus ipso facto an antiphony between otherworldly speculation and the hard, practical business of making it in this world.

If one only looks at high literary expressions, the history of Yiddish literature is heartbreakingly short. It only became a literary language in the late nineteenth century, first in the writings of Mendele Moycher-Sforim (1836–1917), whom Sholem Aleichem called the grandfather, *zeyde*, of Yiddish letters. Before then it was used in written form for biblical translations and prayer books, mainly for the use of women, some folk tales and dramas, and some Hasidic writings. Sholem Aleichem published his first stories in Yiddish in 1883 (when he also adopted the pen name under which he is known today). In 1978 the

Nobel Prize was awarded to Isaac Bashevis Singer (who died in 1991), in all likelihood the last important Yiddish writer. From 1883 to 1978, less than a century for a flowering literature, cut off, along with most of those speaking its language, by the greatest tragedy of Jewish history!

Sholem Aleichem was born as Sholem Rabinovitch in a Ukrainian *shtetl*.[6] Although he subsequently lived in Kiev and Odessa, both as a writer and a businessman, the world of the *shtetl*, the small Jewish village in the provinces, remained the locale of most of his work. He left Russia in 1906 and moved to the United States via Geneva. He died in Brooklyn. Toward the end of his life he was a revered figure and his funeral was a major event.

Since so much of Sholem Aleichem is full of comic characters and situations, it is important to keep in mind under what terrible conditions Jews lived in the so-called Russian Pale of Settlement (the areas of the country in which Jews were allowed to live), practically up to World War I. They were restricted not only in terms of residence but of occupation, officially classed as inferior subjects of the tsar, periodically attacked physically by anti-Semitic mobs as well as government authorities. Most of them lived in grinding poverty. In 1881 a series of bloody pogroms were directly incited by the government under the notorious minister K. P. Pobedonostsev, whose avowed aim was that one-third of Russia's Jews should die, one-third convert to Christianity, and one-third emigrate. This aim was not reached, but not for want of trying on the part of the tsarist government. In 1882 the so-called May Laws further restricted the areas in which Jews were allowed to live, specifically forbidding them to live in rural areas where they had been living for generations. There were widespread expulsions. In 1905, after the failed revolution, there were more pogroms. It was, of course, during this period that there was massive Jewish emigration out of Russia, some of it to Austria-Hungary and Germany, most of it to the United States. Sholem Aleichem himself became part of this wave of migration.

Sholem Aleichem saw as his mission to give voice to what he called an "orphaned people," to be their *folks-shtimme*. And he also expressed his aim of creating laughter in a wretched world (*a paskudneh velt*—the adjective derives from the Ukrainian and Polish words for dirt).

Sholem Aleichem's best known stories are those about Tevye the Milkman (they were that long before the American musical *Fiddler on the Roof*, which is based on them). They are told in Tevye's own voice, an unforgettable blend of resignation, irony, and the determination to survive against all odds. They deal with an endless series of misfortunes, mostly involving Tevye's daughters (whose number is sometimes given as seven, sometimes as five). Any one of them would serve to illustrate

Sholem Aleichem's unique expression of tragicomedy. Take the one about Tevye's daughter, Hodl.[7]

As in earlier stories, Tevye is telling this one to Sholem Aleichem (whom he addresses with the Polish honorific *Pani*): "Whenever something goes wrong in this world, it's Tevye it goes wrong with." Hodl is his second daughter, beautiful like Queen Esther and clever too, and she can read and write in Yiddish and in Russian. Tevye was on his way home from Boiberik, a nearby hamlet where he had been peddling his dairy products. It had been a good day.

> As usual I was thinking about the world's problems, such as why in Yahupetz they had it so good, whether Tevye ever would, what my horse would say if it could, and so on and so forth. It was summertime, the sun was shining down; the flies were biting; and the whole world seemed such a delicious place that it made me want to spout wings and fly off into it.

An offhand comment on Tevye's worldview: Even when things are as delightful as they can be, one is bitten by flies! In any case, as Tevye proceeds on this journey he sees a young man walking on the road and gives him a ride. They engage in a bantering conversation. (Given what happens as a result of Tevye's act of charity, one is vividly reminded of the joke told in an earlier chapter about the Jewish traveler who refuses to engage in conversation with a fellow-passenger on a train, because he does not want a son-in-law who cannot afford a watch!) The young man's name is Pertchik, but he is called Peppercorn, because that is what he looks like. This individual of unprepossessing appearance is a student and also, as it turns out, a revolutionary. Tevye invites the young man into his home. One thing leads to another (just as the reluctant traveler in the joke imagined). Peppercorn keeps on visiting Tevye's family. He makes a living as a tutor, at eighteen kopecks an hour. He begins to tutor Tevye's daughters (it is not clear in what he tutors them, but at least in Hodl's case, it is not only in academic subjects).

Some time later Tevye is told by a local matchmaker (a very important profession in the *shtetl* culture) that a rich young bachelor in Boiberik is interested in marrying Hodl. Tevye fantasizes about this:

> I can't tell you what sweet dreams that gave me. I imagined Hodl trailing smoke in a droshky, and the whole world burning up too, but with envy— and not just for the droshky and the horses, but for all the good I would do once I was the father of a rich woman. Why, I'd become a real philanthropist, giving this beggar twenty-five rubles, that one fifty, that one over there an even hundred; I'd let everyone know that a poor man is a human being too.

One is not in danger of being overly moved by Tevye's fantasized virtue: if he became a rich man, he would engage in wildly generous philanthropy, but this would be at least partly motivated by the desire to arouse envy and finally be one-up on all those rich Jews who had shown little respect for Tevye all those years. A saint Tevye is not! As he tells this fantasy to his horse (in "Horsish"), again on his way home from one of his trips, he comes on Peppercorn and Hodl slipping out of a forest. They tell him that they will get married. Worse than that, they inform him that they are "as good as married already" (there goes Hodl's image as a virginal Queen Esther) and that they want to "make it official," because Peppercorn must leave on a "confidential" mission. Tevye's droshky-driven fantasy goes up in smoke. He argues and argues against this project, all in vain. Finally, since there is no alternative, he agrees to a wedding ("a funeral would have been jollier"). But he does not dare to tell the truth to his wife, Golde, who is made to believe that Peppercorn is coming into a huge inheritance and must travel to manage these financial affairs.

Soon after the wedding Tevye takes Peppercorn to the railroad station, where he meets the latter's friends. They look more like Russians than Jews, with long hair and shirts hanging out over their trousers. Hodl stays behind, pining away. Then comes the news that Peppercorn is in prison, then that he is being sent to Siberia. Hodl decides to join him there. Again, Tevye tries to argue her out of this:

> I answered as usual with a verse from Scripture. "I see, Hodl," I told her, "that you take the Bible seriously when it says, *al keyn ya'azoyv ish es oviv ve'es imoy*, therefore a child shall leave its father and its mother. . . . [8] For Peppercorn's sake you're throwing your papa and your mama to the dogs and going God only knows where, to some far wilderness across the trackless sea where even Alexander the Great nearly drowned the time he was shipwrecked on a desert island inhabited by cannibals. . . . And don't think I'm making that up either, because I read every word in a book." You can see that I tried to make light of it, though my heart was weeping inside me. But Tevye is no woman; Tevye kept a stiff upper lip.

Here indeed is the essence of Tevye as a tragicomic hero—making light of things, even as his heart is weeping inside him. Of course, his arguments are of no avail, not even with the scriptural quotations (this one, ironically, actually undercuts his argument) and the learned references to obscure classics. Hodl is determined to leave. Once again Tevye lies to his wife, telling her that Hodl too must travel because of the fictitious inheritance. At the station, bidding Hodl farewell, Tevye cries after all, "like a woman." The story ends with an expression of sublime irony:

You know what, *Pani Sholem Aleichem*? Let's talk about something more cheerful. Have you heard any news of the cholera in Odessa?

The last of the Tevye stories, *"Lekh-Lekho"* ("Go, Go Out"), deals with the infamous May Laws, which, among other oppressive measures, decreed that Jews must leave rural areas.[9] Tevye tells the story with reference to the third chapter of Genesis, where God tells Abraham to go out from his home to the country that God will show him. Again, the scriptural reference is ironic: Abraham goes out to the Promised Land in obedience to God's command; Tevye must go out to nowhere, in obedience to the cruel and corrupt authorities of tsarist Russia. And this occurs after all the other disasters: Hodl having married and gone off with her mad revolutionary; Beilke's rich husband having to run away to America after having experienced financial ruin; the death of Tsaytl's virtuous but poor husband, forcing Tevye to forgo his intended move to the Holy Land in order to take care of her and her children; worst of all, Chava's conversion to Christianity. Once again Tevye is coming home from a trip to Boiberik. He finds the entire village assembled in front of his house. The village elder, Ivan Paparilo, tells him that they must have a pogrom:

> Look, Tevel, it's like this. We have nothing against you personally . . . A pogrom is a pogrom, and if the village council has voted to have one, then that's what must be. We'll have to smash your windows at least, because if anyone passing through here sees there's been no pogrom yet, we'll be in hot waters ourselves.

In the event, after having tea with Paparilo and discussing what sort of pogrom seems viable, Tevye is allowed to smash his own windows: "They're your windows . . . and you might as well smash them yourself."

But worse is to come. Just as Tevye thinks of the Messiah coming on a white horse to rescue the Jews from their oppressors, the village policeman comes on horseback. He brings an order of expulsion. Tevye knows well that, on this occasion, no argument could possibly prevail. He sells his house to Paparilo for a song, but convinces himself that he has outwitted the village elder. Yet, as the remnants of Tevye's family are leaving the village where, as the only Jews, they have lived all their lives, there is a great consolation. Chava, the convert, has decided to return to Judaism and to leave with them:

> I ask you, *Pani Sholem Aleichem*, you're a person who writes books—is Tevye right or not when he says that there's a great God above and that a man must never lose heart while he lives? And that's especially true of a

Jew, and most especially of a Jew who knows a Hebrew letter when he sees one . . . No, you can rock your brains and be as clever as you like—there's no getting around the fact that we Jews are the best and smartest people. *Mi ke'amkilo yisro'eyl goy ekhod,* as the Prophet says—how can you even compare a goy and a Jew? Anyone can be a goy, but a Jew must be born one.

Is this an expression of genuine religious faith in the face of adversity? Or is this too ironic? Perhaps Sholem Aleichem himself was not sure. Tevye declares that he is actually lucky to have been expelled. This, he thinks, is the lesson of *lekh-lekho,* because Tevye can now move about anywhere without being tied down to a permanent home. This is fine—unless, of course, God finally decides to send Messiah: "I don't even care if He does it just to spite us, as long as He's quick about it, that old God of ours!"

Two more examples from outside the Tevye cycle of stories may serve to round out a picture of Sholem Aleichem's distinctive version of tragicomedy. The first is from the so-called railroad stories. Railroads have always played an important role in Russia, not only among Russian Jews, and there is a whole genre of literature dealing with them. Probably their importance derives from the vastness of the country. Journeys by rail took a long time, and passengers got to know each other quite well, for better or for worse. Be that as it may, this one, called "Two Anti-Semites," is unmistakably Sholem Aleichem.[10] Here is how it begins:

> Max Berlliant is a lost cause. He travels from Lodz to Moscow and from Moscow to Lodz several times a year. He knows all the buffets, all the stations along the way, is hand in glove with all the conductors, and has visited all the remote provinces even the ones where Jews are only allowed to stay twenty-four hours. He has sweated at all the border crossings, put up with all kinds of humiliations, and more than once has been aggravated has eaten his heart out, in fact—and all because of the Jews, not because the Jews as a people exist, but because he himself—don't shout, whisper it—is also a Jew. And not even so much because he's a Jew, as because—if you'll forgive me for saying it—he looks so Jewish. That's what becomes of creating man in God's image! And what an image! Max's eyes are dark and shining, his hair the same. It's real Semitic hair. He speaks Russian like a cripple, and, God help us, with a Yiddish singsong. And on top of everything he's got a nose! A nose to end all noses.

Here once more, even if this time without the full Hebrew text, is a bizarre, Tevye-like implication of a Biblical reference: The suggestion is that God, in whose image Max Berlliant was created, has dark eyes and hair, and a big Jewish nose! Perhaps he also speaks with a Yiddish singsong. Theological speculation aside, Max is a traveling salesman, moves about all the time, even eats nonkosher food. On this occasion he is traveling in Bessarabia. He has a long trip ahead of him and is thinking of how to assure for himself enough room to stretch out over several seats. An explanation is called for here: Russian railways had three classes. The Russian upper classes traveled first-class, the peasantry in third-class; the second, "bourgeois" class was mostly frequented by Jews. This explains Max's ingenious stratagem.

Just before the train enters the region, Max goes out at a station stop and buys a copy of the *Bessarabian,* a fiercely anti-Semitic newspaper. He goes back to his seat, stretches out, puts the paper over his face. He is sure that this will keep away any Jews who might want to share the compartment with him and thus prevent him from stretching out. Thus decked out as a dangerous anti-Semite, Max goes to sleep. Unfortunately, as he sleeps, the newspaper slips off his nose, freeing it to display its full Semitic magnificence. Another Jewish passenger comes into the compartment, one Patti Nyemchick, a man notorious for his practical jokes. He quickly takes in the scene, smiles, and goes out to buy another copy of the same newspaper. He too puts it over his face and goes to sleep. For a while, the two putative anti-Semites sleep peacefully, having the compartment to themselves. (One may assume that any other Jew tempted to join them would have been quickly cured of the temptation by the presence of not just one but two obvious anti-Semites!)

Max wakes up first. He notices the other traveler:

> He wonders: "Where did the fellow come from and why is he lying on the seat opposite? And why is he covered with a copy of the *Bessarabian*?" . . . He starts stirring, rattling his newspaper until he hears that the person on the seat opposite is also stirring and rattling his newspaper. He keeps still for a minute, then takes a quick look and sees the other fellow regarding him with a half-smile. Our two *Bessarabian* customers are lying there across from each other, staring but not talking. Although each anti-Semite is dying to know who the other is, they hide their curiosity and keep mum.

Then, very quietly, Patti starts whistling a well-known Yiddish children's song. Quietly at first, Max joins in:

> Then, slowly, slowly both anti-Semites sit up, throw off the *Bessarabians,* and together burst into the familiar refrain. This time they don't don't whistle it, but sing the words with loud abandon:
> The rebbe sits
> with little children and recites with them
> the Hebrew alphabet.

Classical Greek drama is famous for its great scenes of recognition, or *anagnorisis*. In this story Sholem Aleichem has given a marvelously trag-icomic twist to this tradition—indeed, an *anagnorisis* in Yiddish singsong!

The final example of Sholem Aleichem's opus, a story entitled "Eternal Life," is somewhere on the borderline of tragicomedy and the macabre, indeed could be described as a sort of *danse macabre*.[11] The central character is a young man living on the support of his in-laws, "as the custom was," engaged full-time in studies. He has to travel to the town of his origins to obtain an exemption from military service and a passport, and for this purpose hires a sleigh with a taciturn peasant driver. He prepares for the trip: "prayer shawl and phylacteries, cakes made with butter, and three pillows: one to sit on, one to lean on, and one for my feet." Thus equipped, he takes off quite happily. Some time into the journey he decides to stop at a country tavern. Here the story turns.

A desperate scene awaits the young man. A corpse is lying on the floor, the wife of the tavernkeeper, surrounded by crying children. The tavernkeeper is desperate: How can he take his dead wife into town for burial and leave the children unattended? The young man (who is the narrator) takes pity on the bereaved tavernkeeper, offers to take the corpse on his sleigh. The widower is deeply grateful:

> He threw his arms around me and almost kissed me. "Oh, long life to you for this good deed! You'll gain Eternal Life! As I am a Jew, Eternal Life!"

They take off again. The narrator has memorized the name of the dead woman: Chava Nechama, daughter of Raphael Michael. He keeps repeating the name, but in the process he forgets the name of the husband. It grows darker and a snowstorm begins. They lose their way. The peasant starts to curse. After some time they come to a village. Everyone is sleeping. The narrator knocks at the door of the inn, but the innkeeper refuses to let them in with the corpse. The scene is macabre indeed: The narrator spends the night outside, shivering in a snowstorm, with a raging peasant and a corpse for company. As dawn breaks, the inn-keeper directs them to the officers of the burial society. Again they have to wait in the cold, until these pious gentlemen are finished with their prayers. Finally, the narrator gets to talk to the chief officer, one Reb Shepsel, who demands payment. The narrator instead offers him Eternal Life, which provokes a diatribe:

> Is that so! You are a young man representing Eternal Life? Go and make a little inspection of our town. See to it that people are prevented from dying of hunger and *you* will win Eternal Life. Eternal Life indeed! A

young man who trades in Eternal Life! Go, take your goods to the shiftless and the unbelievers, and peddle your Eternal Life to them.

Other officers of the burial society take a more positive view of the matter, arguing with Reb Shepsel, quoting the Bible and discussing legal arguments as to whether the poor of one's own town must always take precedence over the needs of outsiders. Finally it is agreed that they will take the corpse, though only with payment and proper documentation. After all, the dead woman could be the narrator's own wife, whom he might have murdered. The narrator, desperate, offers them all his money, seventy rubles, just to take the corpse and let him go. They come to an agreement and a splendid funeral ensues. Now a rumor spreads through the *shtetl* to the effect that the narrator is a wealthy man, who is burying his mother-in-law. A huge swarm of beggars is now besieging him. This draws the attention of the local police inspector. With this, things take another turn for the worse.

As this fearful representative of tsarist authority interrogates the narrator, an officer of the burial society advises him to stick to the story about his mother-in-law. He invents various names, but falters when asked what the woman died of. He says what comes into his mind first—she died of fright. "What sort of fright?" asks the policeman.

> I decided that, since I had begun with lies, I might as well continue with lies, and I made up a long tale about my mother-in-law sitting alone, knitting a sock, forgetting that her son Ephraim was there, a boy of thirteen, overgrown and a complete fool. He was playing with his shadow. He stole up to her, waved his hands over her head, and uttered a goat cry, *Mehh!* He was making a shadow goat on the wall. And at this sound my mother-in-law fell from her stool and died.

This story is too much even for the *goyishe kopp* of a Russian policeman. He lets the funeral proceed, but detains the narrator for further inquiries. After a stint in prison, he is put on trial, on suspicion of murder. He is acquitted on the testimony of the bereaved tavernkeeper and his in-laws. They too are furious, especially his mother-in-law: "What did you have against me that you wanted to bury me while I was still alive?" The narrator concludes the story: "From then on, when anyone mentions Eternal Life, I run."

There is no need to repeat here what was said on Jewish humor earlier in this book. It has taken different forms in Europe and North America, though its distinctive comic sensibility very probably originated in the Yiddish-speaking culture of Eastern Europe. Jewish humor presumably ranges across all the categories of the comic, but its central tragicomic motif faithfully represents the appalling conditions of Jewish life in Russia and elsewhere in that part of the world. If it evoked laughter amid tears, there was certainly enough reason for tears. But, as remarked before, there are limits to tragicomedy and its consolations. There are sorrows before which no form of laughter is possible and where even language breaks down. It is impossible today to read an author like Sholem Aleichem and his descriptions of Jewish life in Eastern Europe without thinking about the horror that was to engulf European Jewry not long afterward. Is any laughter still possible after this horror? Does it not mark the end of this particular comic sensibility? It is one of the several triumphs of Jewish survival that, apparently, the answers to these questions are, respectively, yes and no. In this connection it is interesting to look at the work of Isaac Bashevis Singer, who may well have been the last Yiddish writer of any importance.[12] In fairness one should point out that Singer himself would not have agreed with this characterization. Once, when asked why he continued to write in a language that soon would have no more speakers let alone readers, he replied that on the Day of Resurrection tens of thousands of individuals would wake up and immediately ask what new books are available in Yiddish.

Singer (1904–1991) was born in Russian Poland, grew up and lived in Warsaw, where his father was a Hasidic rabbi, and in Bilgoroy, his mother's *shtetl*. He worked as a Hebrew teacher, translator, and proofreader, and started to write in the 1920s. He was strongly influenced by his brother, Israel Joshua, who also became a widely read author. Isaac Bashevis Singer became well-known through his novel *Satan in Goray,* which was first serialized in a Yiddish newspaper, then published as a book in 1935. Throughout his career, Singer continued this practice of first publishing his work in newspaper serials. In 1935, he followed his brother to America, where he first found it very difficult to adjust. There came a period of literary inactivity, broken in the 1940s. Singer's work was now published in the Yiddish daily *Forward*. In 1953 Saul Bellow translated his story "Gimpel the Fool," which appeared in *Partisan Review*. With this, Singer became an important figure in American literature, in translation after translation. The Nobel Prize awarded him in 1978 was a bitter-sweet recognition not only of him as an outstanding writer but of the entire vanished culture whose principal voice he had become. He died in Miami, suffering from Alzheimer's disease.

If one compares Singer with Sholem Aleichem, a number of differences come into view. There are, of course, the American and Israeli settings of many of the later works. There is also a strong preoccupation with sexuality (one can think of Singer as John Updike in a yarmulke in that portion of his work), a preoccupation almost completely absent in Sholem Aleichem. There is also a more overt rebellion against God. But above all there is a deepening darkness—the overwhelming shadow of the Holocaust. This, needless to say, is most dominant in works actually dealing with Holocaust survivors. What is remarkable is that, even there, one finds eruptions of a tragicomic sense very much in line with earlier Yiddish literature. Tevye's voice has become more strangled, but it has not been completely stilled!

The novel *Enemies, A Love Story* is a good example of this.[13] It is the story of one Herman Broder and his women: his wife, Yadwiga, a Polish peasant girl and former family servant, who saved his life during the German occupation by hiding him in a hayloft; Masha, another Holocaust survivor, his volatile mistress; and finally Tamara, his first wife and mother of his murdered children, whom he had believed to be dead and who suddenly reappeared. Even before Tamara's reappearance, Broder's life was one of hectic deceptions. He is constantly on the move across the expanse of Greater New York: from Coney Island, where he lives with Yadwiga, to the Bronx, where Masha lives with her mother, to Manhattan, where Broder works for a fashionable and basically fraudulent rabbi.

The novel is full of absurd scenes. Broder lives in a tangle of complicated lies. He tells Yadwiga that he has to travel as a book salesman, calls her from Masha's apartment pretending to be out of town. His lies explode at a party in Manhattan where his bigamy (if not polygamy) is exposed. There are the pathetic steps by which Yadwiga tries to become Jewish. There is a surreal rendezvous with Masha's former husband. Taken at face value, this would make a perfect bedroom farce. But the farce is overcome by an escalation of tragic events: the death of Masha's mother, followed by the suicide of Masha herself (who is pregnant with Broder's child); the pregnancy of Yadwiga (Broder's fertility is absurd in itself), an innocent trapped in two equally alien worlds, that of Judaism and that of America, with which she is trying to cope with courage and dignity; Broder's flight from all these amorous entanglements and his disappearance, leaving Yadwiga and Tamara to raise his sole surviving child. Over these contemporary tragedies is the all-pervasive tragedy of the Holocaust, which leads to reiterated repudiations of God by several of the characters. Yet the bedroom farce remains just that, despite these somber undertones, and the novel can also be read as a defiant affirmation of the validity of sexual passion. The ending is absurd as well as benign, as Tamara decides to move in with Yadwiga to help take care of the baby.

There are very similar themes in the posthumously published novel *Meshugah*.[14] This is the story of another survivor, Aaron Greidinger, who lives with his mistress Miriam in a *maenage-à-trois* with Max Aberdam, an aged speculator. Again, the novel is full of absurd scenes, many of them in a sexual context, the most absurd being an episode in which Miriam's husband breaks in on the couple with a revolver and forces them to engage in a prolonged conversation during which they remain naked. Another bedroom farce, with the same tragic undertones. But a short story, "Brother Beetle," may serve to illustrate Singer's tragicomic sensibility very succinctly.[15]

The locale this time is not New York but Tel Aviv. The narrator, who normally lives in Brooklyn, is aged fifty, and is also a Holocaust survivor, visits Israel for the first time. He meets old friends and acquaintances from Warsaw, and he does all the things he expected to do in Israel. But "after a week of seeing everything a tourist must see in the Holy Land, I had my fill of holiness and went out to look for some unholy adventure." He did not have far to look. In a café he runs into Dosha, an old mistress of his from Warsaw. Both feel the old attraction. Dosha complains about her present lover (she also has a husband, her third, who lives in Paris). This lover, an engineer, is very intense and insanely jealous. At the moment, as luck would have it, he is not in town.

After having dinner together, the narrator and Dosha walk toward her home. This allows Dosha to complain about Israel and the narrator to make some sardonic observations about it:

> This climate sickens me. The men here become impotent; the women are consumed with passion. Why did God pick out this land for the Jews? When the Khamsin begins, my brains rattle.

Here is a nice Israeli version of the Yiddish question as to why God, of all the peoples in the world He could have chosen, decided to pick on the Jews. And why this country? Dosha's complaint reminds one of the Israeli joke that God, who had good reason to be annoyed at the Jews, gave them the only country in the Middle East without oil. And here are some thoughts of the narrator on the Tel Aviv urban scenery:

> We walked through dim streets, each bearing the name of a Hebrew writer and scholar. I read the signs over women's clothing stores. The commission for modernizing Hebrew has created a terminology for brassieres, nylons, corsets, ladies' coiffures, and cosmetics. They had found the sources for such worldly terms in the Bible, the Babylonian Talmud, the Jerusalem Talmud, the Midrash, and even the Zohar.

But now another bedroom farce is about to begin. During the evening the narrator has to go to the toilet. It turns out that the toilet is on the roof. The narrator climbs up there, still naked (Singer seems to have a penchant for trapping his characters in a state of embarrassing nudity). It is a primitive affair. There is no light and, instead of toilet paper, torn pieces of newspapers hang from a hook. Then the narrator sees the silhouette of a man in Dosha's room. Evidently the mad lover is back! The narrator is trapped on the roof—naked, cold, feeling utterly ridiculous. A large beetle crawls by. It too seems to have lost its way on the roof.

> I had never felt so close to a crawling creature as in those minutes. I shared its fate. Neither of us knew why he had been born and why he must die. "Brother Beetle," I muttered, "what do they want of us?"

Did Singer intend a Franciscan allusion with this "Brother Beetle" business, a Jewish Francis of Assisi, addressing all the creatures of this world as brothers and sisters? One is also reminded of Sholem Aleichem's Tevye talking "Horsish." In any case, soon after the appearance of the philosophically pregnant beetle, the narrator has a sort of religious experience:

> I was overcome by a kind of religious fervor. I was standing on a roof in a land which God had given back to that half of his people that had not been annihilated. I found myself in infinite space, amid myriads of galaxies, between two eternities, one already past and one still to come. Or perhaps nothing had passed, and all that was or ever will be was unrolled across the universe like one vast scroll . . . I asked God's forgiveness.

Forgiveness for what? It is not made clear. But before the narrator can have any more mystical ecstasies, Dosha comes up on the roof with his clothes. She opens a trapdoor to the stairs.

The narrator dresses hastily (Dosha's potentially homicidal lover might wake up at any moment). He finds his American passport and his money, climbs down the stairs. He walks through unknown streets. When he asks an elderly man, in English, how to get to his hotel, he only gets the rude reply, "Speak Hebrew!" He stands on the street, lost once more. Then he feels something moving in the cuff of his trousers. A big beetle crawls out and runs off:

> Was it the same beetle I had seen in the roof? Entrapped in my clothes, it had managed to free itself. We had both been granted another chance by the powers that rule the universe.

### Notes

1. *Meister Eckhart: Ein Breviarium aus seinen Schriften* (Wiesbaden: Insel, 1951), 60. My translation.

2. Cited in Ruth Wisse, *The Schlemiel as Modern Hero* (Chicago: University of Chicago Press, 1972), 47.

3.  I owe. this illustration to Ruth Wisse (who teaches Yiddish language and literature at Harvard).

4.  Cited in Leo Rosten, *The Joys of Yiddish* (New York: Pocket Books, 1970), xxif.

5.  Also told by Rosten, *Joys of Yiddish*.

6.  Cf. Joseph Butwin and Frances Butwin, *Sholom Aleichem* (Boston: Twayne, 1977). The first part of the writer's pen name is sometimes rendered by the Butwins, as Sholem, sometimes as Scholem. Since Yiddish is written with Hebrew characters, the forms of transliteration are rather a matter of taste.

7.  Hilliel Halkin, ed./trans., *Sholem Aleichem: Tevye the Dairyman and the Railroad Stories* (New York: Schocken, 1987), 53ff.

8.  Tevye, of course, uses the Ashkenazi pronunciation, not the Sephardic one used in Israel today.

9.  Halkin, *Sholem Aleichem*, 116ff.

10.  Irving Howe and Ruth Wisse, eds., *The Best of Sholom Aleichem* (Washington: New Republic Books, 1978), 115ff. See note 6 above on the variant spellings of the author's first name.

11.  Ibid., 43ff. The translator was Saul Bellow.

12.  Cf. Paul Kresh, *Isaac Bashevis Singer: The Magician of West 86th Street* (New York: Dial, 1979); Lawrence Friedman, *Understanding Isaac Bashevis Singer* (Columbia: University of South Carolina Press, 1988); Israel Zamir, *Journey to my Father* (New York: Arcade, 1995).

13.  Isaac Bashevis Singer, *Enemies, A Love Story* (New York: Farrar, Straus and Giroux, 1972).

14.  Isaac Bashevis Singer, *Meshugah* (New York: Farrar, Straus and Giroux, 1994).

15.  In *The Collected Stories of Isaac Bashevis Singer* (New York: Farrar, Straus and Giroux, 1982), 497ff.

# 9

# The Comic as Game of Intellect
## *Wit*

As an argument is developed over a period of time, insights emerge, at first seem very clear, then show themselves to be in need of modification. This is especially the case here, when the argument concerns a phenomenon as elusive as that of the comic. Again and again one finds oneself on Bergson's beach, so to speak, trying to hold in one's hands a bundle of foam. But the exercise is not futile. Not everything escapes one's grasp. Some kernels of insight remain reasonably solid. And, of course, there is intrinsic pleasure to the journey of exploration, quite apart from the results to be expected at the destination.

In an earlier part of this argument the point was made that there is an important cognitive dimension to the comic. That is, the comic perspective discloses aspects of reality over and beyond the subjectivity of the individual holding the perspective. More specifically, the comic perspective discloses incongruences that are not perceived in the serious attitude. It is important to add to this the further statement that not all perceptions resulting from the comic attitude are equally valid. Put simply, laughter can be an opening for truth, but there are instances when this opening is deceptive.

The intellect is always involved in perceptions of the comic. If wit is simply understood as intellectually informed humor, then a measure of it will be present in all experiences of the comic. It is naturally most evident in highly sophisticated humor, but intelligence is involved even in quite primitive humor. Take the following joke, which, it will be readily agreed, deserves the label "primitive":

> It seems that this man owned a parrot that kept using obscene language. When all efforts to change this failed, the man put the parrot in his refrigerator and told it, "You will stay in here until you learn how to speak decent." After an hour or so the man opens the refrigerator door. The parrot sits there, shivering, obviously unhappy. "Well," says the man,

"will you speak decent from now on?" "Yes, yes, I promise," replies the parrot. "But what bad thing did this chicken do?"

This joke was told to two five-year old children. One understood it and laughed, the other was puzzled. The first child was the more intelligent one, and was by the same token ready for wit of a kind.

The interest in this chapter is in more or less pure wit—that is, wit as a game of intellect and language, possibly also of behavior. Wit in this form has no interest beyond itself, is dispassionate, detached from any practical agenda. This type of wit can be distinguished from witty satire, which always springs from a practical motive—that of injuring an individual, a group, or an institution. In satire the comic is employed as a weapon, in disinterested wit as a toy. Wit always employs paradox and irony. It paradoxically conjoins aspects of reality that are understood to be separate in the serious attitude. It ironically hides its meanings, saying one thing but meaning another. Paradox and irony need not be comic, but they are inevitably involved in the comic experience, ever more so as this experience becomes intellectually sophisticated.[1]

Freud, as was seen earlier, correctly emphasized the importance of economy in expressions of wit. The most effective wit employs sparse means to achieve a rich result. Wit is sharp, pithy, pointed—all the adjectives suggest economy. This is true of the most casual witticism, of good jokes, and most especially of the epigram—by definition, a brief comment that pretends to encapsulate a startling insight. Witticisms, in the sense of witty observations made in the course of everyday conversation, are the most common expressions of wit. There have been virtuosi of this art form, some of whom achieved fame far beyond their own lifetime. Samuel Johnson and Winston Churchill are two cases of this. (In the case of Churchill, if all the witticisms ascribed to him had actually been spoken by him, he would hardly have had the time to engage in any other activity.) But less awe-inspiring producers of witticisms can be found in almost everyone's circle of acquaintances. Depending on the degree of malice accompanying their wit, these individuals may be eagerly sought out and invited to gatherings for the entertainment of all, or alternatively shunned as threats to any kind of *Gemuetlichkeit*. In other words, depending on circumstances, an accomplished wit may be either the boon or the nightmare of a hostess planning invitations to a party.

The joke is one of the most common expressions of wit, at least in Western cultures.[2] Jokes can be described as very short stories that end with a comically startling statement. In English, the term "punch line," denoting this concluding statement, graphically indicates the comic strategy involved here; so does the German term *die Pointe*, "the point," which even suggests the sharp end of a dagger. Economy here is of the essence. To be sure, there is a cognitive intentionality in jokes. The punch line pretends to deliver some sort of insight. Is the insight necessarily valid? Clearly, it is not. One only has to recall the all too many jokes that seek to denigrate this or that ethnic, racial, or religious group, ascribing to it patently false and misleading characteristics. Put simply, it is just as possible to wittily tell a lie as it is to reveal a truth by means of wit. Put differently, the capacity of a statement to arouse a comic response cannot settle the question of its validity. Having voiced this caveat, though, it remains the case that jokes can summarize an often complex situation in wondrously economical ways, simplifying and illuminating and definitely providing some cognitive benefit. A good way of illustrating this cognitive function is by looking at jokes that people in a group tell about themselves. This was done earlier in this book in looking at Jewish humor. The following bevy of jokes may provide further illustrations from different parts of the world:

The point: The much aspired-to "stiff upper lip" of the English

> In the days of the British Raj in India this patrol was ambushed by fierce tribesmen on the Northwest Frontier. A young English officer is lying wounded on the ground, an enormous spear sticking out of his chest. As he is being lifted onto a stretcher, one of the stretcher-bearers leans over him: "Does it hurt, lieutenant?"
> "Only when I laugh."

The point: The tragic incongruence of the African-American experience

> This black man is talking with God: "Lord, why's I got dark skin?"
> "This is because of the hot sun in Africa. With your dark skin you don't get sunburned. The white man, with his light skin gets sunburned all the time."
> "Lord, why's I got long legs?"
> "In Africa, in the jungle, when wild animals are charging after you, your long legs let you get away. The white man, with his short, stubby legs gets caught and eaten."
> "Lord, why's I got curly hair ?"
> "Same reason. In the African jungle, when these wild animals are after you, you get away. The white man's long hair gets caught in the trees and the animals catch him."
> "Lord, why's I in Cleveland?"

The point: The feelings of Québécois, on their French island in the midst of an English-speaking ocean

> In a village in Quebec a little girl goes out to collect mushrooms when the Virgin Mary appears to her. The little girl sinks to her knees and says: "Ah, vous êtes Notre Dame! Vous êtes si belle. Vous êtes magnifique. Je vous adore. Je vous aime."
> And the Virgin Mary replies: "I'm sorry. I don't speak French."

The point: The craving of the Swiss for an orderly world

> The phone rings at midnight in a pharmacy in the town of Chur. A man's voice asks: "Is this the Amann pharmacy?"
> "Yes, pharmacist Amann speaking."
> "Do you carry baby pacifiers?"
> "Yes,"
> "Do you carry red baby pacifiers?"
> "Yes."
> "Good. Take one and stick it up your behind."
> The next day, at eight in the morning, the phone rings again. A different man asks: "Is this the Amann pharmacy?"
> "Yes, pharmacist Amann speaking."
> "This is the cantonal police. Did you get a call last night to ask whether you carried red baby pacifiers?"
> "Yes."
> "And was it then suggested to you that you should insert a red baby pacifier in your posterior?"
> "Yes."
> "You may take it out again. We have determined that the call was a boys' prank."

The point: The resentment of Catalans about their situation in Spain

> On a train out of Barcelona there are four people in a compartment: an older Catalan woman with her very attractive daughter, a Catalan man not related to them, and a Spaniard. As the train goes through a tunnel, the compartment is in complete darkness for a few moments. Then a resounding slap is heard. What does each of the passenger think after this?
> The older woman: "Well, I have raised my daughter to take care of herself very satisfactorily."
> The daughter: "This is a little annoying. If a pass was made, why at mother and not at me?"
> The Spaniard: "These Catalan women are completely crazy. You only look at them and they start hitting you."
> The Catalan man: "Four more tunnels to Madrid!"

Even more than the joke, the epigram delivers a highly economical kernel of alleged insight. Oscar Wilde and H. L. Mencken were masters of this, in English and American letters respectively. Wilde's famous novella, *The Picture of Dorian Gray*, begins with a preface containing a list of epigrams.[3] Here are two of these:

> The nineteenth century dislike of Realism is the rage of Caliban seeing his own face in a glass. The nineteenth century dislike of Romanticism is the rage of Caliban not seeing his own face in a glass.

> We can forgive a man for making a useful thing as long as he does not

admire it. The only excuse for making a useless thing is that one admires it intensely. All art is quite useless.

Wilde's plays are full of witticisms, some actually in the form of epigrams, others that could easily be converted into such. Following are some exchanges between characters in one of Wilde's best-known plays, *Lady Windermere's Fan*.[4] A comment by the Duchess of Berwick, one of those formidable upper-class dowagers who haunt modern English literature (P. G. Wodehouse created an army of them):

> I'm afraid it's the old, old story, dear. Love—well, not love at first sight, but love at the end of the season, which is so much more satisfying.

A comment by another character, Mrs. Erlynne, on her accepting the proposal of marriage by Lord Augustus, the brother of the Duchess:

> There is a great deal of good in Lord Augustus. Fortunately it is all on the surface. Just where good qualities should be.

An exchange between Graham and Dumby, two dandies who carry on with their witty observations throughout the play:

Graham:    *Gossip is charming. History is merely gossip. But scandal is gossip made tedious by morality. Now, I never moralize. A man who moralizes is usually a hypocrite, and a woman who moralizes is invariably plain. There is nothing in the whole world so unbecoming to a woman as a Nonconformist conscience.*

And a little later:

Dumby:    *How marriage ruins a man It's as demoralizing as cigarettes, and far more expensive.*

The following are by Mencken:[5]

> **Conscience** is the inner voice which warns us that someone may be looking.
> **Alimony**—The ransom that the happy pay to the devil.
> Adultery is the application of democracy to love.
> **Puritanism**—The haunting fear that someone somewhere may be happy.
> To believe that Russia has got rid of the evils of capitalism takes a special kind of mind. It is the same kind that believes that a Holy Roller has got rid of sin.

Any reader of these passages will readily agree that they are witty. Readers will undoubtedly differ on the question as to whether the punch lines of these witticisms convey correct insights into reality, that is, whether they convey witty truths or witty lies.

The two aforementioned authors are helpful in exploring the nature of pure or disinterested wit. Despite great differences in temperament, style, and, of course, historical context, there are significant similarities between them. Both took a posture antagonistic to their own society (or perhaps more accurately, to what they perceived that society to be). Witty detachment was a central component of this posture. Both carefully cultivated a persona to go with the posture: in Wilde's case, the persona of the dandy, legitimated by a rather nebulous philosophy of estheticism: in Mencken's case, the persona of the thoroughgoing skeptic, a marginal man in bourgeois America (he used the term *Tory* to describe his dissent from American democracy), legitimated by a dubious claim on the philosophy of Nietzsche. There are strong satirical strands in the work of both authors, but both lack an element of satire— moral passion motivating the satirical attack. Both Wilde and Mencken took pride in being without any sense of moral outrage and both despised moralists of any stripe. The question of whether either or both of these authors could be characterized as moral nihilists is beyond the scope of the present argument. But the very absence of a moral agenda makes Wilde and Mencken appropriate examples of disinterested wit, of the comic as a pure game of the intellect.[6]

Oscar Wilde (1854–1900), perhaps more than anyone else in modern English literature, represents the cultivation of wit for its own sake. In this, there is great symmetry between his work and his life. Coming from a Protestant middle-class background in Ireland, he moved to London, where he became a literary celebrity. His fame spread to America, which he visited as a wildly popular lecturer. His writings—essays, fiction, and above all plays—were elegant and deliberately provocative of all the values of Victorian society. So was his life. It is actually evidence of the considerable tolerance of that society that it not only allowed these provocations but celebrated their author and rewarded him richly. His tragic downfall was not so much due to his homosexuality, which Victorian England would also have tolerated if practiced discreetly, but by his forcing that issue into the open with his ill-advised libel suit against the Marquess of Queensberry, the father of his lover Lord Alfred Douglas. The Marquess had publicly denounced him as a "sodomite" and, when Wilde sued him for this allegation, the inexorable machinery of English justice had to go into action and was able to demonstrate that the allegation was all too accurate. Prosecution and conviction followed inevitably, under the laws of that time. Wilde was imprisoned, at first under barbarous conditions, and upon his release he went abroad, never to return to England. Except for the eloquent "Ballad of Reading Goal," a *cri de coeur* against the brutality of capital punishment, Wilde was never able to write anything of note after his imprisonment. He died in France, a sick and broken man, in dire poverty. Very rightly so, Wilde's case has become a prime example of the persecution of homosexuals in Western societies. But this topic is beyond the scope of the present argument, as is the rather sophomoric philosophy of estheticism, which Wilde presented in essays and lectures as a revolutionary view of the world. The concern here must be the character of his wit, most notably expressed in his plays.

A commentator of Wilde's opus has summed this up very succinctly:

> It is neither characterization nor plot construction that endows Wildean comedy with its unique flavor, which is derived above all from the language and the dialogue. . . . This observation applies first and foremost to the conversations conducted by the dandies. Instead of communicating ideas by elucidating viewpoints, exchanging opinions or discussing problems, they formulate for the sake of formulating. Their reluctance to be pinned to content or to any sort of commitment is both result and evidence of their use of language as an intellectual game.[8]

The characters of the plays are flat and the plots are thoroughly implausible. The fluffiness of these productions strongly remind of the most mindless Viennese operettas. But where the triviality of the latter is transcended by the music, Wilde's plays are redeemed by the glittering dialogue, especially as carried on by (if a neologism be permitted) an ever-present flurry of dandies. The critics at the time were both annoyed and seduced by this. George Bernard Shaw commented as follows on the critics' reactions to one of Wilde's premieres in the London theater:

> They laugh angrily at his epigrams, like a child who is coaxed into being amused in the very act of setting up a yell of rage and agony.[9]

Wilde himself stated his dramatic credo in these words:

> No artist desires to prove anything. . . . No artist has ethical sympathies. . . . All art is quite useless.[10]

To illustrate Wilde's wit at work, it makes sense to look at his most successful play, still staged today all over the English-speaking world, *The Importance of Being Earnest*.[11] The play opened at St. James's Theatre in February 1895 and was an instant triumph. Its opening also coincided, poignantly, with the beginning of Wilde's catastrophic legal duel with the Marquess of Queensberry (who had to be prevented from entering the theater, where he had intended to make a scene). The title was ironic: The very last thing that this play, or any other by Wilde, sought to convey was earnestness. Rather, the title refers to the name Ernest, which has an important part in the play. One critic observed that any serious review of this play would be like investigating the ingredients of a soufflé after dinner. The plot is at the same time very complex and unspeakably trivial. It revolves around the amorous adventures of two ineffably silly dandies, John Worthing and Algernon Moncrieff, both of whom are wooing two equally silly young ladies whose mind has been set on the idea that they only want to marry a man by the name of Ernest. Little purpose would be served in elaborating on the plot any further. As always with Wilde, the dialogue does all the work—*le ton qui fait la musique.* A few samples will do here. The following is an exchange between Moncrieff and his manservant Lane, at the very beginning of Act One:

Moncrieff: *Why is it that at a bachelor's establishment, the servants invariably drink the champagne ? I ask merely for information.*
Lane: *I attribute it to the superior quality of the wine, sir. I have often observed that in married households the champagne is rarely of a first-rate brand.*
Moncrieff: *Good heavens! Is marriage so demoralizing as that?*
Lane: *I believe it is a very pleasant state, sir. I have had very little experience of it myself up to the present. I have only been married once. That was in consequence of a misunderstanding between myself and a young person.*
Moncrieff: *I don't know that I am much interested in your family life, Lane.*
Lane: *No sir; it is not a very interesting subject. I never think of it myself.*

When Lane goes out after this agreement between master and servant that the quality of wine is an appropriate measure to evaluate the institution of marriage, Moncrieff observes to himself:

Lane's views on marriage seem somewhat lax. Really, if the lower orders don't set us a good example, what on earth is the use of them? They seem, as a class, to have absolutely no sense of moral responsibility.

Somewhat later, another kernel of wisdom from Moncrieff about the nature of marriage; he explains to Worthing why he does not wish to dine with his Aunt Augusta:

I know perfectly well whom she will place me next to, tonight. She will place me next to Mary Farquhar, who always flirts with her own husband across the dinner-table. That is not very pleasant. Indeed, it is not even decent . . . and that sort of thing is enormously on the increase. The amount of women in London who flirt with their own husbands is perfectly scandalous. It looks so bad. it is simply washing one's clean linen in public.

Moncrieff has invented an ailing friend, whom he calls Bunbury, who supposedly must be visited whenever Moncrieff wants to avoid this or that engagement. This is a comment on a relapse by Bunbury on the part of Lady Bracknell, another one of those intimidating upper-class ladies of the aristocracy:

I think it is high time that Mr. Bunbury made up his mind whether he was going to live or to die. This shilly-shallying with the question is absurd. Nor do I in any way approve of the modern sympathy with invalids. I consider it morbid. Illness of any kind is hardly a thing to be encouraged in others. Health is the primary duty of life. I am always telling that to your poor uncle, but he never seems to take much notice . . . as far as any improvement in his ailment goes. I should be much obliged if you would ask Mr. Bunbury, from me, to be kind enough not to have a relapse on Saturday, for I rely on you to arrange my music for me.

Some of Lady Bracknell's most trenchant views on life come out in her interrogation of Worthing, after she finds out that he intends to marry her daughter Gwendolyn. When he admits that he smokes,

I am glad to hear it. A man should always have an occupation of some kind. There are far too many idle men in London as it is.

She then opines that a man who marries should either know everything or nothing. Which, she wants to know, is Worthing's case? After some hesitation, he admits that he knows nothing. Lady Bracknell:

I am pleased to hear it. I do not approve of anything that tampers with natural ignorance. Ignorance is like a delicate exotic fruit; touch it and the bloom is gone. The whole theory of modern education is radically unsound. Fortunately in England, at any rate, education produces no effect whatever.

All of Worthing's other answers are equally satisfactory—about his income, his property both in town and in the country, his Tory politics. The difficulty arises when asked about his parents. He admits that he has lost them (Lady Bracknell: "Both? . . . That seems like carelessness."), or rather was lost by them. He was raised by the late Thomas

Cardew, who gave him the name of Worthing because he was found in a leather handbag at Victoria Station when Cardew was on a trip to Worthing. Lady Bracknell:

> I confess I feel somewhat bewildered by what you have just told me. To be born, or at any rate bred, in a hand-bag, whether it had handles or not, seems to me to display a contempt for the ordinary decencies of family life that reminds one of the worst excesses of the French Revolution. And I presume you know what that unfortunate movement led to?

Under these circumstances, she cannot allow her daughter, "a girl brought up with the utmost care," "to marry into a cloak-room, and form an alliance with a parcel."

Moncrieff, pretending to be Worthing's brother Ernest (like Bunbury, an invention), calls upon Cecily (who is Worthing's ward). Worthing has let it be known that his brother is a very disreputable character, which leads Cecily to say the following when his arrival is announced:

> I have never met any really wicked person before. I feel rather frightened.
> I am so afraid that he will look just like every one else.

When she greets Moncrieff as "my wicked cousin Ernest," he demurs that he is really not wicked at all, which makes Cecily say:

> If you are not, then you have certainly been deceiving us all in a very inexcusable manner. I hope that you have not been leading a double life, pretending to be wicked and being really good all the time. That would be hypocrisy.

Later on, when Moncrieff must admit his deception, Cecily asks him why he undertook it. He answers, truthfully, that he wanted to meet her. Gwendolyn (the young lady being wooed by Worthing) asks her whether she believes this explanation:

> Cecily: *I don't. But that does not affect the wonderful beauty of his answer.*
> Gwendolyn: *True. In matters of grave importance, style, not sincerity, is the vital thing.*

Perhaps a little more of Lady Bracknell's pithy comments may serve to round out the picture. Close to the climactic scene, when it turns out that one Miss Prism, Cecily's governess, is the individual who long ago lost baby Worthing at Victoria Station, Lady Bracknell is interrogating the local vicar, one Reverend Chasuble, about Miss Prism:

Lady Bracknell: *Is this Miss Prism a female of repellent aspect, remotely connected with education?*

Chasuble: *She is the most cultivated of ladies, and the very picture of respectability.*

Lady Bracknell: *It is obviously the same person.*

As it becomes increasingly clear that Worthing is the son of Lady Bracknell's sister, who had been lost in the aforementioned circumstances, he wants to know his name. Lady Bracknell assumes that he was named after his father, a general, but cannot at the moment remember it:

Lady Bracknell: *I cannot at the present moment recall what the General's Christian name was. But I have no doubt he had one. He was eccentric, I admit. But only in later years. And that was the result of the Indian climate, and marriage, and indigestion, and other things of that kind.*

A military directory is consulted and, lo and behold, the general's name was Ernest John. This, of course, removes the last barrier to marriage with Gwendolyn (Cecily's longing for a husband named Ernest as well is left unresolved at the end of the play): Worthing's name really was Ernest:

Worthing: *Gwendolyn, it is a terrible thing for a man to find out that all his life he has been speaking nothing but the truth. Can you forgive me?*

Gwendolyn: *I can. For I feel that you are sure to change.*

A soufflé indeed![12]

H. L. Mencken (1880–1956) at first glance would seem to be a very different case than Wilde.[13] Yet, as maintained earlier, their comic stance (if this phrase be permitted) was rather similar—in its detachment from the society targeted by their wit, in its lack of moral passion, and, last not least, in its malice. Mencken's literary output far exceeded Wilde's, largely explained by the facts that he was primarily a journalist and that he had more years of productive work. Although he did not write plays, he produced volumes of straight journalistic pieces, essays, book reviews, and full-blown books ranging in topic from the nature of religious belief to that of his periodically revised masterpiece, *The American Language.* He was also a prodigious letter-writer and diarist, and he made sure in his will that the products of the latter two activities were to be released seriatim on several carefully spaced dates after his death, with the effect of timed poison capsules. A recent release of diary materials led to an extensive controversy as to whether Mencken really was as anti-Semitic as some of the entries would lead one to believe, but his catalog of dislikes was truly ecumenical. He had nasty observations not only about Jews but about every other ethnic group in America, with the possible exception of German-Americans (of which he was one). He had utter contempt for the South (exempting only its alleged aristocracy) and the Middle West, and he disliked every American city except Baltimore (his own) and San Francisco. He detested England. He cultivated the image of a philosophical skeptic and political iconoclast. In the words of a biographer, although in his private life he was led by a code of honor, applying rather exclusively to family and close associates, Mencken played a "role of *public* immoralist, the heaver of dead cats into the sanctuaries of America."[14] In his own words:

> Having lived all my life in a country swarming with messiahs, I have been mistaken, perhaps quite naturally, for one myself, especially by the others. It would be hard to imagine anything more preposterous. I am, in fact, the complete anti-Messiah, and detest converts almost as much as I detest missionaries. My writings, such as they are, have had only one purpose: to attain for H. L. Mencken that feeling of tension relieved and function achieved which a cow enjoys in giving milk. Further than that, I have had no interest in the matter whatsoever.[15]

Perusal of Mencken's writings provides no grounds to challenge this self-assessment. While Wilde's wit primarily expressed itself in the dialogue between his imagined characters, Mencken was at his best in descriptions, be it of individuals, groups, or of situations. The following is from a book review:

> Dr. Henrik Willem van Loon, in his acute and entertaining history, *The Fall of the Dutch Republic,* more than once describes (sometimes, alas, with a scarcely concealed sniff) the salient trait of his fellow Netherlanders. It is an abnormal capacity for respecting respectability. Their ideal, it appears, is not the dashing military gent, gallantly leaping for glory down red-hot lines of fire, nor is it the lofty and ineffable artist, drunk with beauty. No, the man they most admire is the virtuous citizen and householder, sound in politics and theology, happily devoid of all orgiastic tendencies, and with money in the bank. In other words, the ideal of Holland is the ideal of Kansas. . . . One thinks of that identity on reading *The Americanization of Edward Bok,* an autobiographical monograph by the late editor of the *Ladies' Home Journal.* Edward was born in Holland and his parents did not bring him to America until he was already in breeches, but he had not been here a year before he was an absolutely typical American boy of the '70s. Nay, he was more: he was the typical American boy of the Sunday-school books of the '70s. By day, he labored with inconceivable diligence at

ten or twenty diverse jobs. By night he cultivated the acquaintance of all the moral magnificos of the time, from Ralph Waldo Emerson to Henry Ward Beecher, laboring with what remained of his steam to penetrate to the secret of their high and singular excellence, that he, too, might some day shine as they shined and be pointed out to good little boys on their way to the catechetical class and to bad little boys on their way to the gallows. Well, he got both wishes. At thirty he was sound in theology and politics, happily free from all orgiastic tendencies, and with money in the bank. At forty he was a millionaire and the foremost American soothsayer. At fifty he was a national institute.[16]

The passage shows Mencken's rhetorical artillery going full blast. In one paragraph, he manages to put down the entire culture of the Dutch and to let loose one of his innumerable barrages against American moralism (it is Mencken who made the term "Puritan" permanently pejorative) before he starts to do a job on the unfortunate Mister Bok. In the rest of the review he disparages the magazine edited by Bok and then praises the latter for what he terms his one un-American characteristic, namely his passion for artistic excellence. One is reminded here of the question habitually asked by the comedian Mort Sahl during his performances in the 1950s and 1960s: "Is there any group that I have not offended yet?" But it would be difficult to deny the wit of Mencken's multiple demolition job.

Here is Mencken's description of the teaching profession:

There was a time when teaching school was a relatively simple and easy job, and any young woman who has no talent for housework was deemed fit for it. But that time is no more. The pedagogue of today, whether male or female, must not only undergo a long and arduous course of preliminary training; he (or she) must also keep on studying after getting an appointment. The science of pedagogy has become enormously complicated, and it changes constantly. Its principles of today are never its principles of tomorrow: they are incessantly modified, improved, revised, adorned. They borrow from psychology, metaphysics, sociology, pathology, physical culture, chemistry, meteorology, political economy, psychiatry and sex hygiene. And through them, day and night, blows the hot wind of moral endeavor. Thus the poor gogue (or goguess) has to sweat incessantly. In Summer, when the rest of us are lolling in the cool speakeasies, he suffers a living death in Summer school, trying to puzzle out the latest arcana from Columbia University. . . . It is a dreadful life.[17]

For Mencken to say that any activity is blown upon by moral endeavor, of course, is to condemn it utterly. This piece was written in 1931 and the cool speakeasies that Mencken contrasts with the sweaty torments of summer school were, of course, the illicit refuges from that ultimate moral endeavor known as Prohibition, an exercise in Puritanism for which Mencken reserved particular venom. (It is interesting to reflect what Mencken, who rarely went anywhere without his cigar, would have said about his beloved state of Maryland when in 1995 it enacted the most stringent antismoking regulations in the country).

The "gogues" and "goguesses" in the preceding passage, ridiculous though they are, must still be seen as victims rather than villains. Mencken, who never went to college, had nothing but contempt for higher education. The true villains are the professors, those who produce the arcana, at Columbia and elsewhere, which are then promulgated as the latest wisdom to the practitioners of the lower education. One of Mencken's loving comments on this breed:

> Ever and anon another so-called radical professor is heaved out of a state university, always to the tune of bitter protests in the liberal weeklies. The usual defense of the trustees is that the doctrines he teaches are dangerous to the young. This puts him on all fours with Socrates—surely a somewhat large order. The real objection to his ideas, nine times out of ten, is that only idiots believe such things. But that objection has to be kept quiet, for it is saying nothing apposite against a professor in the average State university to prove that he is an idiot.[18]

This too was written in the early 1930s. Now, some sixty years later, radical professors are not thrown out of American universities; they often run them. It is unlikely that Mencken would have thought more highly of their doctrines.

Probably Mencken's most famous piece of journalism is his account of the so-called monkey trial in Dayton, Tennessee, where in 1925 one of those "gogues," by the name of Scopes, was prosecuted for teaching evolution, contrary to state law. Mencken made a rather brief visit to the place as a reporter for the *Baltimore Sun*. The trial, of course, reached dramatic heights in the confrontation between William Jennings Bryan and Clarence Darrow, who appeared, respectively, for the prosecution and the defense. In his dispatch Mencken expressed surprise that Dayton was not as fervently Puritanical as he had expected:

> On the courthouse green a score of sweating theologians debated the darker passages of Holy Writ day and night, but I soon found that they were all volunteers, and that the local faithful, while interested in their exegesis as an intellectual exercise, did not permit it to impede the indigenous debaucheries. Exactly twelve minutes after I reached the village I was taken in tow by a Christian man and introduced to the favorite tipple of the Cumberland Range: half corn liquor and half Coca-Cola. It seemed a dreadful dose to me, but I found that the Dayton illuminati got it down with gusto, rubbing their tummies and rolling their eyes. I include among

them the chief local proponents of the Mosaic cosmogony. They were all hot for Genesis, but their faces were far too florid to belong to teetotalers, and when a pretty girl came tripping down the main street, which was very often, they reached for the places where their neckties should have been with all the amorous enterprise of movie actors.[19]

Mencken went South with the mind-set of an old-style anthropologist studying a tribe of savages, but, unlike most anthropologists, he had little empathy with the ways of the natives. In any event, a journalist from Chattanooga explained to him that he must not take Dayton as typical of the local culture. Dayton was "a great capital like any other," "it was to Rhea county what Atlanta was to Georgia or Paris to France," hedonistic and sinful:

> A country girl from some remote village of the county, coming into town for her semi-annual bottle of Lydia Pinkham's Vegetable Compound, shivered on approaching Robinson's drug-store quite as a country-girl from upstate New York might shiver on approaching the Metropolitan Opera House. In every village lout she saw a potential white-slaver. The hard sidewalks hurt her feet. Temptations of the flesh bristled to all sides of her, luring her to Hell.

Mencken was then invited to go up into the hills, where the old-time religion still flourished in pristine form. He was taken out of Dayton to a wooded area where a genuine nocturnal revival was taking place. Mencken described it in ethnographic detail: The preacher, "an immensely tall and thin mountaineer in blue-jeans, his collarless shirt open at the neck and his hair a tousled mop"; the congregation, with the older people sitting on benches, the younger folk in front, a young mother suckling her baby, two scared little girls hugging each other, a dozen babies sleeping on a bed. After the sermon and some hymn-singing, individuals from the congregation got up to testify. Then individuals came forward asking to be prayed over; both the preacher and some others began speaking in tongues:

> From the squirming and jabbering mass a young woman gradually detached herself—a woman not uncomely, with a pathetic homemade cap on her head. Her head jerked back, the veins of her neck swelled, and her fists went to her throat as if she were fighting for breath. She bent backward until she was like half a hoop. Then she suddenly snapped forward. We caught a flash of the whites of her eyes. Presently her whole body began to be convulsed—great throes that began at the shoulders and ended at the hips. She would leap to her feet, thrust her arms in air, and then hurl herself upon the heap. Her praying flattened out into a mere delirious caterwauling. I describe the thing discreetly, and as a strict be-

haviorist. The lady's subjective sensations I leave to infidel pathologists, privy to the works of Ellis, Freud and Moll.

And it goes on in the same vein. Here Mencken had finally come upon authentic southern religion, which "began at the bridge over the town creek, where the road makes off for the hills." He did not leave the reader in doubt as to what he thought of it.

Inevitably, the portion of this book seeking to delineate different expressions of the comic had to contain a good many texts and comments on these. Yet it is important not to lose sight of the main purpose, which is to bring into sharper focus the overall phenomenon of the comic. Have the *explications des textes* of this chapter, apart from defining the category of wit, added anything to the general argument of the book? The reader will have to judge. The author proposes that two not inconsiderable insights have been added, one pertaining to the cognitive dimension of the comic, the other to its moral dimension.

As was already pointed out at the beginning of this chapter, the earlier proposition that the comic has a cognitive dimension must be modified inasmuch as decidedly witty statements about the world can be distortive or outright false. The cases of Oscar Wilde and H. L. Mencken should make this point rather clearly. To be sure, one could have discussed cases of wit less permeated by malicious guffaws. Wit does not necessarily rest on malice. For example, the aforementioned comedian Mort Sahl, while he enthusiastically lampooned every aspect of contemporary American society, did so without taking a stance of supercilious contempt; in that, he is probably closer to Will Rogers than to Mencken. This does not mean that Sahl's shtick provides an accurate picture of America under the Eisenhower and Kennedy administrations, any more than Mencken's commentaries on the America of his time. And someone reading Wilde as a historically accurate account of late nineteenth-century England would put himself in the position of the German intelligence agency that, during World War II, dropped a spy into England dressed according to the descriptions by P. G. Wodehouse of the costume of English gentry (as mentioned earlier, this unfortunate individual was promptly arrested).

More specifically, when wit uses irony (which is much of the time), it seeks to debunk, to unmask. It seeks to show up the pretensions (if one prefers, the false consciousness or the bad faith) of society. But this procedure does not necessarily lead to a more valid view of things than the one that has just been debunked. The same observation, of course, applies to noncomic, serious exercises of debunking. One term just used, false consciousness, comes from the vocabulary of Marxism. One can read Marx and many of his disciples, quite usefully, as being on target in debunking the pretensions of bourgeois society. Yet, as history has made amply clear, the allegedly more valid picture of the world that Marxists have proposed in lieu of the debunked one was at least as distorted as the latter. If there has been bourgeois false consciousness, there certainly has also been Marxist false consciousness, beginning with Marx's own propositions about the dynamics of capitalism, virtually every one of which has been massively falsified by the empirical evidence.

H. L. Mencken savagely debunked William Jennings Bryan.[20] By contrast, he did not make Clarence Darrow an object of ironic deconstruction. The reason, of course, is that Mencken agreed with Darrow's view of the issues raised in the Scopes trial and had nothing but contempt for Bryan's. In this, Mencken is very much a predecessor of the American intelligentsia today, with his/its near-total incomprehension of the beliefs and values of Evangelical Protestantism. The present author is certainly not an Evangelical, but neither does he share Darrow's (and Mencken's) shallow rationalistic worldview. It would not be difficult to draw an ironic portrait of Darrow as mercilessly debunking as Mencken's of Bryan. A good scene to start would be Darrow's defense in the Leopold-Loeb trial, where he spent much time in his summation to the jury arguing that life is nothing but a Darwinian struggle for survival of the fittest and then concluded with a passionate attack on capital punishment. This magnificent non sequitur would illustrate the comic incongruence between Darrow's shallow philosophy and his admirable sense of compassion. As to the Scopes trial itself, leaving aside all questions of biological science, seventy years later it is not so easy to mock Bryan's belief that there are moral costs to the view that man is nothing but a subspecies of monkey and therefore nothing very special.

Witty definitions of reality, then, do not in themselves have a higher epistemological status than nonwitty ones. Both the witty commentator and the serious analyst must be subjected to the same tests of validity (whatever these may be in different instances). And the wit who does not care whether he proposes truth or untruth is, both cognitively and morally, a nihilist (Wilde came very close to advocating a philosophy to this effect). Nevertheless, it would be a mistake to throw out completely the notion that the comic has a cognitive dimension. That dimension, though, must now be defined more narrowly.

If the alleged insight mediated by way of wit is indeed valid, then this mediation can convey it succinctly and persuasively. The economy that Freud emphasized in his analysis of wit is essential to this capacity of comic perception. Beyond this, however, an additional point can be made about the cognitive dimension of wit. While wit (or any other expression of the comic) does not necessarily transmit valid information about *specific* areas of experience, it does provide an insight into *reality as a whole*. At its simplest, this is the insight that things are not as they seem, which further implies that things could be quite different from what is commonly thought. The comic in general, and wit as its most cerebral expression in particular, establish distance from the world and its official legitimations. The intellectual game of wit is best played from a social margin, be it ascribed (as in the case of Jewish humor) or achieved (as in the case of the dandy qua sardonic observer). The marginalization, though, is strangely dialectical. The marginal individual, through the magic of his wit, in turn marginalizes the world that he targets. It is now no longer *the* world, but *a* world—and a ridiculous one at that. This marginalization—or, one could also say, relativization—of the world is what makes wit dangerous, potentially subversive, even if the individual practicing it has no such thing in mind. The comic in general, and wit in a very intellectual manner in particular, disclose the *Doppelboedigkeit* of the world—its multiple realities, its dichotomy of facade and that which lies behind the facade, indeed the fragile nature of what appears to be its reality.

Wit debunks. Most of the time this is, as it were, a sociological exercise. That is, it is directed against the pretensions of particular social institutions, conventions, or customs. As has become clear, what results from this may be good or bad sociology; if it is the former, there is certainly a cognitive gain from it being expressed in a witty form. (One could put it this way: other things being equal—that is, criteria of validity having been satisfied—one would rather hear about 1950s America from Mort Sahl than, say, from Talcott Parsons.) But, be that as it may, the debunking action of wit goes beyond the concretely sociological into the realm of…—what should one call it?—let it be called the realm of metaphysics. Society is not what it seems. And the whole world is not what it seems. In its sociological aspect, the comic may lead to an ironic worldview. In its metaphysical aspect, the irony moves, at least in a preliminary way, toward religious experience. Kierkegaard, as was pointed out in an earlier chapter, understood this very well. For him, irony was a stepping-stone to faith. These considerations will have to be pursued further in a later chapter.

It follows from all of this that humorlessness is a cognitive handicap: It shuts off the possibility of certain insights, perhaps prevents access to an entire sphere of reality. For this reason, the humorless person is to be pitied. Could it also be a moral fault? If humorlessness is a character trait, it is presumably congenital. In that case, an individual can no more be blamed for humorlessness than for being color-blind, unmusical, or bereft of mathematical ability. Conversely, the ability to see things in comic terms is not necessarily a morally admirable quality. The comic

ability may be employed for any number of morally reprehensible purposes. Indeed, as this chapter should have illustrated, wit may be exer-
cised in malice and it can be linked to an attitude of moral nihilism.

On the other hand, an individual who does have the comic ability and
refuses to employ it in his perception of certain aspects of his existence
may indeed be morally culpable. There is the egomaniac who refuses to
laugh at his delusions of grandeur, the fanatic who cannot stand the
comic relativization of his precariously achieved dogmas, the tyrant who
must suppress anyone who dares to be witty about his regime. In these
cases, and in others one could think of, humorlessness is not a fate but a
choice, and this choice is part and parcel of the self-serving bad faith
sustaining this particular existence. Egomania, fanaticism, and tyranny
are morally reprehensible; so will be the deliberate humorlessness de-
ployed in their defense. In English (and in German) certain individuals
are described as deadly serious (*toternst*). Some of them, perhaps, were
born that way; these are the ones to be pitied. But others have made
themselves such; they can be condemned for it.

Like other forms of cognition, comic perception is in itself morally
neutral. In this, as a number of philosophers have recognized, it is
similar to esthetic perception.[21] The beautiful is not necessarily good;
the good is not necessarily beautiful. But the manner in which comic
perception is used in the lives of individuals, groups, or societies may
have significant moral implications. Sometimes it may actually be morally neutral—"good, clean fun"—and nothing else. At other times it
may be morally reprehensible, as when it is used cruelly or in the service
of evil. At other times yet it may be morally admirable, as when wit is
directed against the injustice and hypocrisy of a particular social order.

As we walk around and around the comic, it becomes a little clearer.
It also becomes more complex. Who said that this journey would be
easy?

## Notes

1.   Irony has sometimes been interpreted as a subcategory of the comic.
This is probably a misinterpretation. One can be ironic without being comic,
though it is difficult to imagine the comic without some elements of irony. Cf.
Uwe Japp, *Theorie der Ironie* (Frankfurt: Klostermann, 1983).

2.   If there is one thing that is clear from the historical and social-scientific
explorations of the comic, it is that it is universal: comic laughter can be found in
every human culture. As has been argued earlier, the comic is an anthropological constant; *homo sapiens* is always also *homo ridens*. But the joke, as defined
here, is probably not universal. Thus it is my impression that East Asian cultures, though they are full of the comic, have not cultivated the joke as has been

the case in Europe and the Middle East. (Some time ago I was given a book by one Lu Yunzhong, entitled *100 Chinese Jokes through the Ages*. Some of the brief episodes in the book certainly have the form of the joke, but it is unclear whether they originally circulated in this form or were parts of longer narratives.) Are there jokes in traditional African cultures? Or in Mesoamerica? The cultural diffusion of the joke would be a worthy topic for historians and ethnographers. This form of the comic must have originated somewhere. I have no real knowledge, but if I were asked to guess, I would opt for the Middle East or India. My colleague Ali Banuazizi suggests Iran. I would wish this footnote to launch a stampede of doctoral dissertations

3. *The Complete Oscar Wilde* (New York: Crescent, 1995), 11.

4. Ibid., 364ff.

5. Alistair Cooke, ed., *The Vintage Mencken* (New York: Vintage, 1956), 231f.

6. I may as well admit that I dislike both authors. Both, I think, proudly displayed a cynical *Weltanschauung* that I find offensive. Wilde, it appears, was personally the kinder of the two. As far as I am concerned, each had a redeeming feature that mitigates the offensiveness. Not, let me quickly say, their unquestionable wit; as I have argued, that is a morally neutral quality. Wilde's sardonic detachment, the pose of the invulnerable dandy, was all along put in jeopardy by the double life imposed by his sexual urges. I find this very much humanizing. Mencken's equally sardonic detachment and his much-paraded disdain for the common people of America was punctured by his passion for the American language. Here, if nowhere else, the pseudo-Nietzschean anti-democrat comes close to being a sentimental populist. That too is humanizing. At the risk of offending this or that group (Mort Sahl, where are you when we need you?) I would say that Wilde is redeemed by his homosexuality and Mencken by his love of the language of America.

7. Cf. Richard Elman, *Oscar Wilde* (New York: Knopf, 1988); Norbert Kohl, *Oscar Wilde: The Works of a Conformist Rebel* (Cambridge: Cambridge University Press, 1989).

8. Kohl, *Oscar Wilde*, 227.

9. Ibid., 245.

10. Also from the preface to "The Picture of Dorian Gray," in *Complete Oscar Wilde*, 11.

11. Ibid., 315ff.

12. The question has been raised whether there is an intrinsic connection between Wilde's comic style and his homosexuality. it is correct that, at least for a while and at least in English-speaking societies, there has been a linkage between homosexuality, a certain dandylike estheticism, and a clever, sardonic wit. It seems to me, however, that this linkage is accidental rather than intrinsic. Dandyism in England is considerably older than Wilde. The term *dandy* was applied to elegant young men in London in the early nineteenth century; Beau Brummel was an early prototype; as far as I know, there was no necessary implication of homosexuality at that time. Conversely, there have been homosexual subcultures since then and in other places that had none of these estheti-

cist features. The dandy style has a historical connection with the English upper class (at any rate its urban life-style), to which Wilde did not belong though he aspired to it. A commentator on Wilde's work has argued, persuasively, that Wilde was important in the construction of a cultural type of "queerness," which did influence the homosexual subculture in England and America for much of this century. In other words, *au contraire*, it is not the Wildean style that came out of the homosexual subculture, but a particular version of the latter was at least partially shaped by the influence of Wilde. The same commentator argued that this version of "being in the world homosexually" (my phrase, not his) has increasingly disappeared with the more recent (post-Stonewall) appearance of gayness. Cf. Alan Sinfield, *The Wilde Century: Effeminacy, Oscar Wilde and the Queer Moment* (New York: Columbia University Press, 1994).

13.   Cf. Fred Hobson, *Mencken: A Life* (New York: Random House, 1994).

14.   Ibid., 478.

15.   Terry Teachout, ed., *A Second Mencken Chrestomathy* (New York: Knopf, 1995), 490f.

16.   Ibid., 439f.

17.   Ibid., 378f.

18.   Ibid., 392.

19.   The dispatch was entitled "The Hills of Zion." Cf. Huntington Cairns, ed., *H. L. Mencken: The American Scene* (New York: Knopf, 1969), 259ff.

20.   Mencken wrote a savagely debunking obituary on the day after Bryant's death. Cf. Cairns, *H. L. Mencken*, 227ff. Among the many moral maxims that Mencken evidently did not accept was *de mortuis nil nisi bonum*.

21.   There is the further question whether morality is not in itself a form of perception or cognition. This question, alas, cannot be pursued here. But in any event, even if moral judgment is based on a certain perception, it is a different perception from either the comic or the esthetic one.

# 10

# The Comic as Weapon
## *Satire*

Broadly put, satire is the deliberate use of the comic for purposes of attack. If it is thus broadly defined, satire is present in almost all forms of comic expression. It can weave in and out of comic communication, and it can be at least momentarily present even in the most innocuous forms of the comic. Thus satirical elements can be found in P. G. Wodehouse, Will Rogers, or Sholem Aleichem, most certainly in Oscar Wilde and H. L. Mencken. In view of this, it would seem plausible to define satire somewhat more narrowly, namely, as the comic used in attacks that are part of *an agenda* on the part of the satirist. Put differently, in satire, the aggressive intent becomes the central motif of comic expression. All elements of the comic are then, as it were, welded together into the shaping of a weapon. Most often the attack is directed against institutions and their representatives, notably political or religious ones. It may also be directed against entire social groups and their cultures—say, against the bourgeoisie and its mores. Or it may be used against individuals, or against theories or literary modes. Its emotional tone is typically malicious, even if the motive for the attack is this or that high principle. In this, it differs rather clearly from wit. It is possible to be both witty and benevolent, perhaps even innocent. Benevolent satire is an oxymoron.

There is a variety of critical theories about satire.[1] There would be little point discussing these here. For the present purpose it should suffice to follow the conceptualization of satire made by Northrop Frye, which has gained wide acceptance by literary scholars.[2] Frye characterizes satire as "militant irony." This is very close to the definition suggested just now. Militancy is a term derived from war, it is an attitude of attack that is part of a campaign against someone or something. Irony, understood as saying one thing when one means another, need not be militant, can be quite gentle. One can certainly differentiate between cases of satire in terms of their degree of ferocity, but satire that is overly gentle liquidates itself. Frye lists a number of essential elements in satire: fantasy (often grotesque); a standpoint based on moral norms; and an object of attack. He also emphasizes that satire is always dependent on a particular audience, in a particular social context: the satirist and his audience must agree on the undesirability of the object of attack. This assertion by Frye may be questioned. To be sure, there must be a commonality of social context between satirist and audience. A satirical attack on, say, some intricacies of American politics will not be understood by an audience of foreigners who know none of the references. But it is not necessary that the audience agree with the satirist to begin with. Satire can also be educational: it may be a *result* of the satirist's labors that the audience comes to understand the undesirability of what is attacked.

All the same, satire, more than other expressions of the comic, is bound by its social context, and this fact gives it a distinctly fugitive character. A great effort, indeed an exercise in scholarly exegesis, is required if a modern reader is to understand the satire of Aristophanes or of Rabelais. But an American listening in the 1990s to a 1950s recording of Mort Sahl, even if he is old enough to have been an adult at the time, will miss a good many cues. If satire, then, is time-bound, at its best it leads beyond the immediate object of attack and gives a sense of liberation beyond the particular historical moment. Frye makes this point in discussing the satirical aspect of Dante's depiction of Satan as standing upside down when the poet moves out of Inferno and once more sees the stars:

> Tragedy and tragic irony take us into a hell of narrowing circles and culminate in some such vision of the source of all evil in a personal form. Tragedy can take us no further, but if we persevere with the *mythos* of irony and satire, we shall pass a dead center and finally see the gentlemanly Prince of Darkness bottom side up.[3]

There is some scholarly disagreement over the etymology of the term *satire*. [4] The conventional view has been that the term is derived from the satyrs, those half-human/half-animal beings that played an important part in the Dionysian myth. That derivation is attractive, since it links satire with the magical folly that, at least in the Western tradition, has its origins in the Bacchanalian orgy. There is another possible etymology, deriving the term from the Latin *satura*, which refers to a dish with many components. It is this etymology that allowed Roman writers to claim that satire was a Roman rather than a Greek invention. One may point out that the two etymologies are not necessarily contradictory. After all, the Roman Bacchus stood in a sort of apostolic succession from the

Greek Dionysus, as did his cult. Be this as it may, satire has an ancient lineage, both in Western civilization and elsewhere. Folly almost always has a satirical element, and the discussion of that phenomenon in an earlier chapter has already touched upon the near-universality of this manifestation of the comic. Thus, for instance, the tricksters described by Paul Radin in his work on American Indians were genuine satirists in their own right, as were court jesters and fools in Asia.

The earliest Greek satirist on record was Archilochus, who lived on the island of Paros in the seventh century B.C.E.[5] He was betrothed to the daughter of Lycambes, a nobleman. When it became known that Archilochus was the son of a slave mother, Lycambes forbade the marriage. Archilochus thereupon composed satirical poems against Lycambes and kept reciting them in public. Lycambes was so shamed by this that he and his daughter committed suicide. Robert Elliott has taken this story as paradigmatic in his interpretation of satire. At its birth, satire was invective intensified to the quality of a curse—that is, invective with magical power. The object of the invective is ridiculed, but the effect of this went far beyond social embarrassment, attaining the destructive power of black magic. Elliott claims wide cross-cultural diffusion of this phenomenon, including the interesting fact that very frequently there are set rituals within which these curses are uttered. A case he discusses at some length is that of the ancient Irish bards known as *filid*, who pronounced both praise and blame. Both the blessings and the curses had magical potency, and, not surprisingly, these individuals were greatly feared. It seems that they had something like a professional code of ethics, regulating at least in theory how they were to exercise their power. Like professionals in all ages, they did not always live up to their code. Thus one of the most renowned *filid*, aptly named Aithirne the Importunate, traveled around Ireland threatening kings and other notables with shaming verses unless they met his demands. These were not exactly ethical at all times. On one occasion Aithirne demanded to sleep with a king's wife; the king, terrified of the alternative, agreed. In the end Aithirne got his comeuppance: He and his entire family were murdered by outraged victims of his satire.

According to Elliott, satire in the Western tradition became progressively divorced from its magical and ritual origins. One might call this a kind of secularization. In this process, satire becomes an art form. Yet it has never lost some of its original qualities. In a sense, satire is always a curse, and its effects on the targeted individuals can be very destructive indeed. Dictators have very good reasons to suppress satire directed against them. As an art form, satire can use very different means.[6] It is not necessarily verbal. Satire can be behavioral, as in the mimicry practiced by clowns, and not only by professional ones (envisage a group of disgruntled employees miming the pompous gait and gestures of their boss). Satire can be expressed in visual art. The caricature is a pure case of this, which, in modern times, has become an effective instrument of political attack. Most commonly, of course, satire manifests itself verbally and as a form of literature. As observed earlier, it always involves irony. Like the martial arts, it always uses the adversary's strengths against himself and thus turns them into weaknesses. A particularly effective version of this is parody, in which the adversary's own words are used against him.

A survey of satirical literature, even if limited to Western cultures, would necessitate a book many times the length of this one. Suffice it to say that literary satire can take many different forms. A classical form is that of drama, possibly originating with Aristophanes and having such latter-day masters as George Bernard Shaw. It can take the form of fable, using animals to satirize their human counterparts, in a line of works stretching from Aesop to George Orwell's *Animal Farm* . Perhaps there never was a more trenchant criticism of socialist egalitarianism than Orwell's satirical sentence to the effect that some animals are more equal than others. There is the satirical novel, from Cervantes to Evelyn Waugh, more recently in Tom Wolfe's masterpiece *The Bonfire of the Vanities*. Wolfe, of course, perfected his satirical style in many essays long before he wrote that novel. Some would argue that late-sixties radicalism never recovered from Wolfe's essay "Radical Chic," in which he satirized a party given by Leonard Bernstein for the Black Panthers; indeed, the title of this essay has become a category used effectively to discredit an entire political and cultural movement. (The fact that political and cultural movements survive despite being discredited need not concern us here.) Essays and pamphlets have long been vehicles of satire. Jonathan Swift's "Modest Proposal," in which he suggested the export of Irish children for the purpose of cannibalism as a solution to the problem of Irish famine, is probably the most famous case of this in English literature. But satire can even be shorter than the essay. There is the aphorism or epigram, as practiced by such masters as Samuel Johnson, as in his famous statement, "Second marriages represent the triumph of hope over experience." Perhaps the briefest use of satire is one frequently employed by Englishmen to deflate a pompous interlocutor: After the latter has divested himself of a particularly objectionable sentiment, uttered at great length, one leaves a longish pause and then only says the one word—"Quite."

For the rest of this chapter the focus will be on one author who embodies satire in a total way, both in his work and his life. This is the Austrian writer Karl Kraus (1874–1936), a man who would certainly have deserved the title "the Importunate." The social context within which Kraus lived and worked is by now somewhat distant (even for an Austrian reader, let alone an American one), but this very distance also permits a more objective view of the satirist as an ideal type.

Karl Kraus was born in Jičin, Bohemia, the son of a prosperous Jewish businessman. In view of Kraus's later career, it is somewhat ironical that his father's business was a paper factory. As was normal among upper-middle-class Jews in that region of the Austro-Hungarian monarchy, the language of the family was German. When Kraus was three years old the family moved to Vienna, a city in which he lived all his life and to which he was bound in a (for Viennese) not atypical love-hate relation-ship. He developed an early passion for the theater. There is a charming episode from Kraus's childhood. When the family first moved to Vienna he and his brother were taken to play in public parks. Both little boys were afraid that they might be lost in the big city and would have difficulty finding their way home. To prepare for such a contingency, Kraus's brother always took along a provision of sandwiches; little Karl clutched his most prized possession, a miniature puppet theater.

Kraus studied for a while at the university, though he spent most of his time in theaters and literary cafés. He acted briefly, then decided to become a journalist. For a period he worked as the correspondent of the *Neue Freie Presse*, the leading liberal newspaper, in the fashionable spa Bad Ischl. In 1898 the editor, Moritz Benedikt, offered Kraus a position as chief satirical writer for the newspaper. In the decisive act of his life, Kraus declined what was a most attractive offer, and instead, a year later, started his own periodical, *Die Fackel* (the *Torch*). He continued to put out this periodical from 1899 until his death in 1936. After 1911, he was its only author. He also started a practice of public readings, both from his own works and from the (rather limited) number of other authors he admired. Needless to say, it was a most unusual career, possibly a unique one. Satire was at its core.

Equally unusual was Kraus's periodical. *Die Fackel* appeared irregu-larly, whenever Kraus felt that he had enough material for an issue. Its appearances, in dark-red booklets, had the character of exploding time bombs. Contemporaries report riding on streetcars just after an issue had appeared, with seemingly every other passenger eagerly reading his copy and exclaiming either with pleasure or in anger. *Die Fackel* did not make for light reading, but it had a large public from the beginning: the intelligentsia both in Vienna and in other centers of the Dual Mon-archy, as well as a large segment of the educated bourgeoisie. Among young intellectuals Kraus soon became a cult figure, and his public readings had a virtually ritual character. Most of Kraus's writings first appeared in his own periodical. A major portion of his opus consists of polemic and satire, though he also published favorable reviews of the

works of other authors. He was instrumental in the revival of the plays
of Johann Nestroy, the nineteenth-century Viennese writer, and of the
operettas of Jacques Offenbach. There is also a sizable body of lyrical
poetry by Kraus, surprisingly gentle, at times sentimental, in an author
whose prose frequently dripped with venom.

Kraus's polemics seem to go in two different directions—one linguistic, the other sociological. He attacked the corruption of language,
and he attacked the corruption in all the major institutions of his society.
It was his passionately held belief that the two corruptions were intimately related, indeed were essentially the same. Both, he believed,
were symptoms of a profound dehumanization. On the, as it were,
sociological level he targeted both cultural and social institutions. Literary figures were attacked and satirized both for their sins of language—
mistakes in grammar, even in punctuation, sloppy formulations, generally bad German—and for their political sins—such as the glorification
of war and mindless patriotism. Kraus reserved a particular animosity
against the press, which he regarded as epitomizing both the corruption
of language and the corruption of public life. He carried on a lifelong
feud with the *Neue Freie Presse,* its editor, and major writers, who retali-
ated by never mentioning him in the pages of the newspaper. Other
newspapers followed this practice as well, with the notable exception of
the *Arbeiterzeitung,* the organ of the new Social Democratic party (which
was only founded in 1890). He also attacked commercial corruption and
the inhumanities of the criminal justice system. He had a special dislike
for psychoanalysis, which was becoming fashionable in the Vienna of
his time, defining it as "that mental disease of which it believes itself to
be the cure."

Kraus carefully cultivated a persona of himself as the implacable polemicist, almost as a prophet. He claimed to sleep through most of the
day, working only by night (which was close to the truth, but not altogether true). He claimed to disdain both criticisms and flattery (again,
not altogether true). Essentially, this persona was that of a marginal
man, friendless and not in need of friends, totally devoted to his work in
defense of civilization. He also claimed to be totally antagonistic to the
Viennese culture in which he lived. There is some truth in this, yet his
life-style was not all that peculiar by Viennese standards, and it is difficult to imagine Kraus apart from that most Viennese of institutions, the
coffeehouse. Just like other Viennese literary luminaries, Kraus held
court in the coffeehouses he favored, and everybody who was anybody
knew when to find him there. Those who knew Kraus well (and he did
have close, lifelong friends) describe an individual very different indeed
from the cold, sardonic persona of Kraus the polemicist: a warm, consid-
erate individual, who was deeply moved by people in distress and who

would go to great lengths to help them. He did indeed fiercely defend his privacy and never wrote about his personal life. He had a number of intense love affairs, the longest with a Bohemian aristocrat, Sidonie von Nadherny, for whom he wrote some of his most moving poems and whose family estate was a place of refuge for him.

Kraus had a complicated and changing relationship both to religion and politics. As a young man he officially resigned from the Jewish community, was later baptized as a Catholic, but left the Catholic church after World War I, basically because he was repelled by its passive support for the murderous patriotism of both sides in the war (though, characteristically, the immediate cause was the support given by the church to the Salzburg Festival, which Kraus despised as a debasement of culture). He wrote a satirical piece on Zionism, whose founder, Theodor Herzl, was unforgivably a correspondent for the *Neue Freie Presse*. Jews were very often the targets of Kraus's polemics and satires, as were the lapses in German language that were characteristic of Austrian Jews. Understandably this gave rise to the charge of Jewish self-hate against Kraus, and it is correct that some of his writings border uncomfortably on anti-Semitism (some of them were actually used by the anti-Semitic press). However, Kraus always denounced every form of anti-Semitism, and he wrote with deep respect for Judaism as a religion and of the Yiddish culture of Eastern European Jewry (which assimilated Jews in Austria generally looked down upon). He said in his own defense that it was not his fault that Jews played a prominent role in the institutions he felt necessary to attack, especially the press. Defining his relationship to Judaism, he wrote that he was willing to go along with the journey into the wilderness but not with the dance around the golden calf. His general relation to religion is best caught in another statement of his, that the true believers are those who miss the divine.

Prior to World War I, Kraus's work was largely apolitical. This changed with the outbreak of the war. Kraus was passionately opposed to the war, profoundly shocked by its brutalities, and he particularly despised the intellectuals (the overwhelming majority on both sides of the conflict) who defended and glorified it in their writings. He became a consistent, lifelong pacifist. During the war he played a cat-and-mouse game with the military censorship, but both in his writings and his public readings he left little doubt as to where he stood. He was probably saved from prison by the collapse of the Central Powers. After the war, he published the gigantic play, *The Last Days of Mankind*, which has been called one of the greatest antiwar manifestos of the century. In 1918 he wrote with enthusiasm about the departure of the Habsburgs, whom he held responsible for the war, and he welcomed the new republic. He supported the Social Democrats, who formed the first republican government, but was soon disillusioned by their failure to achieve the deep changes he desired. In the 1930s, much to the chagrin of his friends on the left, he supported the authoritarian Dollfuss-Schuschnigg regime, which he saw as the only bulwark left against the Nazis. Hitler's advent to power in Germany shocked Kraus to such an extent that for a time he wrote nothing about it. He then published a long, curious essay on Nazism, "The Third Witches' Sabbath" (*"Die dritte Walpurgisnacht"*). Very characteristically, it mainly dealt with the Nazis' language, which, with a good deal of justification, he understood as a perfect mirror of the underlying barbarism.

Kraus embodies satire as the organizing principle of both a life and a life's work. If he resembles any other figure in European literary history, it would be Søren Kierkegaard, whose work he knew well and greatly admired. Both men had an agenda that inspired everything they wrote and did. In Kierkegaard's case, of course, it was a religious agenda, and his principal target was the Danish Lutheran church and the debased Christianity he believed it to represent. Kraus's agenda was not religious, at least not overtly. The agenda was twofold: the defense of language and the defense of suffering humanity. As remarked before, in Kraus's mind this was really one single concern. Much has been written about Kraus's so-called language mysticism. Suffice it to say here that it is very difficult to agree with Kraus on this linkage of language and morality, and in any case his understanding of language is well-nigh irreproducible other than in German (a fact that in itself throws doubt on Kraus's peculiar view of language). Some of the most admirable individuals who lived in Central Europe in Kraus's times spoke and wrote in abominable German; some Nazis, alas, had a perfect command of the German language. In any case, in what follows the focus will be on Kraus's use of satire to defend suffering humanity, specifically in his great antiwar drama. If one asks what party Kraus stood for in this agenda, one could best reply in a phrase used by Edward Timms, an English biographer of Kraus: the party of human dignity.

To illustrate the nature of Krausian satire, the focus in what follows will be on the great antiwar drama, *The Last Days of Mankind* (*Die letzten Tage der Menschheit*). Portions of it had been published or read publicly during the war, but most of it could not have been published as long as military censorship was in force. The entire play was first published in 1922; suppressed during the Nazi period, it was republished immediately after the end of World War II.[8] The work is huge, filling over seven hundred pages in the standard German edition. It has never been and could not possibly be performed in its entirety; only selected scenes have been performed in various theaters of the German-speaking countries. The scenes move from the home front to the different battle lines of the war, with hundreds of characters, some of them appearing only once. The dramatic scenes are interspersed with direct quotations from newspaper stories and with Kraus's own poetry. The horrors portrayed escalate as the drama proceeds, culminating in apocalyptic scenes depicting the final destruction of the world. In a short preface Kraus observes that the play, which would take some ten evenings to perform as a whole, is intended for a theater on Mars presumably after mankind has destroyed itself. No human audience could stand it. But the author must bear witness to those years, preserved in blood-soaked dreams, "when figures out of operettas played out the human tragedy." In the first edition of the play, the frontispiece was the reproduction of a picture postcard actually sold during the war. It was a photograph of the execution of Cesare Battisti, an Austrian citizen of Italian ethnicity who deserted, joined the Italian army, and was captured and hanged as a traitor. The photograph showed the corpse of Battisti hanging from a gibbet, surrounded by smiling Austro-Hungarian officers, with the hangman standing over the gibbet, grinning jovially from ear to ear. The picture has the subtitle, "The Austrian Face." The scene recurs in the final pages of the play, with a poem by Kraus suggesting that it discloses the true nature of that *Gemuetlichkeit* of which Austrians have always been proud.

The Battisti photograph represents Krausian satire at its most ferocious and prophetic, in almost unbearable protest against inhumanity. But the play contains examples of every form of satire: direct satire, in scenes that only slightly but all the more tellingly distort what could have been actual events; parody; simple citation of actual texts; contrasting citations, side by side; the invention of satirical prototypes; and finally, especially at the end of the play, satire that takes on the quality of apocalypse. Quite apart from its contents, the play thus serves as a kind of lexicon of satirical forms.

The play opens with a scene on the famous Sirk Ecke in Vienna, a street corner across from the opera house that was favored by boulevardiers out to have a good time. A newspaper vendor calls out the news that Archduke Franz Ferdinand, the heir to the throne, has been assassinated. Three idiotic army officers meet and engage in their usual conversation—where to go for a good dinner, the merits of various ladies of the night walking by—with some passing references to the event in Sarajevo that simply repeat, though incoherently, the official government line. The scene on the Sirk Ecke recurs regularly throughout the play, with the same three officers—named Nowotny, Pokorny, and Powolny—repeating their mindless conversation as the world slides ever more into the abyss. Different characters appear and reappear on the street. With unerring exactness, Kraus reproduces every dialect and nuance of language spoken by different social and ethnic groups. The same ethnographic precision characterizes another early scene, the arrival at the railway station of the coffins containing the murdered archduke and his wife, with the representatives of different groups and interests carrying on conversations grotesquely at odds with the occasion. A religious ceremony begins. The assembled crowd kneels down to pray. The three children of the murdered couple can be heard crying over the voice of the priest. Newspaper correspondents are conversing loudly. An editor (presumably Moritz Benedikt of the *Neue Freie Presse*) deplores the absence of one journalist, who is good with emotional scenes. In a moment of silent prayer, when one only hears the sobbing of the children, the editor tells one of his correspondents: "Be sure to write how they pray!"

In the preface Kraus claims that every line in the play was actually spoken or printed somewhere. This claim is not credible, but it is often difficult to know which texts are parody and which are actual quotations. In one early scene, a text that is almost certainly a quotation is inserted into a fictional dialogue. It is another street scene soon after the outbreak of war. A mob is vandalizing a barber shop whose owner has a name that sounds Serbian. The historians Friedjung and Brockhausen (real names) appear. As the mob in the background attacks the barber and demolishes his store, Brockhausen holds forth:

> Just today I read in the *Presse* some telling observations on this theme. With compelling logic every comparison between our people and the mobs in France and England is rejected. Perhaps, dear colleague, you could use this text in your own work. Let me read it to you: Every person educated in history is comforted and inspired by the knowledge that barbarism never achieves a final victory. The great mass of our people instinctively shares in this knowledge. The streets of Vienna have accordingly been free of the shrill howling of cheap patriotism. Here there has been no sign of short-lived hysteria. This old German state has, from the beginning of the war, manifested the most noble German virtues—steadfast self-confidence and deep faith in the victory of our just cause.[9]

Many scenes deal with the activities of newspaper correspondents during the war. Kraus reserved particular venom in his depictions of the activities of Alice Schalek (again a real person), who was greatly admired as the first woman journalist to visit the frontlines. Again actual quotations from Schalek's dispatches are woven into the text. In one scene, Schalek appears on the Italian front. She insists on going right up on the line.[10] As enemy fire comes in, she engages a reluctant officer in conversation:

> Just tell me, lieutenant, whether even the most able artist could reproduce the passionate drama unfolding here. Those who stay back home may call this war a mark of shame on the century. I too did that when I was in the hinterland. But those who are here are gripped by the fever of experience.

Is it not true, lieutenant? You are in the midst of war. Admit it: Many of you would like the war never to end!

The officer denies this, says everyone wants the war to end. Enemy shells keep coming in, then stop. Schalek apologizes for not yet being able to distinguish the sounds made by different types of artillery, then expresses regret that the shelling has ended. The officer asks: "Are you satisfied now?"

Schalek: *What do you mean, "satisfied"? Satisfaction does not come close to expressing what I have learned here. You idealists may call it love of country, you nationalists hatred of the enemy, you modernists a sport, you romantics an adventure. You psychologists may call it the lust for power. I call it liberated humanity!*
Officer: *What do you call it?*
Schalek: *Liberated humanity.*
Officer: *Ah yes. If one could only get a vacation once in a while.*
Schalek: *But then you are compensated by the hourly danger. That is a real experience! Do you know what I would be most interested in now? What are you thinking now? What are your feelings? . . .*

An orderly enters and reports:

Orderly: *Lieutenant, Corporal Hofer is dead.*
Schalek: *How simply this simple man reports this! He is pale like a white cloth. Call it love of country, hatred of the enemy, sport, adventure, lust for power—I call it liberated humanity. I am gripped by the fever of experience! Well, lieutenant. What do you say? What are you thinking now? What are your feelings?*

In a similar scene a military chaplain visits the front: [11]

Officer: *Look, our good chaplain is coming to visit us. That is really nice of him.*
Chaplain: *God bless you, my brave ones! God bless your weapons And are you shooting busily at the enemy?*
Officer: *We are proud to have a fearless chaplain who visits us despite the dangers of enemy fire.*
Chaplain: *Come on, let me do some shooting!*
Officer: *We are all happy to have such a brave chaplain.*

The officer gives a rifle to the chaplain, who fires it several times:

Chaplain: *Boom! Boom!*
Soldiers: *Bravo! What a noble priest! Long live our dear chaplain!*

Even when Kraus is not directly quoting texts from the press, he produces texts that could easily have been published. Parody becomes difficult when the reality exceeds the most inventive satirical imagination. In the repeated conversations between two satirical prototypes, the Subscriber and the Patriot, they mostly quote press reports to each other; sometimes they converse only in headlines:

Subscriber:  *Defeatism in France.*
   Patriot:  *Discouragement in England.*
Subscriber:  *Despair in Russia.*
   Patriot:  *Regrets in Italy.*
Subscriber:  *Generally, what a climate in the enemy countries.*
   Patriot:  *The walls are shaking.*
Subscriber:  *Poincaré is consumed by anxiety.*
   Patriot:  *Grey is disgruntled.*
Subscriber:  *The Czar tosses on his bed.*
   Patriot:  *Troubled Belgium.*
Subscriber:  *What a relief! Demoralization in Serbia.*
   Patriot:  *What good feeling! Despair in Montenegro.*[12]

Two other prototypes, whose lengthy conversations continue throughout the play, are the Optimist and the Complainer; the latter is the persona of Kraus himself. In one of these conversations the Complainer produces a number of press reports so tasteless that the Optimist keeps on exclaiming that they could not possibly be true.[13] First is the report of a theatrical performance in Vienna to commemorate a battle on the eastern front at a place called Uszieczko. It is to honor all those who were killed in this battle. The performers were actual members of the regiment who had fought the battle, many of them wearing decorations earned there. Part of the audience consisted of widows and orphans of those who died at Uszieczko. The battle is reenacted on stage, where the landscape of the region has been carefully reconstructed. At the conclusion of the performance the soldiers on stage kneel in prayer and then sing the national anthem, joined in this by the audience, which included high military and civilian officials as well as representatives of the best social circles. Another text is an advertisement from Germany. For the price of one mark one may purchase a memorial plate with the inscription, He Died a Heroic Death for the Fatherland. A photograph of the deceased can be affixed to the plate, which is suitable for hanging on the wall. Surrounding the photograph are scenes of battle, a replication of the Iron Cross (the highest German decoration), and pictures of the German emperor as well as founding figures of the Second Reich. The Optimist again exclaims that this could not be true and begs the Complainer to admit that he invented it. The Complainer so admits, but the reader is left in doubt: the advertisement could well be real; there were many very similar ones.

There is also the technique of contrasting citations (real or invented), which Kraus often employed in *Die Fackel*. In one scene of the play two Benedicts appear: first Pope Benedict praying, then Moritz Benedikt, editor of the *Neue Freie Presse*, dictating:

> The praying Benedict: In the holy name of God, our heavenly father, and for the sake of the blessed blood of Jesus shed for the redemption of men, I implore you whom divine providence has put in charge of the warring nations to put an end to the terrible slaughter. It is the blood of brothers that is being spilled on land and on the sea. The most beautiful regions of Europe, that garden of the world, are full of corpses and ruins. Listen to the voice of the vicar of the eternal judge, for you will have to stand before the final judgment.
>
> The dictating Benedict: The fish in the Adria have never had such good times as now. In the southern Adria they have been able to dine on almost the entire crew of the "Leon Cambetta," sunk by our fleet. The fish of the middle Adria have been fed by those Italians that we could not save from the sinking "Turbine," while the fish of the northern Adria have been having a regular feast, having been able to dine on the crews of the submarine "Medusa," two torpedo boats and now also the cruiser "Amalfi."[14]

In a subsequent conversation between the Subscriber and the Patriot the above editorial is cited to show the Austrian humanitarian spirit, which even in times of war shows concern for the welfare of Adriatic fish life.

The major satirical prototypes (reminiscent, incidentally, of the stock characters of the *commedia dell'arte*) have already been mentioned: the Complainer and the Optimist, the Subscriber and the Patriot, the military imbeciles of the Sirk Ecke. Another such figure is Old Biach, introduced as the oldest subscriber of the *Neue Freie Presse* and representative of the enlightened Jewish bourgeoisie. Biach says nothing except citations from his newspaper. His last appearance is on the esplanade in Bad Ischl, together with the Subscriber and the Patriot.[15] Biach joins the latter, very upset because he has found a discrepancy between the daily military bulletins from Vienna and Berlin, both reporting on a meeting of the Austrian and German emperors. The Vienna bulletin states that the two monarchs "reaffirmed" their alliance, while the Berlin bulletin had them "noting the same faithful interpretation of the alliance." Could this imply a divergence of views? Biach, more and more agitated, quotes various newspaper texts to reassure himself that there is no discrepancy.

He collapses. With great difficulty he pronounces a number of famous headlines. His last words are, "This is the end of the editorial." He dies, surrounded by a group of deeply moved fellow subscribers.

As the play goes on, the scenes become more and more brutal, finally macabre. Scene: In a police station.[16] A prostitute is brought in. She has lice, is syphilitic, has a record of theft and vagrancy. She is seventeen. The inspector asks her contemptuously about her family. Her father is in the army, her mother has died. How long has she been on the streets? Since 1914. Scene: A military court in Austrian-occupied Serbia.[17] An officer attached to the court asks the clerk whether the three death sentences have been written up, sentences imposed on boys found to own rifles:

| | |
|---|---|
| Clerk (hesitatingly): | *Yes . . . but there is one little problem that I have just discovered. They are only eighteen years old.* |
| Officer: | *Well, so what ?* |
| Clerk: | *Yes . . . well, according to military law they cannot be executed, the sentence would have to be changed to imprisonment.* |
| Officer: | *Let me see. Aha. What we will do is change the age, not the sentence. Anyway, they are sturdy boys. Here, I'm writing—twenty-one instead of eighteen. So. Now we can go ahead and hang them.* |

Kraus wrote a number of scenes ridiculing the megalomania and the stupidity of the German emperor, others portraying members of the house of Habsburg as hopelessly idiotic. He spared the old emperor, Franz Joseph I, although after the war he blamed him as well as the entire dynasty for the war. Also, Kraus did not imply that the brutalities of the war were limited to the side of the Central Powers. In two successive scenes, a German officer named *Niedermacher* (Killer) orders the killing of wounded prisoners of war, followed by a French officer named de Massacre, who reports how he made his men bayonet 180 captured enemy soldiers.[18]

The play ends with a banquet in an officers' club.[19] German and Austrian officers are celebrating, popular music is being played, while artillery fire is heard in the distance. The officers exchange trivial gossip, sentimental assurances of mutual esteem, and insouciant stories of atrocities they have committed. Various messengers appear with reports of military disasters, none of which stop the festivity. The artillery fire stops. In the silence a series of pictures appears on the wall, every one filled with the horror of war—refugees fleeing in the snow, a military court sentencing teenage soldiers to death, the execution itself, massacres of prisoners of war, and so on. A number of characters appear and recite poetry—a chorus of gas masks, a song of soldiers who froze to death, the last words of a Serbian peasant whose children have been murdered, and so on. Here satire stops to give way to relentless lamentation. Arguably the best of Kraus's poems in this series is one entitled "The Dead Forest," an accusation by nature itself against the human beings who have destroyed it. The pictures end with the entire horizon being filled with flames. There is yet another escalation in the apocalyptic prophecy, in an epilogue entitled "The Last Night."[20] There are more scenes of horror, more poems depicting outraged humanity. Hyenas with human faces appear and dance, singing, around piles of corpses. Mysterious signs appear in the sky, crosses and swords.

As a sea of flames envelops the world, there still are voices repeating the banalities of wartime editorials. The world ends with cosmic thunder. A voice from heaven announces that God's image has been destroyed. There is a great silence. Then God's own voice is heard: "I did not will it." And that too is a final irony: these are the words that Emperor Franz Joseph is supposed to have spoken at the outbreak of the war.

Kraus's play is in itself a clear illustration of the thesis mentioned earlier, to the effect that all satire is at its core an act of cursing. The play illustrates the grandeur and near-prophetic power of which satire is capable when it is motivated by moral passion. Nor is one likely to quarrel with the target of Kraus's moral condemnation: the bestiality of which human beings are capable. This was already an object of Kraus's polemics in peacetime, as in his attacks on the criminal justice system, but war is of necessity an enormous amplification of all the cruelties already present in a society. Yet the play, and indeed Kraus's entire opus, also shows the limitations of satire. These limitations also serve to explain Kraus's political uncertainties after the war, and in a curious way lend credibility to the objections made by the Optimist against the Kraus persona in the play. For what was Kraus's curse mainly directed against? One would have to say: Against the Austrian society of his time as a whole, and in particular against the political system of the final years of the Habsburg monarchy. The Optimist's objections can be summed up in one sentence: Come now, you are exaggerating! *Did Kraus exaggerate?*

A fair answer would be both no and yes. On the one hand, no, Kraus did not exaggerate. The horrors he depicted really occurred, there were many individuals in the ruling classes of both Austria-Hungary and Germany as stupid and as inhuman as he depicted them, and the press did play the despicable role he described. But also, yes, he did exaggerate—or at least his satirical attacks were based on an absolute morality that had no room for the ambiguities and the relativity of history. One may leave aside here the moral absurdities into which his mysticism of language led him—as in the notorious case when, after the Nazis had already come to power in Germany, he sued an emigré paper published in Czechoslovakia for quoting him with an omitted comma. We may also leave aside the rather grandiose and humorless vision Kraus had of his own mission in the world. The more general issue here is what perhaps one might call the moral precision of satire.

In retrospect, the regime of Austria-Hungary was more decent than most of the successor regimes in Central Europe. In retrospect, the group that was most frequently satirized by Kraus, the liberal Jewish bourgeoisie and its press (emphatically including the *Neue Freie Presse*), was one of the pillars of this decency. One cannot blame an author for not anticipating the retrospective insights of a later period, but Kraus did not fundamentally change his views as late as the 1930s. There is a more basic issue, though. Every human society has its share of horrors, even the most decent one in times of peace. There is always that line which, in the words of *The Threepenny Opera* of Bertolt Brecht, divides those who walk in darkness from those who walk in the light. Morally inspired satire must necessarily focus on those regions of darkness. In that sense Kraus's attacks on the criminal justice system, from the very beginnings of *Die Fackel*, were well chosen: The law and its enforcement agencies are the mechanisms by which society administers its regions of darkness—or, more precisely, processes those who are forced to inhabit it. The incongruence of the sentimentality of Viennese operetta and the cruelties of the Viennese police has its counterparts in every society, always with the modifications made by the genius of the local culture. Yet satire, if it is to be morally precise, must weigh these dark spots against the moral status of the society as a whole. To be sure, this is not an easy task, but not an impossible one.

These considerations lead back to an observation made in the preceding chapter about wit. Satire too is, so to speak, epistemologically neutral. Its rhetorical power does not necessarily mean that its portrayal of reality is accurate. Satire, like wit, can distort reality, can even lie. In this case, one can appreciate the eloquence and the moral fervor with which Kraus attacked the liberal press of his time, one can even concede the validity of some of his moral condemnations (as those made of the journalists who lent themselves to the bloodthirsty propaganda of the war). And, nevertheless, one can conclude that, in the final analysis, Kraus's attack was unjust.

## Notes

1. Cf. Brian Connery and Kirk Combe, eds., *Theorizing Satire* (New York: St. Martin's, 1995).

2. Northrop Frye, *Anatomy of Criticism* (Princeton, N.J., Princeton University Press, 1957), 223ff.

3. Ibid., 239.

4. Cf. Gab Sibley, "Satura from Quintillion to Joe Bob Briggs," in Connery and Combe, *Theorizing Satire*, 58ff.

5. Cf. Robert Elliott, *The Power of Satire: Magic, Ritual, Art* (Princeton, N.J., Princeton University Press, 1960), 3ff.

6. Cf. Matthew Hodgart, *Satire* (New York: World University Library, 1969).

7. On Kraus's life and work, cf. Caroline Kohn, *Karl Kraus* (Stuttgart: Metzlerscbe Verlagsbuchhandlung, 1966); Frank Field, *The Last Days of Mankind: Karl Kraus and His Vienna* (London: Macmillan, 1967); Edward Timms, *Karl Kraus: Apocalyptic Satirist* (New Haven: Yale University Press, 1986).

8. Karl Kraus, *Die letzten Tage der Menschheit* (Zurich: Pegasus, 1945).

9. Ibid., 76f. All translations from the play are my own.

10. Ibid., 174ff.

11. Ibid., 230f.

12. Ibid., 105.

13. Ibid., 644ff.

14. Ibid., 177ff.

15. Ibid., 565ff.

16. Ibid., 520.

17. Ibid., 518.

18. Ibid., 574ff.

19. Ibid., 678ff.

20. Ibid., 725ff.

# 11

## Interlude
### The Eternal Return of Folly

It is time to take another look at Lady Folly, whose demise has often been announced. Anton Zijderveld, one of the very few sociologists to pay sustained attention to the phenomenon of the comic, quotes a French poem dating from around 1513, which denies the demise. Freely translated: "You tell me that Lady Folly is dead? By my faith, you lie. Never has she been as great, and as powerful, as she is now!"[1] But Zijderveld too thought that she had died, only a couple of centuries later. One can state with some confidence that he was mistaken as well. He could, of course, show how particular social roles, like that of the court jester, came to disappear. But folly itself returns again and again, in ever-new incarnations. If there is any merit to the present argument, this could not be otherwise, for the perceptions that lead to the upside-down view of reality that folly represents spring from the human condition as such. Put differently, folly is anthropologically necessary.

A powerful example of this recurrence of folly is the so-called theater of the absurd, which exploded (the word applies) in Paris in the years following World War II with the plays of Samuel Beckett, Eugène Ionesco, Jean Genet, and others. But Martin Esslin, who wrote the definitive work on this episode, also speaks of "the tradition of the absurd."[2] More of this in a moment. But just what does the term *absurd* refer to?

Etymology is not always useful in clarifying a concept. In this case it is. The Latin, *absurdum*, literally means out of deafness. A possible explanation is that the absurd is what people say who are deaf to reason. The term would in that case be more or less synonymous with the irrational. But a more interesting interpretation suggests itself: The absurd is a view of reality that comes out of deafness itself—that is, an observation of actions that are no longer accompanied by language. Such actions are, precisely, meaningless. Individuals with normal hearing can easily replicate this experience by turning off the sound on television: The actors on the screen now go on busily as before, but much of the time it is impossible to say what their actions mean. The effect usually is comic. By the same token, actions that had self-evident meaning when accompanied by language suddenly appear to be problematic. Deafness *problematizes*. Some psychologists have suggested that deaf people tend to be suspicious. They learn willy-nilly what Nietzsche recommended as a philosophical discipline: the "art of mistrust." If Nietzsche was right, one might conclude that deafness, because of its problematization of ordinary reality, carries with it a certain cognitive gain (which, of course, would not make the condition any less unfortunate).

The absurd is an outlandish, a grotesque representation of reality. It posits a counterworld—just what Zijderveld intended when he described folly as "reality in a looking-glass." Not so incidentally, the etymology of the word *grotesque* is of some interest too. The word comes from the Italian, *grottesca*, and refers to strange paintings that appeared on the walls of grottoes. This etymology suggests a picture: One leaves the ordinary world of sun-lit reality and enters a dark grotto, and then, suddenly, one is confronted with startlingly strange visions. If this experience is of sufficient intensity, one is enveloped in this other reality and, at least temporarily, the ordinary world outside loses its accent of reality. The picture of a grotto graphically conveys what Alfred Schutz called a finite province of meaning.

Most of the links mentioned by Esslin as part of the tradition have been encountered earlier in this book. There is the, as it were, apostolic succession going from the Dionysian orgy through the medieval celebrations of folly to the court jesters and clowns of more recent times, and that is just within Western civilization. If the tradition is taken more narrowly as referring to the stage, there is a chain going back to classical Greek comedy through the *commedia dell'arte* and vaudeville to such heroic clowns of motion pictures as Charlie Chaplin (whose absurdity, true to the aforementioned etymology, comes through more clearly in silent films—that is, under the aspect of deafness).

There is one important feature that recurs in the long history of the absurd: an assault on language. The experience of the absurd beats against the limits of taken-for-granted language, which is simply not made for expressing it. In this, once again, the absurd as a manifestation of the comic resembles both religion and magic. Ordinary language cannot convey the reality of religious experience and, again and again in the history of religion, special languages (such as the *glossolalia* of Pentecostalism) are invented to overcome this difficulty. These special languages, like the language of magic, typically strike the uninitiated as plain nonsense. Thus Esslin includes in the tradition of the absurd such phenomena as the distorted Latin of the *goliards*, the peculiar language of Rabelais and Villon, but also such modern creations as the looking-glass logic of Lewis Carroll's *Alice in Wonderland*, the nonsense verse of Edward Lear in English and Christian Morgenstern in German, and some parts of Franz Kafka's novels. As immediate precursors of the theater of the absurd in France one must count the literary and artistic products of surrealism (the term was coined by Guillaume Apollinaire) and dadaism. Over and beyond the movement that gave itself that name, all expressions of the absurd are surreal—that is, they literally transcend what is taken for granted as real in normal, everyday life.

An important precursor of the theater of the absurd in France was Alfred Jarry (1873–1907), an eccentric bohemian, whose varied works attracted a good deal of attention during his short and unhappy life, but who also underwent a posthumous renascence in the immediate post–World War II period. He was notorious for his penchant for elaborate practical jokes; his entire opus could well be described as a gigantic practical joke, buttressed by an impressive erudition. Jarry is best known for a cycle of plays featuring the character of Ubu, former king of Poland, a grotesque figure surrounded by equally grotesque companions. Arguably, though, Jarry's later work is more interesting, notably the presentation of the supposedly revolutionary new science of "pataphysics."

It is almost impossible to convey the effect of Jarry's plays through their written texts. Everything depends on the actual dramatic performance. As in the later theater of the absurd, the effect lies in the deadly serious enactment of perfectly preposterous actions and dialogues (not so incidentally, the same effect as is achieved by successful clowns and stand-up comedians). This is the case, for example, in the perfectly absurd dialogues between Ubu and his conscience, a tall thin fellow, who is dressed in nothing but a shirt and lives in a suitcase. It is significant that the figure of Ubu was based an a play composed as a parody of a teacher at the *lycée* attended by Jarry; he was fifteen years old at the time. An American commentary on Jarry's work refers to his "free-wheeling and adolescent nihilism."[4] His nondramatic writings, many of them published in newspapers as what he called "speculative journalism," contain such pieces as an application by Ubu for patents on his alleged invention of the umbrella, the carpet slipper, and the glove (each carefully and accurately described), detailed instructions for building a time machine, and the proposal by a priest to transform all statues of the Virgin and Child into machines, designed to imitate the famous Brussels depiction of Manneken-Pis, whereby the infant Jesus would urinate holy water. But Jarry's *magnum opus* was what he called a "neo-scientific novel," *Exploits and Opinions of Doctor Faustroll Pataphysician* . The work is best described as a sort of encyclopedia of nonsense, much of it ex-

tremely difficult to understand. After Jarry's death a College of Pataphysics was founded, in whose publication some of France's most
illustrious writers continued to interpret the new science, only half
tongue-in-cheek.

This is how the protagonist of the neoscientific novel is introduced:

> Doctor Faustroll was sixty-three years old when he was born in Circassia
> in 1898 (the 20th century was (−2) years old). At this age, which he
> retained all his life, Doctor Faustroll was a man of medium height . . . with
> a golden-yellow skin, his face clean-shaven, apart from a sea-green mus-
> tachio, as worn by King Saleh; the hairs of his head alternately platinum
> blonde and jet black, an auburn ambiguity changing according to the sun's
> position; his eyes, two capsules of ordinary writing-ink flecked with gold-
> en spermatozoa like Danzig schnapps.[5]

And this is how Doctor Faustroll's new science is defined:

> An epiphenomenon is that which is superinduced upon a phenomenon.
> Pataphysics . . . is the science of that which is superinduced upon meta-
> physics, whether within or beyond the latter's limitations, extending as far
> beyond metaphysics as the latter extends beyond physics. Ex: an epi-
> phenomenon being often accidental, pataphysics will be, above all, the
> science of the particular, despite the common opinion that the only science
> is that of the general. Pataphysics will examine the laws governing excep-
> tions, and will explain the universe supplementary to this one; or, less
> ambitiously, will describe a universe which can be—and perhaps should
> be—envisaged in the place of the traditional one, since the laws that are
> supposed to have been discovered in the traditional universe are also
> correlations of exceptions, albeit more frequent ones, but in any case acci-
> dental data which, reduced to the status of unexceptional exceptions,
> possess no longer even the virtue of originality.
>
> **DEFINITION:** *Pataphysics is the science of imaginary solutions, which symbol-
> ically attributes the properties of objects, described by their virtuality, to their
> Lineaments.*[6]

Is this purely a spoof? Perhaps. Yet it is understandable that some
very intelligent commentators tried to find interesting insights in the
midst of what at first seems to be an accumulation of witty nonsense.
After all, Doctor Faustroll is not the first great thinker to go out in search
of a "universe supplementary to this one"! In any case, the possibilities
of pataphysical thought are endless. Thus Dr. Faustroll is accompanied
on his journeys (in a boat which is a sieve) by a baboon named Bosse-de-
Nage, whose only linguistic expression is the exclamation "ha ha."
There is a detailed analysis of this phrase, trying to reconstruct from it
the baboon's view of the world:

Pronounced quickly enough, until the letters become confounded, [ha ha] is the idea of unity. Pronounced slowly, it is the idea of duality, of echo, of distance, of symmetry, of greatness and duration, of the two principles of good and evil. But this duality proves also that the perception of Bosse-de-Nage was notoriously discontinuous, not to say discontinuous and analytical, unsuited to all syntheses and to all adequations. One may confidently assume that he could only perceive space in two dimensions, and was refractory to the idea of progress, implying, as it does, a spiral figure.

It would be a complicated problem to study, in addition, whether the first A was the efficient cause of the second. Let us content ourselves with noting that since Bosse-de-Nage usually uttered only AA and nothing more (AAA would be the medical formula *Amalgamate*), he had evidently no notion of the Holy Trinity, nor of all things triple, nor of the indeterminate, nor of the Universe, which may be defined as the Several.[7]

There is even a pataphysical theology. A passage entitled "Concerning the Surface of God" begins as follows:

God is, by definition, without dimension; it is permissible, however, for the clarity of our exposition, and though he possesses no dimensions, to endow him with any number of them greater than zero, if these dimensions vanish on both sides of our identities. We shall content ourselves with two dimensions so that these flat geometrical signs may easily be written down on a sheet of paper.

Based on the vision of a mystic, Anne-Catherine Emmerich, of the cross in the shape of a Y, it is then postulated that God has the shape of three equal straight lines of length $A$, emanating from the same point and having between them angles of 120 degrees. There follows an impenetrable sequence of algebraic formulas, culminating in the definition that "God is the shortest distance between zero and infinity," or alternatively "the tangential point between zero and infinity."[8]

Put simply, Jarry's pataphysics is the construction of a counterworld by means of a counterlanguage and a counterlogic. In this, it is a faithful replication of the key features of classic folly. And this, precisely, is what the theater of the absurd sought to accomplish a half-century later.

Eugène Ionesco (1912–1994) not only produced some of the best-known plays in this genre, but also explained repeatedly how he came to do this and how his intentions are to be understood. The world of folly, or the world of the absurd, is entered as the ordinary world is relativized by means of some sort of shock (one may recall here once more what Alfred Schutz had to say about the entry into finite provinces of meaning). A sudden loss of confidence in the reliability of language is one such shock. In 1948, Ionesco set out to learn English. At the hand of

the textbook he was learning from, he "discovered" such startling insights as that there are seven days in a week, or that the floor is down
and the ceiling up. He experienced, by his own account, a sudden shift
in the sense of reality: What previously was taken for granted is now,
through the medium of a foreign language, made problematic. He then
wrote his first play about the "tragedy of language," *The Bald Soprano* (a
title that has nothing to do with the contents of the play). The entire play
consists of a number of absurd conversations between two couples, the
Smiths and the Martins, their maid Mary, and a visiting fire chief. After
a long conversation between the Smiths (a middle-class English couple,
sitting on English chairs on an English evening) they are visited by the
Martins, who are left alone while the Smiths go to change. For a while
they sit quietly, smiling timidly at each other. Then their dialogue
begins:

| | |
|---|---|
| Mr. Martin: | *Excuse me, madam, but it seems to me, unless I'm mistaken, that I've met you somewhere before.* |
| Mrs. Martin: | *I, too, sir. It seems to me that I've met you somewhere before.* |
| Mr. Martin: | *Was it, by any chance, at Manchester that I caught a glimpse of you, madam?* |
| Mrs. Martin: | *That is very possible. I am originally from the city of Manchester. But I do not have a good memory, sir. I cannot say whether it was there that I caught a glimpse of you or not!* |
| Mr. Martin: | *Good God, that's curious! I, too, am originally from the city of Manchester, madam!* |
| Mrs. Martin: | *That is curious* |
| Mr. Martin: | *Isn't that curious! Only, I, madam, I left the city of Manchester about five weeks ago.* |
| Mrs. Martin: | *That is curious! What a bizarre coincidence! I, too, sir, I left the city of Manchester about five weeks ago.* |
| Mr. Martin: | *Madam, I took the 8:30 morning train which arrives in London at 4:45.* |
| Mrs. Martin: | *That is curious! How very bizarre! And what a coincidence! I took the same train, sir, I, too.* |

They then discover that they traveled in the same compartment, that
they are residing at the same address in London, in the same flat, and
that they both have a little daughter named Alice, who is two years old
and has one white eye and one red eye. At the end of this long conversation, after a period of reflection, Mr. Martin gets up slowly and announces ("in the same flat, monotonous voice"):

Mr. Martin:    *Then, dear lady, I believe that there can be no doubt about it, we*
               *have seen each other before and you are my own wife . . . Eliz-*
               *abeth, I have found you again!* [9]

What is at work here is a kind of demented Cartesian logic, elaborately demonstrating what was obvious to begin with. This, of course,
is comic. Yet at the same time a doubt is introduced as to whether the
obvious is all that obvious after all. Indeed, as the Martins happily
embrace after this rediscovery of their being married to each other, Mary
the maid declares that they are quite mistaken, that they are really
different people, and that her own real name is Sherlock Holmes. One is
reminded of the exercises assigned to his students by Harold Garfinkel,
the founder of the ethnomethodology school in American sociology. For
example, a student would be instructed to go home and ask his parents
or his wife for directions to the bathroom, for instructions on how to use
the refrigerator, or the like. This would naturally upset the student's
interlocutors, but that was not the purpose of the exercise. Rather, it was
to disclose the web of taken-for-granted assumptions underlying normal
social interaction. Be it in ethnomethodology or in the theater of the
absurd, the basic proposition here is quite simple: the obvious becomes
less obvious as it is repeatedly asserted (especially if that is done in a
"flat, monotonous voice").
Ionesco has eloquently expressed this experience:

All my plays have their origin in two fundamental states of consciousness:
now the one, now the other is predominant, and sometimes they are
combined. These basic states of consciousness are an awareness of evanescence and of solidity, of emptiness and of too much presence, of the unreal
transparency of the world and its opacity, of light and of thick darkness.
Each of us has surely felt at moments that the substance of the world is
dream-like, that the walls are no longer solid, that we seem to be able to see
through everything into a spaceless universe made up of pure light and
color; at such a moment the whole of life, the whole history of the world,
becomes useless, senseless and impossible. When you fail to go beyond this
first stage of *depaysement*—for you really do have the impression you are
waking to a world unknown—the sensation of evanescence gives you a
feeling of anguish, a form of giddiness. But all this may equally well lead to
euphoria: the anguish suddenly turns into release; nothing counts now
except the wonder of being, that new and amazing consciousness of life in
the glow of a fresh dawn, when we have found our freedom again. [10]

He goes on to say that, in this new freedom, it is possible to laugh at
the world. And in another passage Ionesco formulates the relation of the

comic to this experience of emigration (*depaysement*) from ordinary reality:

> To feel the absurdity of the commonplace, and of language—its falseness is already to have gone beyond it. To go beyond it we must first of all bury ourselves in it. What is comical is the unusual in its pure state; nothing seems more surprising to me than that which is banal; the surreal is here, within grasp of our hands, in our everyday conversation.[11]

The experiences of the absurd and of the comic are not coterminous. Rather, they overlap. But where they do overlap they reveal the most profound aspect of the comic—namely, a magical transformation of reality. In order to achieve this, ordinary reality must first be problematized— if one prefers, deconstructed. Just as language constructs the order of reality, so it can be used to tear down this construction, or minimally to breach it. Non-sense actions and non-sense language are thus vehicles to induce a different perception of the world. This is a methodology very familiar to anyone who has studied mysticism. Perhaps the closest religious analogy to the theater of the absurd is the way in which Zen techniques of meditation break down the ordinary, "normal" mode of attending to the world.

Absurd comedy releases a curious dialectic. It puts before one a reality that is both strange and familiar, and that evokes the response that it is impossible. But as one exclaims, "That is absurd!"—that being the magical counterworld one has just entered—another exclamation immediately suggests itself, "This is absurd!"—and this, of course, is the world of ordinary, everyday experience. It is this dialectic that is implied in Anton Zijderveld's characterization of folly as reality in a looking-glass. The Vedanta used the phrase *neti, neti* (not this, not that) to indicate the impossibility of describing the ultimate reality. One could say that absurd comedy applies the same phrase to ordinary reality— not this, not that—and thereby, however tentatively, adumbrates the possibility that there may be a reality beyond the ordinary. This does not as yet make it a religious phenomenon. But it comes dangerously close (and the adverb here is quite appropriate). Martin Esslin, in the concluding chapter of his book on the theater of the absurd, makes an argument about its relation to religion that at first seems self-contradictory.[12] On the one hand, he puts the experience it sought to convey in the context of the decline of religion: A world bereft of any divine presence must appear absurd, meaningless. But on the other hand, Esslin suggests, the experience of the absurd also opens up the possibility of transcendence that is, of a reality beyond the absurd realities of this life.

The Latin church father Tertullian is famous for his statement, "*Credo quia absurdum"* (I believe because it is absurd). Much has been made of this both by advocates and by critics of Christianity, to show the power of faith or, alternatively, its irrationality. The correct interpretation of Tertullian must be left to experts in patristics. But a most nonexpert— perhaps a pataphysical—exegesis may be ventured here: Perhaps Tertullian said more than he intended. For it is not so much that one should believe because something is absurd, but rather that one is led toward faith by the perception of absurdity. Needless to say, there is nothing inevitable about this progression. It remains as an intriguing possibility. In other words (and never mind what Tertullian actually meant): it is not the object of faith that is absurd. The world is absurd. And, therefore, faith is possible.

## Notes

1. Anton Zijderveld, *Reality*, 70:

*Me di toi que dame Folie*
*Est mort? Ma foy, tu as menty;*
*Jamais si grande ne la vy,*
*Ny si puissante comme elle est.*

2. Martin Esslin, *The Theater of the Absurd* (Garden City, N.Y.: Anchor, 1961), 229ff.

3. Cf. Roger Shattuck and Simon Taylor, eds., *Selected Works of Alfred Jarry* (New York: Grove, 1965); Keith Beaumont, *Alfred Jarry* (New York: St. Martin's, 1984).

4. Shattuck and Taylor, *Alfred Jarry*, 13.

5. Ibid., 182f.

6. Ibid., 192f.

7. Ibid., 228f.

8. Ibid., 254ff.

9. Eugène Ionesco, *Four Plays* (New York: Grove, 1958), 15ff.

10. Eugène Ionesco, *Notes and Counter-Notes* (London: Calder, 1964), 169.

11. Cited by Esslin, *Theater of the Absurd*, 93.

12. Ibid., 291ff.

# III

## Toward a Theology of the Comic

# 12

# The Folly of Redemption

In many parts of the world madness has been viewed as a sign of holiness. Folly, as has been seen, is a widely diffused if not universal phenomenon. So are holy fools. And, as with (so to speak) mundane fools, the holy fools have been both real madmen (what today would be called cases of mental illness or retardation) and individuals feigning madness (who could be called holy fools *ex officio*). There are important elements of religiously privileged folly in Taoism and Zen Buddhism, among the wandering *sanyasin* of India, and in primal religions in Africa and the Americas. Holy fools have appeared in Judaism, Christianity, and Islam, often exhibiting very similar behavior, even if the religious rationale of this behavior varied in accordance with the several traditions.

There are examples of holy folly in the Hebrew Bible. A prototypical example is that of King David, in an episode recounted in the Second Book of Samuel (2 Sam. 6): As the ark of the covenant was brought to Jerusalem, David went into a kind of frenzy and started to dance in front of the ark, apparently in a state of nakedness. His wife, Michal (daughter of King Saul), was embarrassed by this very unkingly behavior and rebuked him for it, saying that he was bringing shame on himself even in the eyes of the servant maids present. David replied, "I will make myself yet more contemptible than this, and I will be abased in your eyes; but by the maids of whom you have spoken, by them I shall be held in honor." The text does not tell what further embarrassing acts David undertook, though it informs that, as punishment for her criticism of David, "Michal was afflicted with infertility for the rest of her life" (a severe penalty, one might think, for lacking a sense of humor). A number of important themes in holy folly (at least in Judaism and Christianity) are already explicit in this story: the frenzied absurdity in behavior (including the nakedness), the deliberate surrender of dignity, and the ability of very humble people (here the servant girls) to understand more than the mighty and the wise (here represented by Michal).

The prophetic literature has a number of cases that can properly be described as holy folly. In the Book of Isaiah, the prophet is reported to have walked naked and barefoot for three years (Is. 20). The prophet Jeremiah put on a wooden yoke around his neck (Jer. 27). And Ezekiel was commanded to eat excrement (Ezek. 4). In each instance the seemingly mad behavior was intended to symbolize specific prophecies, but it is safe to assume that such behavior was not limited to these instances. This should not surprise, in view of what is known about the origins of Israelite prophecy—almost certainly to be sought in the phenomenon of wandering ecstatics, whose activities always contained bizarre and seemingly absurd characteristics.

As was observed in an earlier chapter, folly, absurdity, and grotesqueness are closely related. The history of religion, again in many parts of the world, is full of grotesque figures: gods, demons, and others. One may think here of the grotesque divinities abounding in Hinduism or in Tibetan Buddhism, perhaps epitomized in the figure of Kali Durga, the goddess of destruction, depicted as a woman of monstrous appearance dancing on a mountain of skulls. The religious aspect of grotesqueness can be explained. As Rudolf Otto has classically formulated (*The Idea of the Holy*), religious experience involves an encounter with realities and beings that are "totally other" (*totaliter aliter*). This otherness cannot be grasped in ordinary language and imagery, at best can only be adumbrated. It shatters the assumptions of ordinary, everyday experience. This is precisely what the grotesque symbolizes very effectively. Human beings trying to perceive this other are like people submerged underwater looking up at what is above the water: The latter, inevitably, will be perceived in a grossly distorted form. The grotesque expresses such distortion. Holy folly, in its grotesqueness, makes explicit the otherness breaking into ordinary reality, but also the impossibility of containing this otherness in the categories of ordinary reality.

In the teaching of Jesus, as reported in the Gospels, there are no direct references to anything that might be called holy folly. But Jesus' repeated statement that one should try to be like a child and his pronouncement of blessing on those who are poor in spirit convey the similar idea that there is a simplicity that is superior to worldly wisdom. The closest approach to holy folly in the Gospels comes in two events at the very end of Jesus' life: the entry into Jerusalem (Matt. 21) and the events following Jesus' appearance before Pontius Pilate (Matt. 27). Jesus chooses to enter Jerusalem mounted on a donkey. To be sure, the rationale given to this by the evangelist is the fulfillment of a prophecy from the Book of Isaiah to the effect that Zion's king will come riding on an ass (though here too this act is described as being humble). Nevertheless there is the ancient association of the donkey with folly. There is no way of knowing whether Jesus, or for that matter the author of Matthew, knew of this association (Greco-Roman rather than Israelite). It would certainly be known to many who received the Gospels in the Greek language. To them, one must suppose, there came the image of Jesus entering the city of his Passion in a manner suggesting the behavior of a fool. Even more telling is the second episode. After the Roman governor had disclaimed responsibility for the fate of Jesus and just before the latter was taken out to be crucified, the Roman soldiers took him and subjected him to a mock coronation. He was dressed in a scarlet robe, a crown of thorns was placed on his head and a reed in his right hand, and he was hailed as king of the Jews. Here Jesus is mocked by being treated as if he were a bogus royalty of the Bacchanalia, the predecessor of the medieval feast of fools. Indeed, one might say that, just before his crucifixion, Jesus was crowned as a king of folly.

The classical passages in the New Testament that refer to folly, though, are in the Pauline literature, notably the Letters to the Corinthians. The apostle repeatedly states that he speaks "as a fool," and he announces that this is indeed the calling for Christians: "We are fools for Christ's sake" (1 Cor. 4:10). This phrase, "fools for Christ's sake," has been the self-description of holy fools in Christian history ever since. Here are two passages in which Paul explains the meaning of this folly: "For the word of the cross is folly to those who are perishing, but to us who are being saved it is the power of God." And then this description of the one whom the apostle preaches: "Christ crucified, a stumbling-block to Jews and folly to Gentiles." Finally, the climactic theological explanation: "God chose what is foolish in the world to shame the wise, God chose what is weak in the world to shame the strong, God chose what is low and despised in the world, even things that are not, to bring to nothing things that are, so that no human being might boast in the presence of God" (1 Cor. 1:27–28).

There are many layers of meaning in these passages. There is, for one, the explicit relation to Paul's own weakness, described merely as his "thorn in the flesh," which God told him to accept rather than fight against. The Corinthians are asked also to accept the apostle's weakness and to understand that the power of his message comes from God, not from his own strength. There have been different theories (all unproved and unprovable) that Paul's affliction was epilepsy. If so, this would make Paul himself into a figure of holy folly, of which epilepsy has been seen as a manifestation in classical antiquity. Beyond this, however, Paul points to the same mystery of the Incarnation that is suggested in the aforementioned episodes from the Gospels. This mystery is the self-humiliation of God, the *kenosis*, who descends from the infinite majesty of the divinity, not only to take on the form of a human being but of one despised, mocked, and finally killed under the most degrading circumstances. Yet this humiliated Jesus is the same as the triumphant victor of the Resurrection. The central paradox of the Christian message, as preached by Paul, is the immense tension between the kenotic Christ of the Passion and the *Christus Victor* of Easter morning.

To proclaim this paradox is to engage in an act of folly, as perceived by the wise of this world. In speaking as a fool, the apostle does at least two things: He is faithful to the extraordinary character of the message that has been trusted to him, without making concessions to the false wisdom of the worldly. And, in his own weakness, he also imitates the weakness assumed by the kenotic savior, who was crowned and crucified as a royal fool (or, more precisely, as a fool who thought himself a king). From that time on, every fool for Christ's sake both participates in and symbolizes the *kenosis* of God that brings about the redemption of the world.[1]

It is not necessary to be Russian in order to appreciate holy fools. However, it seems to help.

There is a long tradition of fools for Christ's sake in both Western and Eastern Christendom, containing both real fools and fools *ex officio*.[2] In the West, for example, St. Francis of Assisi exhibited some of the characteristics of holy folly, as did the order he founded. But it is Eastern Orthodoxy, especially in Russia, that has produced the richest collection of holy fools.[3] In the case of Russia, the argument could actually be made that holy folly became a major theme in the national culture, both on the popular and literary levels (Dostoyevsky's novel *The Idiot* being the undisputed literary climax of the tradition).

Holy folly in the Eastern church may go back to the early days of the desert saints of Egypt, but the phenomenon became prominent in the sixth century. Famous cases are those of Theophilus and Maria of Antioch, and of St. Symeon of Emesa. Theophilus and Maria came from aristocratic families. They were engaged to be married, instead decided to become fools for Christ's sake. They roamed the streets of the Syrian metropolis, he dressed as a jester, she as a prostitute, outraging the populace with bizarre and often obscene behavior. Gradually, it was recognized that this behavior was an expression of unusual piety. St. Symeon was an anchorite in the lands east of the river Jordan. He too began to roam through the towns and villages of this area. He would throw walnuts at people in church, overthrow the stalls of street vendors, dance with prostitutes in the street, burst into women's bathhouses, and conspicuously eat on fast days. At first, of course, the reaction to this behavior was outrage. Then it came to be accepted that the behavior symbolized great religious mysteries and Symeon was revered as a saintly individual. This greatly disturbed him, as a reputation for saintliness would undermine the whole (let it be called) kenotic program, which was to be an ongoing exercise in humility and humiliation. To prove that he was not a saint, Symeon pretended to make an effort to seduce the wife of the shopkeeper for whom he occasionally worked. The shopkeeper raised an alarm, and Symeon was beaten and chased away, thoroughly humiliated and discredited. Paradoxically, this only enhanced his reputation as a holy fool later on. It is presumably impossible to determine whether Symeon was really mad or only pretended to be—or, for that matter, whether he was a genuine adulterer or only a make-believe one. The significant fact is that by consensus he was deemed to be a fool for Christ's sake, and as such he was canonized by the Orthodox church.

An important figure in the development of the tradition was St. Andrew the Fool, who lived in Constantinople from the end of the ninth to the early tenth century. Born in Scythia, reputedly of Slavic ethnicity, he was brought to the imperial capital as a slave. He too engaged in the by now standardized fool's behavior, adding the personal enhancements of walking around naked and sleeping with stray dogs. He too was canonized. The stories about him were taken to Russia in the course of its Christianization and he was particularly revered there as a fellow Slav.

The first important Russian case, in the eleventh century, was that of St. Isaac Zatvornik, a hermit of the famous Monastery of the Caves in Kiev. The greatest flourishing of holy fools occurred in the sixteenth century. Holy folly was especially associated with the city of Novgorod. Many travelers to Russia noticed the prevalence of the phenomenon. This is how the English traveler Giles Fletcher described what he saw:

> They have certain hermits, whom they call holy men, that are like gymnosophists for their life and behavior, though far unlike for their knowledge and learning. They use to go stark naked save a clout about their middle, with their hair hanging long and wildly about their shoulders, and many of them with an iron collar or chain about their necks or midst, even in the very extremity of winter. These they take as prophets and men of great holiness, giving them a liberty to speak what they list without any controlment, though it be of the very highest himself. . . . If any of them take some piece of salesware from any man's shop as he passeth by, to give where he list, he thinketh himself much beloved of God and much beholden to the holy man for taking it in that sort. Of this kind there are not many, because it is a very hard and cold profession to go naked in Russia, especially in winter. Among other at this time they have one at Moscow that walketh naked about the streets and inveyeth commonly against the state and government, especially against the Godunovs, that are thought at this time to be great oppressors of that commonwealth.[4]

One of the most famous practitioners of this "very hard and cold profession" was St. Basil the Innocent, who died around 1550.[5] He is also known as St. Basil the Blessed; significantly, the Russian word *blazhenny* can mean both innocent (in the sense also of childlike or imbecile) and blessed. He has been associated with Ivan the Terrible. Although he died before that bloody ruler unleashed a reign of terror in the rebellious city of Novgorod, legend puts St. Basil there at the time. Supposedly he lived in a cave under the Volkhov Bridge. He summoned Ivan to come there and, when strangely enough the tsar obeyed the summons, Basil offered him fresh blood and meat. Ivan refused the disgusting gift, whereupon Basil put his arm around him and pointed to the sky, where the souls of Ivan's innocent victims were ascending to heaven. The tsar was terrified and ordered the executions to stop, whereupon the blood and meat turned into wine and sweet watermelon.

The combination of holy folly and political criticism may not have been very common, but even its occasional occurrence explains why the authorities in Moscow became increasingly suspicious of holy fools. Suppressed in Moscow and other urban centers, the institution survived in remoter areas. But the Russian church stopped the canonization of any additional fools for Christ's sake.

A number of themes recur in this Orthodox tradition. Central, of course, is the theme of utter humiliation—first self-humiliation, then humiliation on the part of others that is deliberately provoked. In this the fools for Christ's sake imitate the humiliation of Christ. The worst sin is pride; everything must be done to avoid this. The association with blatant sinners and, a step further, the pretense of actually sinning are intended to make pride impossible. It is not difficult to see that there could be one additional step: *really* sinning, in which case pride would become completely impossible. And there developed indeed an underground current of Russian spirituality in which self-abasing sin, especially of a sexual nature, was understood as an exercise in Christian humility. This underground tradition reached a late and historically important embodiment in the sinister figure of Rasputin, who haunted the court of the last Romanovs.

The recurrent theme of nakedness is also important. Nakedness, in addition to violating normal notions of decency, symbolizes the rejection of all social roles and artificial childlikeness. Also, of course, it invites disgust and vilification—exactly the outcome sought by the holy fools. Religiously motivated nakedness can be found in a number of cultures (prominently, for example, in India), but here it has a specific kenotic meaning.

The fools for Christ's sake were, for the most part, wanderers, pilgrims. This holy vagabondage is also significant. It symbolizes the rejection of worldly ties and security. The holy fool is a perpetual stranger, a man without a home or fixed abode—in this too imitating Jesus. Finally, the holy fool, though typically an individual without formal learning (or one who had such learning but deliberately rejected it), is the repository of superior wisdom. To him are revealed mysteries that remain hidden to the wise men of this world. This theme is nicely illustrated by the following legend: Somewhere in the vastness of Russia lived three hermits, renowned for their saintliness but utterly devoid of the knowledge of religious doctrine and ritual. When the local bishop discovered that the hermits did not even know a single prayer of the church, he sought them out and taught them to say the Lord's Prayer. They memorized the prayer and gratefully said goodbye to the bishop, who returned to his residence by crossing a lake on a ferry. As the ferry was halfway across the lake in the early evening, the bishop was amazed to see the three hermits walking across the water in great haste in order to catch up with him. They told him that they had forgotten one line of the prayer and asked him to repeat it. The bishop, overcome with awe, told them that they need not bother.

In an earlier discussion of folly the point was made that it constitutes a magical transformation of the world, or more precisely, an act of magic by which a counterworld is made to appear. This counterworld serves to illuminate the realities of the ordinary world, typically in a debunking or critical manner. This is why Anton Zijderveld, as previously cited, spoke of folly as reality in a looking-glass. If folly is, as it were, baptized as *holy* folly, then what occurs is what could be called an epistemological reversal: The status of the counterworld comes to be radically redefined. To stay within Zijderveld's image the looking glass becomes a windowpane. That is, instead of the foolish counterworld being understood as a distorted reflection of *this* world, it can now be viewed as a distorted glimpse of *another* world. The apostle Paul actually uses the image of the looking glass in this latter sense, when he says in the Revised Standard Version that in the present aeon "we see in a mirror dimly" (1 Cor. 13:12); the King James Version puts it more poetically: "through a glass, darkly," and only in the aeon to come will we see "face to face."

If we take these images literally—mirror versus window—they are contradictory. But, rightly understood, there is here a metaphor that resolves the seeming contradiction. For one can look at the world consecutively in two ways, providing two perspectives that are not necessarily irreconcilable. The first perspective emerges from an attitude that, at least provisionally, puts aside or brackets the religious possibility that there is indeed a world other than this one. This attitude involves a method aptly described by the scholastics' phrase *etsi Deus non daretur* (as if God is not assumed). In that event, it is perfectly plausible to look at folly as a reflection of ordinary social reality and nothing else, and this perspective does indeed yield useful insights. If one then takes on the attitude of faith, which does indeed assume the existence of God, folly is *also* something else—namely, an uncertain reflection of what lies *beyond* or *behind* this world, a shadow play of the divine reality.

Kierkegaard has used the phrase "knight of faith" to describe an individual who dares to have faith. There is here a deliberate allusion to Don Quixote, who is arguably the most magnificent fool in world literature. The further implication is that, in the perspective of faith, Don Quixote is finally justified: He is more right about the nature of reality than the empiricist Sancho Panza or all those others who mock his folly. Commenting on Don Quixote from a Christian point of view, the German Protestant theologian Helmut Thielicke summed up: "The fool is always right; *only* the fool is right in this world."[6] Cervantes's "knight of sad appearance" and Kierkegaard's "knight of faith" have in common a *rejection* of ordinary reality, a refusal to accept its rules and limitations. *Etsi Deus non daretur,* this refusal, however heroic, must end in defeat (as did Cervantes's hero, who on his deathbed renounced his previous ideas of noble chivalry). However, if God *is* assumed, the refusal is fully justified; it represents a truth greatly superior to all mundane knowledge. Folly is now seen as a prelude to the overcoming of the empirical world. As Miguel de Unamuno put it in his discussion of Don Quixote: "It was by making himself ridiculous that Don Quixote achieved his immortality."[7] One could put it more strongly: Don Quixote is a witness to immortality.

From the standpoint of faith, folly results in the intersection between absolute and contingent reality, between the world *beyond* and this world. This is how Thielicke puts this:

> Don Quixote, although also victorious, is the victim of a law of life: *The absolute is always on the edge of ridiculousness when it collides with the contingent.* Therefore he who represents the absolute does not belong in this world, at least not fully. While he is struggling against it, he also stands outside it; he can never be absorbed by it. Because of this standing outside this world, because of his failure to adjust, he appears in this world in the costume of the fool, the disguise of the clown.[8]

This phenomenon can also be described in Schutzian terms. The act of faith brings with it a shift in the accent of reality. The paramount reality of everyday life is relativized; conversely, the specific finite province of meaning to which faith pertains is absolutized. Needless to say, it is finite only in the perspective of the paramount reality. As the epistemological reversal occurs, it is, on the contrary, the threshold of infinity; conversely, the empirical world, far from being paramount, is disclosed as being very finite indeed. The madness of the fool is now seen to be the infinitely more profound truth. In his analysis of Don Quixote, Alfred Schutz was interested in the way in which the two realities—Quixote's fantasy world and the ordinary world of all the others—related to each other.[9] Schutz proposed that the two realities were connected by a sort of switching system—the "enchanters," as Quixote called them, powerful magicians who made the reality of his world appear as something quite different to his fellowmen. In other words, the enchanters made sure that the reality perceived by Quixote was perceived as fantasy by others. In the Quixotic universe, of course, what the others see is fantasy; the true reality is his own world of chivalry. Schutz was uninterested in religious matters, but this alternation of the real and the fantastic in, respectively, the perceptions of mundaneness and faith accurately applies to any religious perspective on the world: What to faith is the most real (*ens realissimum*) is to the nonbelieving mind a fantasy; conversely, the hard reality of a mundane worldview is, in the eyes of faith, a fleeting fantasy.

Don Quixote believes that the knights-errant are "God's ministers on earth." But at times he too has his doubts and wonders whether he might not be mad after all. In this he is very similar to Kierkegaard's knight, who must again and again repeat his leap of faith. More generally, the epistemological status of the world of folly can only be resolved by the decision to leap or not to leap into the attitude of faith. In the absence of faith, *etsi Deus non daretur*, the fool is finally a tragic figure, as Quixote was on his deathbed: "He finds himself at the end a home comer to a world to which he does not belong, enclosed in everyday reality as in a prison, and tortured by the most cruel jailer: the commonsense reason which is conscious of its own limits."[10] The intrusion of the transcendental into this world of everyday life is either denied or dissimulated by common reason. In the perspective of faith, things look very different. There is no tragedy here. On the contrary, the fool is gloriously vindicated. This was the insight with which Enid Welsford concluded her history of the fool:

> To those who do not repudiate the religious insight of the race, the human spirit is uneasy in this world because it is at home elsewhere, and escape from the prison house is possible not only in fancy but in fact. The theist believes in possible beatitude, because he disbelieves in the dignified isolation of humanity. To him, therefore, romantic comedy is serious literature because it is a foretaste of the truth: the Fool is wiser than the Humanist, and clownage is less frivolous than the deification of humanity.[11]

## Notes

1.   There are non-Christian analogs to the idea of *kenosis*. A notable one can be found in Jewish mysticism, in the school of Isaac Luria, which flourished in the wake of the expulsion of the Jews from Spain. Cf. Gershom Sholem, *Major Trends in Jewish Mysticism* (New York: Schocken, 1946), 265ff. Its doctrine of the "breaking of the vessels" (which had roots in earlier gnostic speculations) maintained that fragments of the divine glory descended into the lower realms of reality in which evil dwells. The redemption of the world, its repair (*tikkun*), consists of rescuing these broken fragments of glory and restoring them to their proper place. The coming of the Messiah will complete the process of "repair," redeeming not only Israel but all of reality. This doctrine is many-layered. It certainly contains an interpretation of the meaning of exile, which had recently been suffered by Spanish Jewry. But far beyond this the doctrine is cosmic in scope, suggesting the self-exile of the divinity: in other words, its kenosis. It received a bizarre transmutation in the heresy of Sabbatianism. Cf. pp. 287ff.; also Sholem, *Sabbatai Sevi* (Princeton, N.J.: Princeton University Press, 1973). This had its origins in the career of the "false Messiah" Sabbattai Sevi, who led a tumultuous mass movement, was imprisoned by the Turkish authorities, and then underwent a forced conversion to Islam. This conversion, a contemptible act of apostasy in the perception of orthodox Judaism, was interpreted as the clue to the Messianic mystery by some Sabbatians: The Messianic light must descend into the lowest darkness for the work of redemption to be completed. This paradoxical *kenosis* became the rationale not only for conversions to Islam and Christianity, but for gross violations of every moral and ritual precept of Judaism. Isaac Bashevis Singer has given a vivid picture of what this involved in his novel, *Satan in Goray*. This is a Jewish analog to the antinomianism represented by various "fools for Christ's sake" in Russian Christianity, dramatically by the case of the "mad monk" Rasputin.

2.   Cf. John Saward, *Perfect Fools: Folly for Christ's Sake in Catholic and Orthodox Spirituality* (Oxford: Oxford University Press, 1980).

3.   Cf. Christos Yannaras, *The Freedom of Morality* (Crestwood, N.Y.: St. Vladimir's Seminary Press, 1984), 65ff.; G. P. Fedotov, *The Russian Religious Mind* (Cambridge, Mass.: Harvard University Press, 1966), vol. II, 316ff.

4.   Cited in Saward, *Perfect Fools*, 22f.

5.   Cf. Fedotov, *Russian Religious Mind*, 338.

6.   Helmut Thielicke, *Das Lachen der Heiligen und Narren* (Stuttgart: Quell, [1974] 1988), 167. My translation.

7.   Miguel de Unamuno, *The Tragic Sense of Life* (New York: Dover, 1954), 306. In this work, written in 1912, Unamuno presented Don Quixote as the quintessence of a "Spanish soul" opposed to the rationalism of Europe. This ideological exercise is of no interest here.

8.   Thielicke, *Des Lachen*, 168f. My translation.

9.   Alfred Schutz, "Don Quixote and the Problem of Reality," in Schutz, *Collected Papers*, vol. II, 135ff.

10.   Ibid., 157.

11.   Enid Welsford, *The Fool* (Garden City, N.Y.: Anchor, 1956), 326f.

# 13

## Interlude
### *On Grim Theologians*

Some religions are more humorous than others. Some gods laugh more than others. In East Asia in particular: Zen monks and Taoist sages seem to be helplessly in the grip of mirth much of the time, and every souvenir store in Hong Kong or Taipei offers a variegated line of laughing Buddhas. The Greek gods laughed a lot, mostly unpleasantly. The so-called Abrahamic religions that emerged from the monotheistic experiences of western Asia—Judaism, Christianity, and Islam—are comparatively underprivileged in the department of mirth. Nietzsche made the renowned quip that he would find Christianity more believable if only the Christians looked more redeemed. He had the same observation in mind, no doubt, when he called his anti-Christian philosophy "the cheerful science." There is in all this an agenda for comparative religion that is clearly beyond the scope of this book. However, the apparent absence of humor in the sacred texts and in the theology of Christianity create an inconvenient problem for a Christian writer who wants to argue for the religious implications of the comic. The problem ought to be faced, at least briefly.

Anyone surfing through the Bible (Old and New Testament alike) or the history of Christian theology in search of the comic is bound to be disappointed.[1] The God of the Hebrew Bible is indeed mentioned as laughing a number of times, but it is virtually always a laughter of derision over the vain ambitions of human beings (as in Psalms 2 and 59). The most strategic occurrence of laughter in the Hebrew Bible is when God informs the aged Abraham and Sarah that they will be blessed with a child. Both Abraham and Sarah greet this announcement with laughter (respectively, in Gen. 17:15–21 and 18:1–15). The idea strikes them as ludicrous, as it would anybody. Their laughter expresses a lack of faith, though God is not reported as having held this against them. When the child was indeed born, they named him Isaac (*Yizchak*, "he laughed" in Hebrew), thus commemorating their doubting laughter (unless the implication was that *God* laughed at their laughter—certainly the Israelite God *always* had the last laugh). One could perhaps, with some effort, find a biblical legitimation of humor in the fact that laughter is in the name of the second of the three great patriarchs of the Jewish tradition. One does not fare much better with the New Testament. The Greek church Father John Chrysostom stated that Jesus never laughed. This may be doubted. Surely, for instance, there must have been laughter at the wedding in Cana. But there is definitely no account of Jesus' laughing anywhere in the Gospels. Laughter is mentioned in Jesus' reported sayings, but it is to berate those who laugh now in godless sinfulness and to announce that they will weep in the fullness of time (as in Luke 6:25). Jesus was, of course, repeatedly the object of sinful mockery, even while suffering on the cross (Luke 23:35). However, as was argued in the preceding chapter, it is by way of folly that the comic makes its most persuasive appearance in the New Testament: Jesus as the ultimate holy fool, from the entrance into Jerusalem to the mock coronation by the Roman soldiers. It is, of course, in the same way—via the metaphor of folly—that the comic appears in the Pauline Epistles. What one does find repeatedly throughout the New Testament is an affirmation of *joy* as a blessing of redemption. One may safely assume that the joy of the blessed includes laughter. But, as was made clear earlier, specifically comic laughter is not the same as laughter that simply expresses joyfulness. By and large, one can fairly say that the search for comic laughter in the biblical literature succeeds only if one engages in rather labored interpretations. At best, it is implicit rather than explicit.

The negative attitude toward laughter continues in the patristic and medieval periods of Christian thought. There is a long line of grim theologians. Repeatedly there are negative comments on laughter, which is understood as expressing worldliness, sinful insouciance, and lack of faith. Conversely, weeping over the wretchedness of this world is praised as a Christian virtue. Christian saints rarely laugh—except, it seems, in defiance of imminent martyrdom. Monastic rules proscribed laughter. One does not have to be a Nietzschean to look upon the history of Christian theology as a depressingly lachrymose affair.

The picture becomes brighter if one looks at Christian behavior rather than Christian theorizing. Mention was made earlier in this book of Mikhail Bakhtin's view of the laughing culture (better, comic culture) of the Middle Ages. Some of Bakhtin's particular interpretations of this have been questioned, but there can be no doubt that there flourished a rich comic culture in medieval Europe and that this culture, while often frowned upon by the ecclesiastical authorities, was emphatically Christian in content.[2] One of the most intriguing manifestations of this was liturgical. This was the so-called Easter laughter (*risus paschalis*). In the course of the Easter mass the congregation was encouraged to engage in loud and prolonged laughter, to celebrate the joy of the Resurrection. To achieve this end, preachers would tell jokes and funny stories, often with quite obscene elements. In some localities this practice continued into modern times.

If one looks at great figures in church history, arguably the one with the most visible sense of humor was Luther.[3] Humor permeates Luther's correspondence and table talk. When he was asked how God occupied himself in eternity, he replied that God sat under a tree cutting branches into rods to use on people who ask stupid questions. When a young pastor asked for advice on how to overcome his stage fright when facing his congregation, Luther suggested that he should imagine them sitting there naked. Sometimes Luther's sense of humor is sufficiently Rabelaisian—that is, rooted in the medieval comic culture—to be a bit hard to take for a modern reader. Thus, in explaining the doctrine of Christ's descent into hell, Luther describes the devil as a monster sitting in hell and devouring all the sinners who arrive there. When Christ arrives in hell, the devil devours him too. But Christ, the only arrival without sin, tastes different and causes the devil to have severe stomach cramps. The devil vomits Christ out again. But the, as it were, purgative power of Christ's purity was so great that with him the devil also spits out all the other sinners he had previously eaten.[4] When Luther attacked the Archbishop of Mainz, who announced that he would exhibit annually his collection of relics, Luther said that a few new ones had just been added—such as three flames from the burning bush of Moses, a piece of the flag carried by Christ into hell, half a wing of the archangel Gabriel, and five strings of David's harp.[5] The same robust sense of humor can even be detected in one of Luther's most famous statements, containing as it does the doctrine of justification by faith in a comic nutshell, when he advised the overscrupulous Melanchthon "to sin forcefully, but to believe even more forcefully" (*pecca fortiter sed crede fortius*)—a sentence that humorless Catholic critics have often used to discredit Lutheranism and that equally humorless Lutherans have reinterpreted to make it inoffensive.

Of important modern theologians, Kierkegaard, as was mentioned previously, had most to say about the comic. His views of irony and humor as marking the boundaries of the esthetic, ethical, and religious perspectives are complicated and need not be developed further here. His basic insight into the religious dimension of the comic is contained in the most lapidary form in one of his journal entries: "But humor is also the joy which has overcome the world."[6] Similar statements can be found in the writings of several other theologians, though typically in the form of asides rather than sustained treatments. Karl Barth, shortly before his death, said that good theology should always be done cheerfully and with a sense of humor. Dietrich Bonhoeffer, the Protestant theologian executed by the Nazis for his involvement in the attempt to assassinate Hitler, wrote from prison how humor sustains Christian faith in adversity. Alfred Delp, a Catholic priest who was another victim of Nazism, joked in the best tradition of Christian martyrdom when he was actually walking toward his execution. He asked the chaplain accompanying him about the latest news from the front, then said "In a half hour I will know more than you!"[7]

Helmut Thielicke, one of the few recent theologians to devote an entire book to the comic, has summed up these insights as follows: "The message, which resides in humor and from which it lives, is the *kerygma* [the proclamation] of the overcoming of the world."[8] Reinhold Niebuhr, the best-known American Protestant theologian in this century, wrote an essay on "Humor and Faith." The following sums up his view:

> The intimate relation between humor and faith is derived from the fact that both deal with the incongruities of our existence. Humor is concerned with the immediate incongruities of life and faith with the ultimate ones. Both humor and faith are expressions of the freedom of the human spirit, of its capacity to stand outside of life, and itself, and view the whole scene. But any view of the whole immediately creates the problem of how the incongruities of life are to be dealt with; for the effort to understand life, and our place in it, confronts us with inconsistencies and incongruities which do not fit into any neat picture of the whole. Laughter is our reaction to immediate incongruities and those which do not affect us essentially. Faith is the only possible response to the ultimate incongruities of existence which threaten the very meaning of our life. . . .
>
> Faith is the final triumph over incongruity, the final assertion of the meaningfulness of existence. There is no other triumph and will be none, no matter how much human knowledge is enlarged. Faith is the final assertion of the freedom of the human spirit, but also the final acceptance of the weakness of man and the final solution for the problem of life through the disavowal of any final solution in the power of man.[9]

The comic as a phenomenon must be distinguished from that of play. Yet the two are related. The Catholic theologian Hugo Rahner wrote a delightful little book on the religious significance of play. What he says there is also relevant for the religious significance of the comic:

> To play is to yield oneself to a kind of magic, to enact to oneself the absolutely other, to pre-empt the future, to give the lie to the inconvenient world of fact. In play earthly realities become, of a sudden, things of the transient moment, presently left behind, then disposed of and buried in

the past; the mind is prepared to accept the unimagined and incredible, to enter a world where different laws apply, to be relieved of all the weights that bear it down, to be free, kingly, unfettered and divine. Man at play is reaching out . . . for that superlative ease, in which even the body, freed from its earthly burden, moves to the effortless measures of a heavenly dance.[10]

If, then, one is to make an argument for the religious implications of the comic from a Christian vantage point, one will find some support in the tradition. Still, the scarcity of this support provokes reflection.

As far as the absence or near absence of explicit humor in the biblical sources is concerned, it is useful to recall the nature of this literature. In a traditional Jewish or Christian understanding, it is through these texts that God revealed Himself. One can put this understanding in more secular terms by saying (using here a term of Mircea Eliade) that the biblical sources report on various hierophanies—that is, powerful manifestations of sacred reality and their human consequences (for instance, moral consequences). What is more, many biblical texts were used in worship—that is, in actions intended to reiterate or even replicate these hierophanies. When the sacred is experienced at such close range (or when there is, at least, the intention of mediating such an experience), all reflection must cease. That is certainly the case with theoretical reflection. There is hardly any theology in the Hebrew Bible, as Jews are prone to point out repeatedly, and modern constructions of a theology of the Old Testament are ex post facto theoretical exercises, usually produced by Christians. The New Testament can more plausibly be said to contain theology, especially in its Pauline and Johannine texts. But here too there is no theoretical interest as such; the interest is always *kerygmatic*—in the authoritative proclamation of the Gospel message. In other words, to engage in the systematic intellectual activity known as theology requires a certain distance from the cataclysmic presence of the sacred. A theologically informed sense of humor—that is, a perception of the comic as a religiously meaningful aspect of reality—also requires a measure of distance.

Al-Ghazali, the great Muslim theologian who made a place for mysticism within the "divine sciences" of Islam, was convinced that reason had no place within the mystical experience itself. That is, an individual cannot simultaneously experience religious ecstasy and engage in systematic intellectual activity. But no one can remain in a state of ecstasy indefinitely. Reason can reassert itself in the wake of ecstasy, when the individual can and, as far as Al-Ghazali was concerned, should ask himself what the experience means in the total order of things. In this context Al-Ghazali coined the wonderful sentence, "Reason is God's scale on earth." Perhaps something very similar can be said about the perception of the comic.

This reflection, of course, does not get one off the hook as far as the lachrymose history of Christian theology is concerned. There, if not in the canonical texts, one would expect more friendly attention to the comic. One may derive some consolation from the fact that, as has been seen, the philosophers, at least in Western culture, have not been much better than the theologians, certainly not before the onset of the modern era. The philosophers of classical antiquity, from Plato to Cicero, tended toward a sour view of laughter. It is plausible to assume that their Christian successors simply took over this attitude, only deepening it by linking it with a religious deprecation of this world and of the human condition. It was only in the "underground" of popular comic culture that a different sensibility, comic *and* Christian, maintained itself. Occasionally, as in the practice of Easter laughter, it erupted into the liturgy of the church.

Very tentatively, a further hypothesis might be ventured. As was seen earlier, the turn in philosophy from a negative to a positive assessment of the comic only came in modern times. Erasmus, with his *Praise of Folly*, marks this turning point (at the same time serving as a bridge between the comic culture of the Middle Ages and modern understandings of the comic). Then, especially in the seventeenth and eighteenth centuries, came a period of intense and generally positive interest in the comic by philosophers. It is possible that modern consciousness, both in its pretheoretical form and then as it is theoretically explicated, produces a comic sensibility all its own. Modernity *pluralizes* the world. It throws together people with different values and worldviews; it undermines taken-for-granted traditions; it accelerates all processes of change.[11] This brings about a multiplicity of incongruencies—and it is the perception of incongruence that is at the core of the comic experience. Sociologists have used the phrase "role distance" to describe the detached, reflective attitude of modern individuals toward their actions in society. This also implies *cognitive* distance—Helmut Schelsky, a German sociologist, has called this "permanent reflectiveness" (*Dauerreflektion*). The same distance may well be the basis of a specifically modern sense of humor. If so, modern theology, despite its frequently frenetic efforts to keep up with the times, has not really caught up yet.

All the same, the comic, like the sacred, has a way of breaking into the most unlikely situations. Helmut Thielicke tells the delightful story of an experience he had toward the end of World War II, when he was preaching in a village church near Stuttgart. Suddenly there was an air raid, without warning, with the most frightening noises of attacking airplanes, machine-gun fire and countering flak. Thielicke shouted from

the pulpit: "Everyone flat on the ground! We sing 'Jesus, my Joy'"
("*Jesu, meine Freude,*" a well-known German hymn). The organist and
the congregation followed this instruction. Thielicke could no longer see
them from the pulpit, as everyone was crouched under the pews, singing. Despite the horrible noise all around the church, and despite the
great danger, the situation impressed Thielicke as acutely funny. He
started to laugh wholeheartedly. In retrospect, he thought that this was
indeed laughter that pleased God.

## Notes

1.   There does not seem to be any overall history of humor in Christian
history. I must confess that I didn't look very hard, since I had reason to be
confident what the result would be. In any case, if this book aspired to completeness, I would need the life expectancy of one of those unpleasantly laughing
Greek gods (as Homer put it *so* well: "He who outlives his reviewers laughs
last"). I have found the following books moderately helpful: Werner Thiede, *Das
verheissende Lachen: Humor in theologischer Perspektive* (Goettingen: Vandenhoeck
& Ruprecht), 1966); Helmut Thielicke, *Das Lachen der Heiligen und der Narren*
(Stuttgart: Quell, [1974] 1988); and Franz-Josef Kuschel, *Laughter: A Theological
Essay* (New York: Continuum, 1994 [orig. in German also 1994]). I suppose that I
should mention Harvey Cox, *Feast of Fools* (Cambridge, Mass.: Harvard University Press, 1969). It makes a number of interesting observations on the relation of
Christian hope and the life of fantasy, but its main thrust is a theological legitimation of the countercultural sensibility of the late 1960s—a less than exciting
exercise a generation later. A more recent book by an American Protestant
theologian—A. Roy Eckardt, *How to Tell God from the Devil: On the Way to Comedy*
(New Brunswick, N.J.: Transaction, 1994)—also contains some acute insights,
but it is marked by an idiosyncratic approach that is often hard to follow.
2.   Cf. Gerhard Schmitz, *"Ein Narr, der da lacht,"* in Thomas Vogel, ed., *Vom
Lachen* (Tuebingen: Attempto, 1992), 129ff.
3.   This comes through in all Luther biographies, recently in Heiko Ober-
man's masterful *Luther* (New Haven: Yale University Press, 1989). One biography, by Eric Gritsch, is actually entitled *Martin—God's Court Jester* (Philadelphia:
Fortress, 1983), but not much is made of this title in the text. An authoritative
work on Luther's humor appears to be Fritz Blanks, *Luthers Humor* (1954, in
German); I was unable to put my hands on this work.
4.   Cf. Thielicke, *Das Lachen,* 98.
5.   Cf. Thiede, *Das verheissende Lachen,* 120.
6.   Howard Hong and Edna Hong, eds., *Søren Kierkegaard's Journals and
Papers* (Bloomington: Indiana University Press), vol. 2, 262.
7.   Cf. Thiede, *Das verheissende Lachen,* 127 ff.
8.   Thielicke, *Das Lachen,* 96. My translation.
9.   Reinhold Niebuhr, *Discerning the Signs of the Times* (New York: Scribner,
1946), IIIff. Niebuhr thought that humor led into the "vestibule of the temple,"

Toward a Theology of the Comic

but that laughter must: cease in the "holy of holies." This, probably not coincidentally, was also Kierkegaard's view. I'm inclined to think that in this both were mistaken.

10.   Hugo Rahner, *Man at Play* (London: Burns & Oates, 1965), 65f.

11.   Cf. my book with Brigitte Berger and Hansfried Kellner, *The Homeless Mind: Modernization and Consciousness* (New York, Random House, 1973). We did not, alas, consider humor at the time.

# 14

# The Comic as a Signal of Transcendence

The term *transcendence* carries a heavy freight of diverse meanings in philosophical and theological discourse, and no useful purpose would be served by untangling all these meanings here. However, the notion of transcendence has appeared at several points in the ruminations of this book, most loudly in the preceding two chapters. It is useful, therefore, to clarify at least two meanings of the term relevant to the phenomenon of the comic: First, the comic transcends the reality of ordinary, everyday existence; it posits, however temporarily, a different reality in which the assumptions and rules of ordinary life are suspended. This is, as it were, transcendence in a lower key; it does not in itself have any necessary religious implications. But second, at least certain manifestations of the comic suggest that this other reality has redeeming qualities that are not temporary at all, but rather that point to that other world that has always been the object of the religious attitude. In ordinary parlance one speaks of "redeeming laughter." Any joke can provoke such laughter, and it can be redeeming in the sense of making life easier to bear, at least briefly. In the perspective of religious faith, though, there is in this transitory experience an intuition, a signal of true redemption, that is, of a world that has been made whole and in which the miseries of the human condition have been abolished. This implies transcendence in a higher key; it is religious in the full, proper sense of the word. There is no inevitable passage from the first to the second kind of transcendence. Of course there is not; otherwise every stand-up comedian would be a minister of God (which is what Don Quixote thought himself to be). There is a secular and a religious mode of comic experience, and the passage from one to the other requires an act of faith.

When we first tried to circumscribe the phenomenon of the comic, we described it as an intrusion. In the terminology of Alfred Schutz, the comic breaks into the consciousness of the paramount reality, which is that ordinary, everyday world in which we exist most of the time, which we share with most of our fellowmen, and which therefore appears to us as massively real. This reality is dense, heavy, compelling. By comparison, the reality of the comic is thin, effervescent, often shared with only a few other people, and sometimes shared with no one at all. As long as it lasts, the comic posits another reality that is inserted like an island into the ocean of everyday experience. It is then what Schutz called a finite province of meaning. As such it is by no means unique. A whole range of human experiences can produce such islands—the worlds of dreams, of intense sexual or esthetic experience, of self-contained theoretical speculation (pure mathematics is an ideal case of this), or, in a very different vein, of physical pain. But religious experience, viewed from the vantage point of everyday life, is yet another such finite province of meaning. The comparison with comic experience is instructive. The two phenomena share certain basic characteristics with all other finite provinces of meaning—discrete structures of reality, discrete categories of space and time, "threshold" sensations as one passes into and again out of these island worlds, discrete experiences of other people and of oneself. Thus, for example, in the world of comedy one senses that one is in a different order of things, one is transported to other places and other times, there is a kind of jolt (here marked by laughter or its anticipation) as one moves into the world of the comedy and a reverse jolt (one stops laughing) as one moves out of it, other people are experienced differently (the threatening tyrant, say, becomes a pathetic figure) and so is one's own self (the victim becomes a victor over circumstance). *Mutatis mutandis*, these characteristics apply to all finite provinces of meaning, including that of religious experience. The latter, however, has some characteristics that are more or less unique. Specifically, these are the qualities of the sacred—the "tremendous mystery," as Rudolf Otto called it, the experience of an otherness that is total, an ambiguity of terror and attraction (the "numinous," in Otto's terminology), and the attitude of awe or reverence that is provoked by the experience. These characteristics are adumbrated in some manifestations of the comic, notably those belonging to the category of folly, but there are large areas of comic experience that show none of these characteristics.

As the preceding pages have documented, the range of the comic is vast—from the howling madness of Dionysus to the subdued irony of Jeeves. Yet it is the former that shows most clearly the full potential of the comic, and thus its proximity to the religious sphere. At least in Western history (and very likely elsewhere as well) the origins of the comic experience are found to be very close to the encounter with the numinous. Both phenomena bring about the perception of a magically transformed world and, for this reason, both are dangerous when they reach a certain degree of intensity. Dangerous to what? Dangerous, precisely, to the maintenance of ordinary, everyday reality or, if you will, to the business of living. Both phenomena produce ecstasies—literally, experiences of *standing outside* ordinary reality. Such ecstasies are tolerable, indeed useful both psychologically and sociologically, if they are temporary and carefully controlled. The danger is that they might escape the efforts at control and thus undermine the social order. Robert Musil, in his great novel *The Man without Qualities*, gives much attention to what he calls the "other condition"—a sort of mystical experience, presented without a theological interpretation. Taken in small doses (such as encountering a whiff of it as one is deeply moved by a theatrical performance), this experience is like going on a vacation from life. The danger is that someone might decide to go on vacation permanently (which is what Ulrich, the protagonist of the novel, would like to do).

To mitigate this danger, both religion and the comic have been confined to specific places or times. In terms of the sociology of religion, one could actually say that one of the primary social functions of religious institutions is the domestication of religious experience. Thus a preacher may say the most outlandish things in church on Sunday morning, suggesting, for instance, that one might actually live every day in accordance with the maxims of the Sermon on the Mount. For a few moments his comfortable bourgeois congregation may be disturbed by this preposterous suggestion. But as they leave church a little later, and move back into the familiar world of everyday living, they can breathe a sigh of relief and say to themselves (if not in just these words), "Well, that was only in church," and then resume their usual habits. There is a close analogy here to the formula "Well, that was only a joke"; after the joke has been duly appreciated and laughed at, one can, "And now, seriously," return to the nonjocular world. The magic, once again, has been left behind.

The comic, however temporarily, brings about what we just called transcendence in a lower key, that is, it relativizes the paramount reality. Suddenly, the familiar is seen in a new light, becomes strangely unfamiliar. In the language of the theater, this is what Eugène Ionesco called *depaysement* (literally, losing one's country): Temporarily, one loses one's citizenship in the ordinary world, one becomes denaturalized. Put differently, what was taken for granted as natural now appears as unnatural. Bertolt Brecht has meant more or less the same thing when he called his own theatrical technique *Verfremdung* (literally, making strange). Now, clearly, this process is not, or not yet, religious in quality. But it is a step in that direction, minimally toward the *possibility* of a religious view of the world.

The comic at its most intense, as in folly, presents a counterworld, an upside-down world. This counterworld is disclosed as lurking behind or beneath the world as we commonly know it (we have previously used another theatrical metaphor to describe this experience, that of *Doppelboedigkeit*—the perception of multiple levels). While the experience lasts, of course, it has the accent of reality. Indeed, its counterworld seems to be more real than the ordinary, empirical world. On the morning after, so to speak, one must reflect about the epistemological status of this counterworld. The presence or absence of religious faith will determine the outcome of the reflection.

Given the fugitive character of the comic phenomenon, we have avoided confining definitions in this book. However, broadly speaking, we have implied a differentiation between the subjective and objective aspects of the phenomenon. The subjective aspect is intended by what is commonly called a sense of humor, or just humor for short. This is the capacity to perceive something as comical or funny. But there is also a putative objectivity in this perception. That is, there is the assumption that there is *something out there*, something outside one's own mind, that is comical. This putative objectivity allows one to speak of the *phenomenon* of the comic. Now, as we have seen, philosophers and others have pondered over just what this something out there may be. Of course, no agreement has been reached (philosophers never reach agreement; if they ever did, the business of philosophy would come to an end). But we have given credence to the view, propounded by Henri Bergson and Marie Collins Swabey among others, that there are real cognitive gains to humor. Put differently, the sense of humor is not simply an expression of subjective feelings (akin to, say, the statement that one is depressed), but rather is an act of perception pertaining to the reality of the world outside one's own consciousness. It is amply clear that this perception is greatly influenced by history and social location: we find it difficult to laugh at Cicero's examples of humor, and we know that our jokes will fall flat if told in social milieus greatly different from our own. Despite these relativities of time and space, there is widespread agreement that the sense of humor leads above all to a perception of *incongruence*, or *incongruity*.

*One may then ask: Incongruence between what* and what? In principle, *any* incongruence may be perceived as comical—between what is alive and what is mechanical (as Bergson proposed), between the demands of censorious morality and the blind urges of our libidinal nature (the Freudian angle), between the pretensions of political authority and its underlying fallibility (the fodder for much satire), and so on. Again, what is perceived as incongruent in one situation may not be so perceived in another situation.

Still, it is possible to ask whether there are some underlying incongruences that can be perceived over and beyond all relativizations. Two answers are possible. One is anthropological, having to do with the nature of man; the other is ontological, having to do with man's place in the overall nature of the universe. The anthropological answer is the one that was brilliantly proposed by Helmuth Plessner: Man is incongruent within himself. Human existence is an ongoing balancing act between *being* a body and *having* a body. Man is the only animal capable of somehow standing outside himself (Plessner calls this his "ex-centric" nature). Put differently, man is the only animal capable of action and not just *behavior*. When this ongoing balancing act collapses, the body takes over. Both laughter and weeping manifest this collapse. This is both a physical and a psychological process. But it is also possible that the sense of humor repeatedly *perceives* the built-in incongruence of being human. It is in this sense that one cognitive gain of humor is anthropological: as one engages in comic laughter, one has a valid insight into a core aspect of human nature. Although Plessner, for reasons of his own, disclaims the notion that he is referring to the traditional distinction between the body and the mind, the incongruence he analyzes is very close to what many philosophers have discussed as the mind/body problem. Be this as it may, we are all familiar with the comic consequences of this incongruence erupting in everyday life: The statesman, in the midst of a solemn patriotic ceremony, has to throw up. The great intellectual, as he is expounding on the meaning of virtue, has an erection. Or, conversely, the seducer on the way to erotic success is arrested by thoughts of mortality. It could even be that, in the midst of seduction, he loses his erection because he finds the solution to a puzzling philosophical problem. None of these things could happen to a dog or even a chimpanzee. Each incongruence is unmistakably, and perhaps endearingly, *human*.

There is another incongruence, rooted not in man's nature but in his location in the universe. Pascal formulated this incongruence by locating man between the nothing and the infinite. Modern science has given us the technical means to experience this incongruence quite easily: We peer into the world revealed by the microscope and we feel ourselves to be immense; then we look through a telescope and we perceive ourselves as specks of nothingness in the vastness of the galaxies. The comic experience points to this ontological incongruence: Man as a conscious being, suspended in this ridiculous position between the microbes and the stars. All human pretensions to wisdom and power are comically debunked as this fundamental incongruence is perceived.

Despite the aforementioned similarities with a specifically religious finite province of meaning, what has been said here on the comic bringing about a transcendence in a lower key does not necessarily lead to a religious interpretation of this experience. It all can be said *etsi Deus non daretur*—that is, without assuming God (or, for that matter, any gods or supernatural entities). After all, the ecstasies of intense esthetic or sexual experience also evince some of these similarities; they too transcend the taken-for-granted reality of ordinary life, but this transcendence need not be understood in religious terms. To pass from the lower to the higher key requires an act of faith, which will be a kind of leap (to use Kierkegaard's term). Leave aside for the moment the question as to *why* one should make such a leap. The point here is that, once it has been made, the comic takes on a very different aspect. To use the phrase suggested earlier, an epistemological reversal takes place. With it, some of the key features of the comic experience take on new meaning.

Specifically, the experience of the comic presents a world without pain. A number of analysts discussed earlier in this book have pointed out the peculiar abstraction that is presupposed in comic perception. It is, above all, an abstraction from the tragic dimension of human existence. There are exceptions to this, for example in so-called black humor, though even there the painful realities dealt with are somehow neutralized as they are translated into comic terms. By and large, from the worlds of benign humor to the counterworlds of folly there is a suspension of tragic facts. This fact can be compactly illustrated by the figure of the clown, who is beaten, knocked down, trampled upon, and generally tormented. Yet the assumption is that he does not really feel the pain. Indeed, the clown's laughing performance through all these tribulations is only possible because of this imputed painlessness. As soon as the assumption of painlessness is left behind, the comedy turns into tragedy: the clown may still pretend to laugh, but we know that he is really weeping, and his performance is no longer funny. Generally, any comedy turns into tragedy as soon as real suffering, real pain is allowed to enter it.

*Etsi Deus non daretur*, every instance of the comic is an escape from reality—healthy physically, psychologically, and sociologically, but an escape all the same. The real world of empirical existence must in the end reassert itself; the counterempirical world of the comic must be seen as an illusion. Comedy is fundamentally counterfactual; tragedy reveals the hard facticity of the human condition. But as soon as all of this is perceived in the light of faith—*etsi Deus daretur*—the assertions of reality and illusion are reversed. It is the hard facts of the empirical world that are now seen as, if not illusion, a temporary reality that will eventually be superseded. Conversely, the painless worlds of the comic can now be seen as an adumbration of a world beyond this world. The promise of redemption, in one form or another, is always of a world without pain. Empirically, the comic is a finite and temporary game within the serious world that is marked by our pain and that inexorably leads to our death. Faith, however, puts the empirical in question and denies its ultimate seriousness. In this it is, strictly speaking, metaempirical. It presents, not an illusion, but a vision of a world infinitely more real than all the realities of *this* world.

The character of this epistemological reversal can be illustrated by looking at some of the primal experiences of the comic, the ones that psychologists have found even among very young children—the pratfall, the jack-in-the-box, and (probably the most primal of all) the game of peekaboo. The pratfall expresses most clearly the incongruence between human pretensions and human reality. Thales of Miletus thought that he understood the stars, but he fell into a ditch, and the Thracian maid's laughter implied an insight into the human condition that went far beyond this particular philosopher's momentary embarrassment. The pratfall represents an anthropological paradigm with that wonderful economy that (as Freud discovered) jokes have in common with dreams. The jack-in-the-box is the reverse figure. He is a mechanical replication of the same denial of the pratfall enacted and reenacted by every clown who keeps jumping back up no matter how often he has been made to fall. Another toy doing this is what in German is nicely called the *Stehaufmaennchen* (the little man who keeps standing up). This is a doll with a rounded bottom into which some weights have been put, so that, however much the doll is pressed down, it will always revert to the upright position. If the pratfall is an anthropological paradigm, the jack-in-the-box is a soteriological one—that is, it is a symbol of redemption. If one understands redemption in Christian terms (and it is always important to remember that there are other notions of redemption), a slightly reckless formulation suggests itself: The jack-in-the-box and the *Stehaufmaennchen* are apt symbolizations of the Resurrection. In this imagery, Christ was the first little man who stood up and, as the Apostle Paul explained, this is the basis of our own hope to put the primal pratfall behind us for ever.

But it is the game of peekaboo that takes on an even more surprising meaning in the wake of the epistemological reversal brought on by the act of faith. Let us recall what this game is all about: The child sees the mother; then the mother disappears, causing the child to be anxious; when the mother reappears after a brief absence, the child smiles or laughs; this laughter expresses a great relief (or, as German psychologists have put it, an *Entlastung*, an "unburdening"). Here, in a wondrous nutshell, is the drama of redemption as seen in the light of faith. *Etsi Deus daretur*, God's dealings with mankind can be seen as a cosmic game of hide-and-seek. We catch a glimpse of Him and then He promptly disappears. His absence is a central feature of our existence, and the ultimate source of all our anxieties. Religious faith is the hope that He will eventually reappear, providing that ultimate relief, which, precisely, is redemption. There is actually a liturgy in Eastern Ortho-

doxy that visually represents the cosmic game of peekaboo. Every Orthodox church contains the *ikonostasis,* the icon screen that separates the
altar from the rest of the sanctuary. The icon screen has several doors,
through which the clergy and their assistants come and go in the course
of the service. In that particular liturgy, as the officiating priest goes in
and out through the icon screen, a deacon intones, "Now you see him,
now you don't see him."

Someone once observed that every new mother is in a morally privileged position: She knows exactly what God wants her to do. That is, of
course, to take care of her child. A universally understood human icon is
the image of a mother protectively cradling her infant. There is further
the primal scene of a mother comforting a crying child. The child, let us
suppose, wakes up from a terrifying dream and starts crying. The mother cradles him and says soothingly, "Don't cry: Everything is alright,
everything is all right." Now, while this scene evokes universal human
empathy, it can finally be interpreted in contradictory terms depending
on the presence or absence of religious faith. In the absence of faith, the
mother is lying to the child. Not, of course, in that particular moment.
Nor is there any implication that what the mother is doing is morally
wrong. However, as modern child psychology has amply demonstrated, these reassuring gestures and words experienced in early childhood build in the child a fundamental *trust in the world.* Yet, speaking
empirically, this trust is misplaced, is an illusion. The world is not at all
trustworthy. It is a world in which the child will experience every sort of
pain, and it is a world that in the end will kill him. Everything is *not* all
right; on the contrary. The mother's reassurance is thus, in the final
analysis, an act of false consciousness. In the presence of faith, the scene
has a sharply different meaning. Now the mother plays what could
actually be called a priestly role. Her words of reassurance reiterate the
divine promise of redemption: In the end, everything will be all right.
False consciousness or promise of redemption: Depending on one's angle of vision, *either* interpretation is valid. We are faced with the option
of leaping either way.

Of course, it is not being suggested here that mothers know this, not
even subconsciously. And, of course, there is no suggestion that children laugh at a clown or a jack-in-the-box in the capacity of kindergarten
theologians. Rather, we have been asking what these events can mean
to us, as observers, who have or do not have faith. Perhaps, though,
Jesus' sayings to the effect that we ought to become like children are
relevant here. The happy child, the one who has known sufficient reas-
surances of the kind just described, does indeed trust the world. If we
have faith, we can again trust the world. Luther described faith (*fides*) as
precisely trust (*fiducia*). Childish faith trusts that the clown will always

jump up again, that the mother will always reappear, and that therefore one is free to laugh. Adults are capable of being born again into a childlike faith in which the world becomes trustworthy once more. Such faith cannot be based on rational proofs, but it is not contrary to reason either. What is more, it can and must be reflected upon. One result of such reflection is the intuition that comedy is more profound than tragedy.

Throughout most of the nineteenth century and all of the twentieth century thus far, modern thought has been heavily influenced by the idea of projection in its treatment of religion. The idea goes back to Ludwig Feuerbach, whose program of (as he put it) transforming theology into anthropology was based on the idea that the worlds posited by religion are simply reflections, or projections, of the empirical world of ordinary human life. This idea has found its most powerful ramifications in the works of Marx (religion as part of the superstructure, which reflects the underlying social realities), Nietzsche (religion, especially Christianity, as the projection of the resentments of the losers in the power game), and Freud (religion as the great illusion that serves to "sublimate" the censored desires of the libido). But many other modern thinkers, including considerable numbers of theologians, have also operated with the concept of projection. Taken as the only possible description of religion, the idea of projection is based upon and in turn reinforces the atheist hypothesis: the gods are symbolizations of human affairs and, apart from that, they do not exist. This, however, is not the only way in which this concept can be understood. One can also take it as a statement about religion *within the parameters of the empirical sciences of man*—such as history, psychology, the social sciences, perhaps even certain versions of philosophical anthropology. If one stays within these parameters, much of what has been said about projection is perfectly valid. Of course, this by no means implies that one must agree with, say, the full-blown Marxist or Freudian theories of religion (these, incidentally, are very dubious on purely empirical grounds). But, empirically speaking, it is perfectly valid to look upon religious experiences and tradition in their historical, social, and psychological settings. When one does that, one invariably finds that these religious phenomena do indeed symbolize—if you will, reflect or project—various human realities. It is futile for theologians to dispute these insights in principle.

Once more, the act of faith introduces a new perspective. It is not, in this case, a complete epistemological reversal, because the insights into religion as a projection remain valid within the limits of the empirical. But faith opens up the possibility of a different, metaempirical way of looking at this phenomenon. In that perspective, man is only capable of projecting the gods because he himself is related to the gods in the first place. In monotheistic terms, God created man in His own image—which, minimally, means that man is capable of conceiving of God. In the acts of projection, man reaches out toward the infinite. But he is only capable of doing this because the infinite reached out to him first. Put succinctly, man is the *projector* because ultimately it is he himself who is a projectile. The symbolizer is himself the symbol. The empirical disciplines will legitimately look for projections of mundane realities in whatever purports to be transcendence. A theological discipline (by which is meant here no more than a systematic reflection about the implications of faith) will, conversely, look for intimations of transcendence within the mundane realities. Once faith has opened up this particular angle of vision, a number of such intimations disclose themselves. It should be emphasized that these are not "proofs" for the existence of God or any other supernatural realities. There are no such proofs that would make superfluous the act of faith. What we are speaking about here are not proofs but signals of transcendence or, if you will, glimpses of Him who is playing the cosmic game of hide-and-seek with us.

Why should one look for such signals? This is not the place to make an argument for religious faith in general or for Christian faith in particular. But this much should be said here: There are people who claim, on whatever basis, to be absolutely certain in their religious beliefs. Perhaps some of them have indeed been chosen for such self-disclosures of the divine that are self-certifying in their reality and durably so. If one has drunk of the bitter wine of modern thought, one will incline toward skepticism concerning most such claims. The capacity of human beings to invent dubious certitudes is awesome, and by no means only when it comes to religion. Be this as it may, those of us who have not been blessed with experiences that substitute certainty for faith have no choice, if we are honest, except to do the best with the uncertainties that we are stuck with. Not *knowing*, we only have the choice to *believe*. The possessors of alleged certitude have no need to go in search of signals of transcendence. The rest of us do, unless we are prepared to resign ourselves with stoic fortitude to the ultimate hopelessness of the world.

The present argument is to the effect that the experience of the comic is one such signal of transcendence, and an important one at that. In Christian terms this means that the comic is one manifestation of a sacramental universe—a universe that, paraphrasing the *Book of Common Prayer*, contains visible signs of invisible grace. Sacraments are not magic. They do not transform the world in its empirical reality, which continues to be full of all the afflictions to which human beings are prone. Also, sacraments are not logically compelling: The grace that they convey cannot be empirically or rationally demonstrated, but is only perceived in an act of faith. In this case, the experience of the comic does not miraculously remove suffering and evil in this world, nor does it provide self-evident proof that God is active in the world and intends to redeem it. However, perceived in faith, the comic becomes a great consolation and a witness to the redemption that is yet to come. There are different ways in which this proposition could be elaborated theologically. The German Protestant theologian Helmut Thielicke has suggested that, if the comic were to be given a place in Christian theology, it would be under the heading of eschatology—that is, the doctrine of the last things, of the final and fully visible establishment of the Kingdom of God in this world. Another German Protestant theologian, Wolfhart Pannenberg, has used the term "proleptic" (taking ahead) to describe the nature of faith in this world, that is, faith anticipates the culmination that is yet to come, and in this anticipation acts now as if the culmination had already occurred. We would contend that the comic is proleptic in just this sense. The so-called Easter laughter of the medieval church was a powerful liturgical expression of this view.

Finally, we would return to some very hypothetical remarks made earlier about a distinctively modern comic sensibility. It could be described as witty, sardonic, very much detached. If so, it is possible to relate it to other characteristics of modernity—notably its intellectualism (a propensity to reflect constantly about everything) and its emotional control (the psychological correlate of role distance). In the history of Western thought it is interesting in this connection to recall two points in time: the time when medieval folly began to wane and the time when philosophers began to take a more positive view of the comic. Both moments of time cannot be dated precisely, but they coincide roughly with the advent of modernity in Europe. Erasmus is a pivotal figure here: He praised folly just as its more exuberant expressions were disappearing from the streets, to be domesticated in the institutions of the court jester and of formal comedy. And his book that praised folly is the first important work of a Western thinker that takes a benign view of the comic. Is this coincidental? Perhaps it is. But it is also possible that the two events are related. Modernity did away with much of the enchantment that medieval man still lived with. The counterworld of folly began to recede and, along with much else, it was secularized, adapted to an age that increasingly considered itself superior to previous ages because of its alleged rationality. But the disenchanted, overly rational world of modernity generated its own incongruences. Modern humor may be one consequence of this development, both an expression of and a reaction against it. As long as modern man can still laugh at himself, his alienation from the enchanted gardens of earlier times will not be complete. The new comic sensibility may be both the Achilles' heel of modernity and its possible salvation.

# Epilogue

## The Donkey

When fishes flew and forests walked
And figs grew upon thorn,
Some moment when the moon was blood
Then surely I was born.

With monstrous head and sickening cry
And ears like errant wings,
The devil's walking parody
On all four-footed things.

The tattered outlaw of the earth,
Of ancient crooked will;
Starve, scourge, deride me: I am dumb,
I keep my secret still.

Fools! For I also had in my hour;
One far fierce hour and sweet:
There was a shout about my, ears,
And palms before my feet.

G. K. Chesterton in *The Wild Knight*, from Robert Knille, ed., *As I Was Saying: A Chesterton Reader* (Grand Rapids, Mich., Eerdmans, 1985).